International Students from Asia in Canadian Universities

This book under the series *Routledge Studies in Global Student Mobility* explores how the recruitment and retention of international students from selected places in Asia intersect with other university priorities in the Canadian context. In situating international students and universities within the broader context of nation-building, notably at the intersection of immigration, economic, and educational policies, its intent is to highlight how postsecondary education institutions frame their engagement with international students in a context in which this group has become an important source of cultural diversification, revenue, and permanent migration. Specifically, this book responds to the growing need for new insights and perspectives on the institutional mechanisms adopted by universities to support international students from Asia in their academic and social integration to university life. One key theme that runs through this book relates to the challenges and limitations of framing the support to this diverse student group at the intersection of two institutional priorities – internationalization and inclusion. This is important for group members, who are known to experience less visible forms of discrimination and differential treatment in Canadian postsecondary education institutions.

There are three main sections in the collection to meet our objectives for examining the intersection of internationalization, inclusion, and racialization. The first section includes five complementary chapters that offer critical assessments of how government and institutional strategies and priorities on internationalization fit with values of inclusion and diversity. The six chapters in the second section differ in focus but overlap on the theme of inclusion and exclusion experiences of students in universities. In the third and final section, we have five chapters that address anti-Asian racism and the politics of race in different but meaningful ways. The volume will appeal to teacher-scholars, researchers, and educators with interest in higher education, international education, and race and ethnic studies.

Ann H. Kim is Associate Professor in the Department of Sociology at York University and Faculty Associate of the York Centre for Asian Research, Canada.

Elizabeth Buckner is Assistant Professor in the Department of Leadership, Higher and Adult Education at the Ontario Institute for Studies in Education at the University of Toronto, Canada.

Jean Michel Montsion is Associate Professor in the Canadian Studies Program at Glendon College, York University, Canada. He is also Director of the Robarts Centre for Canadian Studies and Distinguished Fellow at the Asia Pacific Foundation of Canada.

Routledge Studies in Global Student Mobility
Series Editors: *Krishna Bista and Christopher Glass*

Routledge Studies in Global Student Mobility offers a scholarly forum for original and innovative research which explores, explains, and increases understanding of issues and opportunities relating to international student mobility in K-12, higher education, and beyond. Consisting in peer-reviewed authored and edited volumes, the series advances theoretical understanding and identifies best practices for educators and professionals involved in study abroad.

As an interdisciplinary scholarly venue, the series showcases new ideas and fresh perspectives relating to international student mobility, study abroad, exchange programs, student affairs from the US and around the world, and from a wide range of academic fields, including student affairs, international education, and cultural studies.

This series is produced in collaboration with the CIES SIG Study Abroad & International Students, STAR Scholars Network, and Open Journals in Education (OJED).

Books in this series include:

Chinese Students and the Experience of International Doctoral Study in STEM
Using a Multi-World Model to Understand Challenges and Success
Yibo Yang and Judith MacCallum

International Student Support and Engagement in Higher Education
Exploring Innovative Practices in Campus, Academic and Professional Support Services
Edited by Janet Boyd and Mutiara Mohamad

Unintended Consequences of Internationalization in Higher Education
Comparative International Perspectives on the Impacts of Policy and Practice
Edited by Shahrzad Kamyab and Rosalind Latiner Raby

For more information about this series, please visit: https://www.routledge.com/go/routledge-studies-in-global-student-mobility

International Students from Asia in Canadian Universities

Institutional Challenges at the Intersection of Internationalization, Inclusion, and Racialization

Edited by Ann H. Kim, Elizabeth Buckner, and Jean Michel Montsion

Routledge
Taylor & Francis Group

NEW YORK AND LONDON

First published 2024
by Routledge
605 Third Avenue, New York, NY 10158

and by Routledge
4 Park Square, Milton Park, Abingdon, Oxon, OX14 4RN

Routledge is an imprint of the Taylor & Francis Group, an informa business

Funded by York University, Canada.

ISBN: 978-1-032-36006-5 (hbk)
ISBN: 978-1-032-36007-2 (pbk)
ISBN: 978-1-003-32980-0 (ebk)

DOI: 10.4324/b23160

Typeset in Sabon
by SPi Technologies India Pvt Ltd (Straive)

Contents

Contributors' Biography

Firrisaa Abdulkarim is a doctoral student in Sociology at York University. His research interest revolves around the intersections of inequality and race, particularly within the educational system. Prior to starting his doctoral program, Firrisaa completed MA degrees in economics and sociology, and a BSc in psychology.

Fabiola Melo Araneda is a doctoral student in Education Sciences at the University of Montreal. She completed her Master's degree in Psychology at the Pontifical Catholic University of Chile as well as a Master's degree in Human and Social Sciences at the ÉHESS in Paris.

Kumari Beck is an associate professor, co-director of the Centre for Research on International Education, and co-academic coordinator of the Equity Studies in Education program in the Faculty of Education at Simon Fraser University. Her research interests include internationalization of higher education, international education, and equity issues in education.

Elizabeth Buckner is an assistant professor in the Department of Leadership, Higher and Adult Education (LHAE) at the Ontario Institute for Studies in Education, University of Toronto. One strand of her research program explores the internationalization of higher education.

Daniela Caneo is a master's graduate at York University's Faculty of Environmental and Urban Change. Her research centers on the neoliberalization of universities in Ontario. Daniela graduated with a Bachelor of Arts from the University of Toronto, majoring in Human Geography and Political Science.

Elic Chan is a lecturer in Sociology at the University of British Columbia. His research focuses on the social and economic integration of Asian Canadians and their experiences across Canadian cities. He has published in the *International Migration Review*, *Journal of International Migration and Integration*, and *City and Community*.

Angie Y. Chung is a professor in the Department of Sociology at the University at Albany. She is the author of *Saving Face: The Emotional Costs of the Asian Immigrant Family Myth* (2016) and *Legacies of Struggle: Conflict and Cooperation in Korean American Politics* (2007).

Cynthia Eden is a doctoral student in Higher Education at the Ontario Institute for Studies in Education, University of Toronto and a curriculum development specialist at the University of Guelph. She has decades of experience in international education, primarily as an academic English instructor throughout Asia.

Madison Gateman is a juris doctor student at Osgoode Hall Law School, with a focus on immigration law. Madison completed her Master of Arts at Dalhousie University, focusing on the resettlement of Southeast Asian refugees within Canada in the late 1970s. She currently resides in Tkaronto/Toronto.

Bianca Gomez is an international student pursuing her doctorate degree in Sociology at York University. She explores international student migration and post-graduation settlement in Canada, specifically the interactions between immigration structures, personal experiences, and emotions.

Tania Das Gupta is a professor in the School of Gender, Sexuality and Women's Studies, York University. She is also currently the Affirmative Action, Equity and Inclusivity Officer at York. She has published widely on South Asian diaspora, race and racism, immigration and refugee issues, and community activism.

Mihyon Jeon is an associate professor in the Department of Languages, Literatures and Linguistics at York University. Her research interests include Korean language education as a heritage language in North America and English as second language education in Asia.

Phoebe Kang is a doctoral candidate in Educational Leadership and Policy at the Ontario Institute for Studies in Education, University of Toronto. Her research interests lie with internationalization in higher education, international students' equity and policy analysis in higher education contexts.

Amaan Kazmi is a Master's student in History at Dalhousie University. His interests lie in colonial governmentality, the development of the postcolonial state, identity, self-determination, and the impact of modernity on the people of South Asia. He has found refuge in unceded Mi'kma'ki.

Ann H. Kim is an associate professor in the Department of Sociology at York University. She studies migration, race and ethnicity, and urban sociology, and has a long-standing interest in the Korean diaspora.

Eun Gi Kim is a doctoral candidate in Higher Education at the Ontario Institute for Studies in Education, University of Toronto. Her research focuses on the varied experiences of Korean immigrants and international students in Canadian higher education.

Thomas R. Klassen is a professor in the School of Public Policy and Administration at York University. He is the co-author of *The Essential Guide to Studying Abroad: From Success in the Classroom to a Fulfilling Career* (Routledge 2020). He has published widely on labor market and social policy.

Janine Knight-Grofe is a doctoral student in Higher Education at the Ontario Institute for Studies in Education, University of Toronto and Manager, International Education at Durham College in Ontario. She has decades of experience in international education, including at the Canadian Bureau of International Education (CBIE).

Min-Jung Kwak is an associate professor in the Department of Geography and Environmental Studies at Saint Mary's University. She has conducted research projects on education migration, student mobility, transnational family experiences, and immigrant entrepreneurship.

Yifan Liu is currently a Ph.D. student in Social Justice Education at the Ontario Institute for Studies in Education, with a collaborative specialization in Diaspora and transnational studies. Liu has two Master's degrees in Education from the University College London and the University of Montreal.

Lucia Lo is a professor emerita and senior scholar of Geography in the Faculty of Environmental and Urban Change at York University, Canada. Her general research interest focuses on the role of (im)migrants in economic development and urban transformation. Her latest project is about the dynamics of intellectual migration.

Yazhi Luo is a Master's student in Sociology at the University of Manitoba. Her research interests lie in racism, racial triangulation, and immigration studies. She is a research assistant on the SSHRC-funded Racialization of Asian International Students project and is assigned to the University of Manitoba case study.

Marie-Odile Magnan is Chair in Ethnic Relations and Full Professor in the Department of Administration and Foundations of Education at the University of Montreal. Her research focuses on the voice of racialized groups on the experiences in educational environments and on the practices, processes, and policies implemented by schools.

Brett Matsushita is a graduate student in the Department of Sociology at the University of British Columbia. His research interests include race, ethnicity, networks, and intimate partnerships. His research examines how marriages are associated with a change in ethnic friendship composition among individuals in interethnic marriages.

Jean Michel Montsion is an associate professor in the Canadian Studies Program at Glendon College, York University; Director of the Robarts Centre for Canadian Studies; and Distinguished Fellow at the Asia Pacific Foundation of Canada (2018–2023). He researches on the questions of ethnicity and mobility in gateway cities like Singapore and Vancouver.

Guanglong Pang is a doctoral student in the Higher, Adult, and Lifelong Education Program at Michigan State University. His current dissertation research assesses student learning from online international education. Previously trained as a geographer, Guanglong also studies the experiences of international students and their migration trajectories.

Ajay Parasram is a transnational, multigenerational byproduct of colonialism with roots in South Asia, the Caribbean, and across Turtle Island. He is an associate professor in the Departments of International Development Studies, History, and Political Science at Dalhousie University, unceded Mi'kma'ki on the eastern coast of Turtle Island.

Melissa Payne is Director, Membership, Research, and Learning at the Canadian Bureau for International Education. She is also a faculty member in the communications department at Algonquin College. Melissa has a degree in Communications from the University of Ottawa and a post-graduate diploma from Humber College in International Project Management.

Hyunjung Shin is an assistant professor in the Department of Curriculum Studies at the University of Saskatchewan. Her research examines the construction of social difference and social inequality in the context of language education and sociolinguistics. Her works have appeared in multiple refereed journals as well as international handbook volumes.

Brandon R. G. Smith is a doctoral student in the higher, adult, and lifelong education program at Michigan State University. Brandon's research interests focus on (1) student success and (2) professional success and persistence behaviors of administrators working in postsecondary education, specifically, career buoyancy of this population.

Roberta de Oliveira Soares is a doctoral student in Education Sciences at the University of Montreal. She completed her Master's degree in Sociology and her Bachelor's degree in Social Sciences at the University of

São Paulo. Her qualitative research focuses on the placement procedures in welcoming classes in Montreal.

Vander Tavares is currently a postdoctoral research fellow in the Faculty of Education at Høgskolen i Innlandet (Inland Norway University of Applied Sciences). He is the author of *International Students in Higher Education: Language, Identity and Experience from a Holistic Perspective* (2021).

Patricia Trudel is a doctoral student in Sociology at York University. Her doctoral research focuses on the manifestations of intergenerational and postcolonial memory narratives in the Korean diaspora.

Fotini Vlahos is a Master's student in Higher Education at the Ontario Institute for Studies in Education, University of Toronto. Her research focuses on the experiences of francophone African international students in Canadian universities.

Yun Wang is an assistant professor in Marketing at Mount Saint Vincent University. She obtained her PhD in Management (Marketing) at Sprott School of Business, Carleton University. Her research interest focuses on digital marketing, consumer health consumption and promotion, and internationalization of higher education.

Lori Wilkinson is a professor in the Department of Sociology and Criminology at the University of Manitoba and is Director of Immigration Research West. Her current program of research centers on the resettlement and integration experiences of immigrants and refugees.

Eustacia Yu is a researcher in the Werklund School of Education, University of Calgary, where she also earned her Doctor of Education degree. Her research interests include internationalization in higher education, adult education, intercultural learning and communication, comparative education, and third space in higher education.

Shangcao Yuan is a PhD student in the Higher Education program at the Ontario Institute for Studies in Education, University of Toronto. Shangcao's research interests are in private higher education, organizational studies of higher education, and comparative and international higher education.

You Zhang is a doctoral candidate in Higher Education at the Ontario Institute for Studies in Education, University of Toronto. Her research interests are in higher education internationalization and regionalization. Her work has appeared in the *Journal of International Students*, *Canadian Journal of Higher Education*, and *Higher Education*.

Introduction

The Federalization of Education Migration: Redefining Success

Ann H. Kim, Elizabeth Buckner, and Jean Michel Montsion

Introduction

The purpose of this book under the series *Routledge Studies in Global Student Mobility* is to explore how the recruitment and retention of international students from selected places in Asia intersect with other university priorities in the Canadian context. In situating international students and universities within the broader context of nation-building, notably at the intersection of immigration, economic, and educational policies, its intent is to highlight how postsecondary education institutions frame their engagement with international students in a context in which this group has become an important source of cultural diversification, revenue, and permanent migration. Specifically, this book responds to the growing need for new insights and perspectives on the institutional mechanisms adopted by universities to support international students from Asia in their academic and social integration to university life. One key theme that runs through this book relates to the challenges and limitations of framing the support to this diverse student group at the intersection of two institutional priorities – internationalization and anti-racism. This is important for group members, who are known to experience less-visible forms of discrimination and differential treatment in Canadian postsecondary education institutions (Colomba 2013). In its engagement with these themes, this collection complements our 2022 special issue of *Comparative and International Education/Éducation comparée et internationale* titled, "International Students from Asia in Canada's Postsecondary Institutions: Disconnections and Connections," which examines how students from Asia are situated within internationalization, Indigenization, and decolonization and the equity, diversity, and inclusion (EDI) initiatives in Canadian universities (Kim, Buckner, and Montsion 2022). In this introduction, we set the stage for the chapters ahead that address these critical matters by demonstrating that the international students we presently find in Canada, many from Asia, did not arrive by happenstance or invisible market forces. There are many moving parts to

DOI: 10.4324/b23160-1

enticing and hosting hundreds of thousands of students across borders and university gates. In other words, international students are here undeniably and unquestionably by design.

Whereas Canadian postsecondary institutions and provincial governments have a relatively long-standing interest in recruiting international students from Asia, we are especially interested in the most recent period, which reflects the federalization of education migration, meaning the explicit interest and involvement of Canada's federal government in shaping international education trends in the country, even though education policy and funding continue to be the jurisdiction of provincial governments. Since the unveiling of the first national branding initiative, "Imagine Education au/in Canada," in 2007, the federal government has become increasingly involved in international education (Kim and Kwak 2019). The launch of *Canada's International Education Strategy: Harnessing our Knowledge Advantage to Drive Innovation and Prosperity* by the Government of Canada in 2014 provided a strategic framework to the recruitment and retention of international students, thereby shaping a normative vision to the ongoing efforts in the postsecondary education sector across the country. The intent was to significantly increase the number of international students to support Canada's economic and labour market needs, which was updated in *Building on Success: International Education Strategy 2019–2024* in 2019 with more of a focus on diversifying students' countries of origin. Whereas the 2014 policy was originally published by only one federal department – Foreign Affairs, Trade and Development – five years later, the strategy entailed a partnership among three departments, which were named at the time: Employment, Workforce Development, and Labour; Immigration Refugees and Citizenship Canada; and International Trade Diversification, further entrenching the juncture among the three policy realms of education, immigration, and economy. These strategies structure the discourse and practice of institutional actors and international students to form the ruling relations of internationalization (see Beck). They also provide insights on evolving institutional relationships among the Canadian government, its provincial counterparts, and its postsecondary institutions, all of whom are now involved in the recruitment and retention of international students, the majority of whom are notably from Asia.

The enrolment indicator

By many indicators, such as enrolment, country of origin, and revenue, the federal international strategy has been a resounding success. Canada is now one of the top destinations for international students, third after the United States (US) and the United Kingdom (UK), moving up from the eighth position in 2000 (Institute of International Education 2020). Mirroring the global increase in education migration, the number of international students enroled in Canada has increased over the past two decades to more than 620,000 in 2019 and 2021 with a slight dip to 528,000 in 2020 due to the Covid-19 pandemic (Crossman, Choi, Lu, and Hou 2022). Enrolments of international students in postsecondary institutions, including colleges and universities,[1] have also increased dramatically in absolute numbers over the past two decades from less than 46,000 in 2000 to 136,000 in 2009 to approximately 390,000 in 2019 (Statistics Canada 2022), nearly trebling each decade. This rapid growth is observed in the relative numbers as well, with a gradual increase in international university enrolments as a percentage of total university enrolments from 2000 to 2009 (from 5 percent to 8 percent, respectively) and then a steeper rise during the period covered by the federal strategies to reach 17 percent in 2019. The growth in the colleges was even more remarkable, increasing from 3 percent in 2000 and 5 percent in 2009 to nearly 20 percent in 2019. Figure I.1 presents these relative figures for international university and college students. Noteworthy is the sharp rise in the percentages of international student enrolments in university and college settings but also the general flattening of total enrolments during the same period which shows that any growth in postsecondary enrolments was due to international students (Statistics Canada 2021).

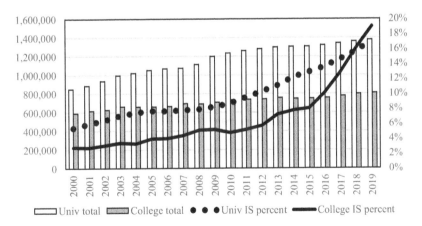

Figure I.1 Postsecondary enrolments in universities and colleges and percent international students, 2000–2019.

Source: Statistics Canada. 2022. Table 37-10-0018-01. Postsecondary enrolments, by registration status, institution type, status of student in Canada and gender. https://www150.statcan.gc.ca/

4 *Ann H. Kim et al.*

The target country indicator

To meet the overall enrolment goals, the 2014 strategy clearly identified specific countries to target for students across all levels and named countries such as France, the UK, Germany, Japan, Korea, and the US as major contributors. It also articulated other countries where resources for recruitment were to be invested: Brazil, China, India, Mexico, North Africa, the Middle East, and Vietnam. Of the 12 target regions, *five* are in East, South, and Southeast Asia. Unsurprisingly, the presence of students from Asia grew exponentially. Four out of the five Asian countries identified in the report are placed in the top ten origin countries of postsecondary international students in 2019 (see Figure I.2). Consistent with the strategy's objectives, the numbers of postsecondary students from the top ten countries increased in the expected direction and pace during the 2010–2019 period, or what we refer to as the "federalization of education migration" period. The numbers of students from France, the US, and South Korea (Korea) increased slightly while those from Brazil, China, India, Iran, and Vietnam grew much faster, noticeably after 2014. Although Japan was not in the top ten in 2019, their numbers of postsecondary international students still rose over the period, from 2,500 to over 3,100 students, as did those from Mexico, doubling from 1,750 to 3,500 (Statistics Canada 2022).

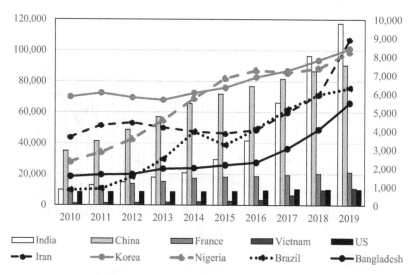

Figure I.2 Postsecondary enrolments of international students, top ten countries by citizenship, 2010–2019.

Note: Bars, left axis: India, China, France, Vietnam, the US. Lines, right axis: Iran, Korea, Nigeria, Brazil, Bangladesh.

Source: Statistics Canada. 2022. Table 37-10-0086-01. Postsecondary enrolments, by status of student in Canada, country of citizenship and gender. https://www150.statcan.gc.ca/

Of the nearly 390,000 international student enrolments in postsecondary institutions in 2019, 60 percent were either South Asian or East Asian; students from South Asia comprised over 127,600 or 33 percent and students from East Asia numbered more than 106,700 or 27 percent. To show the rapid growth of student mobility from Asia during this new period of federal coordination, we present the numbers of postsecondary students from seven Asian countries at two time points, 2014 and 2019, disaggregated by institution type in Table I.1. The largest group of postsecondary international students, at 117,500, came from India. This is an increase of nearly 300 percent from 2014, and approximately 31 percent of them enrolled in universities. They have, by far, the most substantial international presence in colleges, representing over half of all international students in colleges. The second largest group, from China, comprised over 90,000 postsecondary enrolments in 2019 and this group grew 26 percent from 2014 when it was the largest country of origin of students that year. Currently, over 86 percent of students from China enrol in universities, in contrast to their counterparts from India, and they form the most sizable group in universities, representing over 33 percent of international students in universities. Their significant proportions in many institutions explains why they are the focus of most of the chapters in this volume. Together, students from these two countries made up over 53 percent of all postsecondary international enrolments with students from India at 30 percent and students from China at 23 percent.

Vietnam has also risen in the rankings of postsecondary international student numbers and we anticipate this trend to continue. Where there were fewer students from Vietnam than from Korea in 2014, their student population in Canada grew by over 300 percent to stand at nearly 11,000 in 2019. Like India, the majority of students from Vietnam enrolled in colleges (68 percent). The remaining countries on the list, Korea, Bangladesh, Philippines, and Japan, also grew over the period but numbered less than 5,000 each in 2019. In these groups, we also observe a shift toward college enrolment, with students from Korea and the Philippines primarily going to colleges rather than universities. The shift to colleges, which is a clear and recent trend during this federalization period, may be explained by the appeal of the shorter time it takes to completion, the more direct connections to the labour market and subsequent permanent residence, and greater accessibility in terms of admission requirements and lower tuition fees relative to universities. These factors call for more research on international students in colleges, which is an emerging area, as there are indications to suggest that the college route is not consistently the most efficient for obtaining professional licences or permanent residence (Walton-Roberts and Hennebry 2019).

Students from the above seven countries in Asia represented 53 percent of the total postsecondary international student enrolments in 2014 and

Table I.1 Postsecondary enrolments of international students from selected countries in Asia by institution type, 2014 and 2019

	2014			2019			Total Growth (%)
	Total	University	College	Total	University	College	
India	29,487	9,027	11,820	117,477	36,927	80,550	298
China	71,844	53,472	12,069	90,378	78,183	12,198	26
Vietnam	2,625	1,185	1,032	10,881	3,516	7,365	315
Korea	6,324	3,570	2,472	8,421	3,888	4,533	33
Bangladesh	2,157	1,875	123	5,496	4,548	951	155
Philippines	867	375	306	3,624	630	2,997	318
Japan	2,844	1,830	987	3,147	1,974	1,173	11
Column total	116,148	71,334	28,809	239,424	129,666	109,767	165
% of total IS (%)	53	45	50	62	55	72	
Total IS	217,521	159,393	58,125	388,782	235,419	153,360	79

Source: Statistics Canada. 2022. Table 37-10-0086-01. Postsecondary enrolments, by status of student in Canada, country of citizenship and gender. https://www150.statcan.gc.ca/

62 percent in 2019. Among university enrolments, they comprised 55 percent in 2019, up from 45 percent in 2014 (Table I.1). While there is variation in students from Asia across institutions and geographic locations, the federal strategy unequivocally brought greater attention to these countries as important targets for recruitment and retention by educational institutions, including universities.

Notably, the more recent report underscores the need to diversify countries of origin due to this overconcentration of international students from India and China (Government of Canada 2019). The absence of numerical and country targets in the present strategy raises questions about an implicit saturation point, particularly with respect to certain countries of origin. And given the ways in which international students from Asia have been problematically represented or rendered invisible in official institutional documents and promotional materials and the ways in which they experience life inside and outside of these institutions, as illustrated in this collection, "diversify" might be interpreted as code for "less Asian." Thus, prior to embarking on this diversification of international students, we must evaluate where things stand for the students who are here now and who have paid their dues in myriad ways.

The revenue indicator

In terms of overall enrolment figures and specific numbers from identified source countries, Canada's internationalizing initiatives are highly successful. Economic benefits have also exceeded expectations, rising from an estimated $8.4 billion in spending by international students in 2012 to $21.6 billion in 2018, surpassing the goal set at $16.1 billion as well as having a greater impact on the economy than other large industries such as auto parts, lumber, and aircraft (Government of Canada 2014, 2019). This is not difficult to believe when we examine how exorbitantly tuition rose for international students relative to resident[2] students during this federalization period.

Historically, fees were not differentiated for international students, but this changed in 1977 beginning with Ontario and Alberta (Cameron 2006). Since resident fees are subsidized by the government and taxpayers, international student fees are significantly higher, although there are exceptions.[3] Figure I.3 presents the annual average undergraduate tuition fee in Canada from 2007 to 2022 for international and resident students. In 2007, the mean undergraduate fee for international students, which includes professional programs such as law and medicine, was $17,615, compared to $5,322 for a resident student – a gap of $12,293. This mean fee jumped to over $40,000 for international students and $9,000 for resident students in 2022 with a gap of $31,452. To appreciate the effect of federalization on

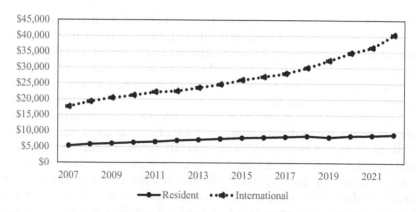

Figure I.3 Undergraduate tuition fees for international and resident students, 2007–2022.

Source: Statistics Canada. 2022. Table 37-10-0003-01. Canadian undergraduate tuition fees by field of study. https://www150.statcan.gc.ca/

Note: "Resident student" refers to within-province students, those who are generally known as "domestic" students. "Resident" is a more appropriate term since many universities also charge a differential fee for out of province Canadian students.

international students from a slightly different angle is to examine the percentage change from 2007, when the national branding campaign began, to 2014, when the first federal strategy was published, and then to present-day. The 2007–2014 period saw a roughly 40 percent rise in tuition fees for both international and resident students. During the federalization of education migration period, from 2014 to the present, we observed the tuition fees soaring 64 percent higher for international students compared to the 19 percent increase for resident students who also started at a lower baseline. It is very difficult to justify this substantial disparity in fees and to not view the growing gap as exploitative. It also provokes questions about all public stakeholders contributing and benefitting from the federalization of education migration, including provincial governments and postsecondary institutions, to ask whether they are doing enough for international students who live in and interact within local communities and are exposed to the day-to-day dynamics of race and other social tensions. This is one of the tasks of this volume and we use the federal strategy's stated objectives and outcomes in enrolment, places of origin, and revenue to provide the backdrop for more critical perspectives on internationalization.

After more than five years since the publication of the 2014 strategy, universities have developed their own institutional approach to increasing their intake of international students. With promises of a high quality and world-class education in a safe and multicultural country, we put forth the argument that institutions bear some responsibility to international students and to create a more welcoming and accepting society for international students, among others. Universities were not welcoming places for international students 40 years ago (Cameron 2006) and they remain lacking in areas shown in the chapters presented here. Inclusion, exclusion, experiences of anti-Asian racism, equity, and Indigenization – these are the measures by which internationalization should also be assessed. The difference between the past and the present is that internationalization plans are now directly put in relation to the work needed to address questions of racial inequities on campuses. However, the tools to address issues relating to discrimination and racialization have been broadly defined through initiatives pertaining to equity and inclusion (Henry, Dua, Kobayashi, James, Li, Ramos, and Smith 2017, 309) and while international students from Asia have been re-defining the Canadian university landscape for many years, the current focus on addressing racial inequities in Canadian postsecondary institutions rarely addresses the intersection between internationalization and anti-racism strategies in Canadian universities.

About the book

This collection is inspired by the Racialization of Asian International Students (RAIS) Project, a multi-institutional study of students from China, India, and South Korea, funded by the Social Sciences and Humanities Research Council of Canada. Most chapters tend to focus on these groups, primarily China, and larger institutions, which is also a convergence of recent demographic history, geo-political dynamics, and scholarly attention. While we strived for representation in terms of regions, institutions, and groups, we recognize there is less attention in the book to smaller institutions and regions and to groups from Asia with fewer international students, all of whom deserve a greater voice, and we expect to hear them in future work. In this collection, we offer some critical analyses of the types of institutions who recruit large numbers of international students and of which groups from Asia are admitted as students. And we advise caution in generalizing the experiences of the groups under study to other international student groups from Asia and elsewhere. We acknowledge the limitations of a book that focuses on specific groups from Asia and Asians and attempts to draw conclusions about Asian experiences; there is no singular Asian experience. At the same time, there are broader lessons to be learned in the experiences of particular groups, and with the diversifying phase of internationalization in which we currently find ourselves, these lessons will prove invaluable. The studies shown here demonstrate shared experiences under the themes but differences across groups and regions are highlighted as well.

There are three main sections in the collection to meet our objectives to examine the intersection of internationalization, inclusion, and racialization. The first section includes five complementary chapters that offer critical assessments of how government and institutional strategies and priorities on internationalization fit with values of inclusion and diversity. Beck sets the scene for examining international student experiences through her critical analysis of federal strategies and policies around internationalization and multiculturalism. She argues that these textual practices construct students as economic assets and create the ideological frame that structures international student lives. Where international students are also written as bearers of culture, this diversity is rendered invisible on campuses. Like Beck, the second chapter, by Buckner, Knight-Grofe, and Eden, offers a discursive interrogation but of the international strategies of 32 colleges and universities to contrast the framing of Asia and Europe. Although many priority activities are similar, they find Asia is often constructed as a source of students while Europe is a source of research partnerships. In the third chapter, Montsion and Caneo also find the erasure of the culture and diversity of students in university settings by examining the role played by the relationships between each institution and their provincial government. They argue that part of the problem is the main focus on international students from Asia as economic assets, which they show through an analysis of Ontario's Strategic Mandate Agreements with three Toronto-based universities: the University of Toronto, Toronto Metropolitan University, and York University. Moving to BC, Chan and Matsushita examine the increasing privatization of the college to university transfer system, particularly among international students and their representation in BCCAT (BC Council on Admissions and Transfers) Articulation meeting reports as being ill-prepared and not diverse enough. This section culminates with an important chapter by Das Gupta and Gomez that reveals how the internationalization of universities, in practice, has been fundamentally inequitable and untreatable by EDI programs, which, they argue, are themselves largely performative. Together, these five chapters tell us that diversity in internationalization and EDI policies appear to be more aspiration rhetoric than praxis and the chapters in the next two sections provide an evaluation of some of these claims. Several of the chapters in this first section also engage, directly or indirectly, with the question of the central location of the university in the policy realms of education, economy, and border control.

The six chapters in the second section differ in focus but overlap on the theme of inclusion and exclusion experiences of students in universities. Kim, Abdulkarim, and Payne find student assessments with respect to inclusion and other features of institutions to vary according to place of origin thereby pointing to the range of experiences of students from Asia.

Using the Canadian Bureau of International Education (CBIE) 2018 International Student Survey, they find students from India and the Philippines to be more positive than those from China, South Korea, and Vietnam. Despite these differences, less than half of all groups strongly agreed with feeling included in classrooms and less than a third strongly agreed that others in the institution demonstrated interest in their country and culture. In Chapter 7, Kwak, Lo, Pang, and Wang compare the distinctiveness of students from China going to Halifax, an intellectual periphery, and to Toronto, an intellectual gateway. Despite these differences, they show barriers to integration to be similar across sites. Turning to a university in Western Canada, Yu's chapter also informs us about social exclusion and experiences of systemic discrimination for Chinese undergraduate students undergoing multiple types of transitions as they go from high school to university. These experiences are also shared by students from China in Quebec, as de Oliviera Soares, Magnan, Yu, and Araneda show in their chapter that highlights a range of barriers to institutional services at four universities in Montreal. Similarly, back in Ontario, Tavares reveals the experiences of academic, social, and linguistic exclusion to be common in the narratives of three undergraduate students, one each from Hong Kong, Macao, and Taiwan. The final chapter in this section, Chapter 11 by Pang and Smith, offers a theoretical contribution in its revision of Alexander W. Astin's *Inputs-Environments-Outcomes* (I-E-O) model that emphasizes the interaction of international students with their institutional environments that results in certain kinds of outcomes related to student success. The chapters in this second section inform us that regardless of whether social inclusion and exclusion occur on or off campus, international students tend to view these experiences through the lens of internationalization and their institutional identity as international students.

In the third and final section, we have five chapters that address anti-Asian racism and the politics of race in different but meaningful ways. In Chapter 12, Buckner, Kim, and Vlahos show there is a contradiction between the University of Toronto's promotion of its international students as multicultural and its reality that a high concentration (65 percent) of international students come from China. The glossing over of the actual composition of the international student body in this way, they contend, suggests the institution fears being perceived as "too Asian," a media-induced marker by which Canadian universities have been pejoratively assessed. The following chapter by Parasram, Gateman, and Kazmi gives voice to six Dalhousie University students from India and China and situates their racialized experiences within the anti-Black and anti-Indigenous racial politics of Halifax and Dalhousie's international strategy. Similarly, Wilkinson and Luo discuss racism at the University of Manitoba in light of broader Indigenization efforts in Winnipeg and reveal the range of institutional issues that impinge on international students from Asia who comprise almost two thirds of international students. Chapter 15 focuses on students in China and elsewhere on their perceptions of anti-Chinese racism in various places, including Canada. The authors, Zhang, Yuan, and Kang, show that Canada is viewed more negatively and that participants attribute anti-Asian racism to geo-political relations. The final chapter in this section, by Kim, Chung, Jeon, Klassen, Kwak, Shin, and Trudel, offers a look at students from South Korea and they find racial incidents across Toronto, Saskatoon, Halifax, and Albany in the US to be similar, often occurring in public spaces with comments and behaviours that illustrate the enduring trope of fear and disease. They also find incidents were recounted in ways that reflected the politics of race in Canada and the US. While the five chapters in this section cover multiple groups, institutions, countries, and regions in Canada, they demonstrate that a deeper understanding of anti-Asian racism requires drawing connections between individual or personal experiences and broader forces of race dynamics linked to places.

The Covid-19 pandemic has resulted in a rise of anti-Asian racism in Canada and questions of racialization in the Canadian context echo other calls for addressing racial inequities in other countries and globally (Gover, Harper, and Langton 2020; Tate and Bagguley 2017). For this reason, we hope the insights from this collection will engage scholars, researchers, teachers, policymakers, and practitioners in a broader discussion on the necessity of connecting internationalization strategies to anti-racist principles.

Notes

1 Colleges in Canada are distinctive from universities. Colleges tend to be shorter, often two-year programs, and offer certificate programs, diplomas, apprenticeships, and degrees. Universities offer undergraduate and graduate degrees and other professional programs. https://www.ontario.ca/page/go-college-or-university-ontario
2 "Resident" refers to within-province students who have previously been labelled "domestic" students, that is students with Canadian citizenship or permanent residence. "Resident (within-province)" is a more appropriate term since many universities charge higher fees for out of province Canadian students, which is still less than the fees for international students.
3 In Quebec, there are study fee exemptions at institutions outside of Montreal and for particular groups: https://www.quebec.ca/en/education/study-quebec/financial-assistance-international-students/

References

Cameron, James D. 2006. International Student Integration into the Canadian University: A Post-World War Two Historical Case Study. *History of Intellectual Culture* 6, no. 1. Retrieved October 5, 2022. https://journalhosting.ucalgary.ca/index.php/hic.

Colomba, Roland Sintos. 2013. "Too Asian?" On Racism, Paradox and Ethno-Nationalism. *Discourse: Studies in the Cultural Politics of Education* 34, no. 4: 579–598.

Crossman, Eden, Youjin Choi, Yuqian Lu, and Feng Hou. 2022. International Students as a Source of Labour Supply: A Summary of Recent Trends. Statistics Canada, Economic and Social Reports 36-28-0001.

Gover, Angela R., Shannon B. Harper, and Lynn Langton. 2020. Anti-Asian Hate Crime during the COVID-19 Pandemic: Exploring the Reproduction of Inequality. *American Journal of Criminal Justice* 45, no. 4: 647–667.

Government of Canada. 2014. Canada's International Education Strategy: Harnessing Our Knowledge Advantage to Drive Innovation and Prosperity. https://www.international.gc.ca/education/assets/pdfs/overview-apercu-eng.pdf.

Government of Canada. 2019. Building on Success: International Education Strategy, 2019-2024. https://www.international.gc.ca/education/assets/pdfs/ies-sei/Building-on-Success-International-Education-Strategy-2019-2024.pdf.

Henry, Frances, Enakshi Dua, Audrey Kobayashi, Carl James, Peter Li, Howard Ramos, and Malinda Smith. 2017. Race, Racialization and Indigeneity in Canadian Universities. *Race, Ethnicity and Education* 20, no. 3: 300–314.

Institute of International Education. 2020. "Project Atlas 2020: A Quick Look at Global Mobility Trends." https://iie.widen.net/s/g2bqxwkwqv/project-atlas-infographics-2020.

Kim, Ann H., Elizabeth Buckner, and Jean Michel Montsion. 2022. Introduction to Special Issue: International Students from Asia in Canada's Postsecondary Institutions: Disconnections and Connections. *Comparative and International Education / Éducation Comparée et Internationale* 51, no. 1. https://doi.org/10.5206/cieeci.v51i1.15481.

Kim, Ann H., and Min-Jung Kwak (eds). 2019. *Outward and Upward Mobilities: International Students in Canada, Their Families, and Structuring Institutions.* Toronto: University of Toronto Press.

Statistics Canada. 2021. Prior to COVID-19, International Students Accounted for the Growth in Postsecondary Enrolments and Graduates. *The Daily* 11-001-X. November 24.

Statistics Canada. 2022. Table 37-10-0086-01 Postsecondary Enrolments, by Status of Student in Canada, Country of Citizenship and Gender.

Tate, Shirley Anne, and Paul Bagguley. 2017. Building the Anti-Racist University: Next Steps. *Race, Ethnicity and Education* 20, no. 3: 289–299.

Walton-Roberts, Margaret, and Jenna Hennebry. 2019. "Bumpy Roads: Tracing Pathways into Practice for International Students in Nursing." In *Outward and Upward Mobilities: International Students in Canada, Their Families, and Structuring Institutions*, edited by Ann H. Kim and Min-Jung Kwak, 246–265. Toronto: University of Toronto Press.

Section I

Institutional Contexts
A Critical View

1 The Ruling Relations of the Internationalizing Canadian University

Kumari Beck

Introduction

Growing up, in Sri Lanka, I was well immersed in the belief that one had to go to a university in the UK or the US for the best education and the most advanced knowledge. The dream was well beyond my reach at the time. Years later, after immigrating to Canada, and in the midst of raising a family, I had the opportunity of working in an international teacher education program and was introduced to the world of international education. I also signed up for graduate school. In this dual capacity, I came to know the cohorts of teachers and administrators who came from elsewhere for professional development and many international students studying at the university. The stories of challenge, resilience, discrimination, accomplishment, isolation, hardship, struggle, and pride fueled my research interests in the experiences of international students, an under-researched topic at the time.

It was about this time that the notion of internationalization of higher education came into its own, with Jane Knight emerging as a leading scholar in the field. Her conceptualization of internationalization has become very influential among institutions, practitioners, and scholars in Canada and globally. The definitions (Knight 2004) held a promise of educating for global citizenship, of intercultural learning and an internationalized curriculum, and of higher education institutions reflecting a global ethos in a globalizing world. The internationalization movement propelled Canadian higher education institutions to host students from other parts of the world who would, by their very presence, diversify the institution and prompt intercultural learning. It was assumed that internationalization was an inevitable progression for higher education and good for everyone. Accordingly, the students were recruited, and they came in their hundreds, and then thousands. As shown in the introductory chapter (Kim, Buckner, and Montsion), 600,000 international students were studying in Canada in 2021 and roughly 65% of them were from

DOI: 10.4324/b23160-3

countries in Asia. They were all promised a high-quality education and a welcoming and safe environment based on Canada being a model of multiculturalism in practice.

Contrary to these aspirations, however, research and media have documented troubling accounts of international student experiences of mental health issues, racism, multiple forms of discrimination, bullying and harassment, and sexual assault, along with other forms of well-recognized challenges faced by international students such as culture shock, loneliness, and so on (Appia 2021; Canada Bound Immigrant n.d.; Dey and Williams 2021; Houshmand, Spanierman and Tafarodi 2014). According to the most recent survey conducted by the Canadian Bureau of International Education (CBIE 2021), 55% of the respondents of which were from Asia, the majority of international students were satisfied with their time in Canada despite many challenges. Some of these challenges were logistical or technical – such as arranging for accommodation, transferring funds, and obtaining a study visa. Regarding safety, well-being and inclusion, however, many respondents felt isolated and unwelcomed. More concerning and of relevance to the topic under study, "[s]tudent respondents from Asia were significantly more likely to report having experienced discrimination, harassment or feeling unsafe, especially in off-campus settings" (5). Furthermore, the COVID-19 pandemic has increased the vulnerabilities faced by international students (Firang 2020; Varughese and Schwartz 2022) and has resulted in a spike in anti-Asian racism and hatred (Appia 2021; Gill 2020; Kurl, Korzinski and Noels 2020). Even prior to the pandemic, some media articles promoted negative views of international students, and, in particular, international students from Asia (Findlay and Köhler 2010; Todd 2016).

International students on our campuses appear to be exercising their educational choices by participating in the internationalization process, and yet are impacted by forces that are outside of their choosing. To understand this better, I have selected concepts in institutional ethnography (IE) (Smith 1987, 1990, 2005) to support this analysis. The attraction of IE is the centrality of people, their actions, their views, and their relations with the world around them and the notion that relations external to them order their lives. In this chapter, I argue that texts central to internationalization and international education, such as definitions of internationalization, and policies of international education have a role in the governance of international student life. I hope to demonstrate that these texts of internationalization and their ideological frames form the ruling relations of the institution (the university) as they order the lives of international students from Asia.

I am turning to IE not as an empirical methodology but rather to employ IE concepts to identify the ordering of the relations of internationalization. In a sense, it is about understanding how the internationalizing university is produced through ideological frames that become the ruling relations of internationalization. In an interview about IE, Smith states: "You are looking at these relations, which have a generalizing, standardizing kind of character. And so you are actually discovering things" (Carroll 2011, 22). As she explains further, *thinking* like an institutional ethnographer "has this capacity to open things up" (24). It is in the spirit of opening things up that I seek, in this paper, to think like an institutional ethnographer and to name some of the texts that contribute to ruling relations that order the lives of international students from Asia studying in Canadian universities. These analyses may be applicable to all international students, but are particularly relevant to international students from Asia.

I will first make a case for how IE thinking informs my sense-making by describing how the conceptual application of IE is useful for my analysis. Next, I will examine selected texts to show how they constitute the ruling relations of internationalization, and, in particular, how they order the lives of Asian international students studying in Canada. The texts I have selected are the prevailing definitions of internationalization that are popular in Canada, the federal policies on international education, and multiculturalism. I conclude this chapter with reflections on how IE thinking and ruling relations inform our understanding of the structural dimensions governing international students from Asia.

IE Thinking

[T]he everyday of our lives is organized by what we have come to call *ruling relations* – relations that, though we participate in them, impose their objectified modes upon us.

(Smith and Griffith 2022, 7)

Smith was interested in social relations and how they are constituted, and in IE, aimed "to create a sociology *for* rather than *of* people that can expand the scope of our knowledge of what we are part of but cannot apprehend directly" (Smith and Griffith 2022, xiv, emphasis in original). As Smith has asserted through many of her publications, IE is not a qualitative method; it is a sociology. "[I]t seeks to discover just how actual people's doings are coordinated with others so that what we might call the ongoing social organizing of our everyday lives actually happens" (Smith and Griffith 2022, 3). IE is primarily used in empirical research, but it offers entry points to textual analysis that accomplish the objective of uncovering ruling relations and the social organizing of everyday lives to which Smith refers.

How, then, might an IE approach in textual analysis be similar to or different from discourse analysis? The notion of 'discourse' is prominent among the concepts used in IE, and Smith follows a Foucauldian usage of the term as being produced, ordered, and distributed (Smith and Griffith 2022). Building on that, discourse in IE refers to translocal relations, "an organization of relations" (Smith and Griffith 2022, 34) that order the practices of people and the institution. Ruling relations brings attention to what Smith calls "a complex of objectified relations, coordinating the activities of many, many people whose consciousness as subjects is formed within those relations" (Smith 1996, 175). Smith acknowledges that these relations are an organization of power but asserts that they are not monolithic nor hegemonic. "They are activities in and in relation to texts, and texts coordinate them as relations" (176). Texts have the property of being replicable, and this replicability makes it possible for them to be active in multiple sites and settings, extending the extent of power: "it is the materiality of the text itself that connects the local setting into the non-local relations that it bears" (176). It is this connection between translocal relations and the ordering of international students' everyday lives that I seek to make in this chapter.

The analysis of the texts of internationalization will illuminate how "ruling knowledge" (Campbell and Manicom 1995, 9) is created, making it possible to create ruling actions in what can be called a "textual technology" (Smith and Turner 2014, 11). In this analysis, I am using Roxana Ng's (1995) analysis of multiculturalism as ideology as the exemplar. Ng follows Smith's (1990 cited in Ng 1995, 36) methods of textual analysis, where text is taken up as "a constituent of a social relation" (36), recognizing that "the interpretive practices which activate it are embedded in a relational process. Textual practices are operative in the work of accomplishing the social relations in which texts occur" (36). Ng uses the notion of "ideological frame" to argue that multiculturalism is "an artefact *produced* by ... administrative processes" (35) and a concept that was "constructed and articulated to a bureaucratic process so that it is treated as a fact" (35). She argues further that when such a frame is in place, it normalizes the ideas contained in the frame so that they are taken for granted, become common sense, and the initiating process itself becomes invisible. It makes it possible for its implementation as an institutional or state policy.

Following this line of thinking, I argue in this chapter that internationalization has become an ideological frame; the ideas within that frame become normalized and common sense. I will demonstrate through selected texts how this has been produced and constructed to form the ruling relations of internationalization. I suggest that definitions of internationalization, federal and provincial and other policy texts of internationalization, and institutional websites and policies, for example, could be considered as the more obvious texts of internationalization (see Buckner, Knight-Grofe, and Eden, as well as Montsion and Caneo). Other texts that are less visible, but as I shall demonstrate are very much connected, are multiculturalism and Canada's various immigration policies that are antecedents for the current climate in which international students from Asia are immersed. As indicated earlier, I will limit the discussion here to definitions of internationalization, two federal policy documents, and the Multiculturalism Act of Canada (1988).

Texts, Ideologies, and Ruling Relations

"[A] central task of ruling is to organize and generate knowledge in a form that is useful for ruling practice".

(Campbell and Manicom 1995, 9)

Definitions of Internationalization

A key text that has been influential in generating initial knowledge about internationalization is the definition of the term over the past two decades. The Jane Knight definition (first described in 1994, subsequently updated in a study in 2003, cited in Knight 2004) has guided the rationale, purpose, and direction of international higher education in institutions across Canada. It reflects what Knight called a "process approach": "the process of integrating an international, intercultural or global dimension into the purpose, functions or delivery of post-secondary education" (Knight 2003, cited in Knight 2004, 11). Others such as Hudzik's (2011) description of comprehensive internationalization have emerged and Knight's definition has been revised (de Wit and Hunter 2015) to denote intentionality and social justice outcomes for internationalization, but the main idea remains undisturbed. These definitions convey the idea that internationalization, the process, is neutral in that it arose naturally and is an inevitable outcome of the interconnectedness of the world as a consequence of globalization. In this way, they contribute to the facticity of internationalization and have become common sense, in the Gramscian way of thinking (Ng 1995). As common sense, internationalization is inevitable, a fact, good for everyone, unassailable, and beyond critique.

There are a number of ways in which these texts could be taken up by institutions. For one, the common sense of internationalization lends legitimacy to the recruitment of international students, particularly from culturally different places. Students becoming a key driver of internationalization is a common-sense strategy as a means of bringing culture and a global or international ethos into the university. Internationalization as common sense becomes more problematic as it hides the asymmetrical power relations and colonial hierarchies that order the geopolitics of international relations. Internationalization is not ahistorical – it has its roots in development assistance programs and activities following World War II, including faculty and student exchanges, technical assistance, and program development and delivery (Trilokekar 2010). Known as humane internationalism (Trilokekar 2010), these activities, supported by federal development assistance policies, have reproduced colonial patterns of mobility and Western knowledges and values. Mobilities were primarily from Global South to the North and the continued establishment of Western expertise constituted "academic imperialism" (de Wit 2002). People from the Global South were constructed as deficient and in need of improvement and this evaluation extended to students who were brought over to campuses in the Global North or to whom educational instruction was delivered.

When international students, especially those from Asian countries, arrive in Canada the identity they take up of 'international student' is, on the one hand, the highly desired bearer of culture, and yet on the other, as "unworthy or inferior participants in the contest for social mobility" (Stein and de Andreotti 2016, 226) in their English or French language and knowledge deficiencies. In the classic colonial trope, they are simultaneously exotic and inferior. As Bhabha (1994) theorizes, relations of power and authority in the colonial context operate ambivalently and marks colonial discourse in terms of inherent contradictions. It "produces the colonized as a social reality which is at once an 'other' and yet entirely knowable and visible" (Bhabha 1994, 70–71), the "'otherness' which is at once an object of desire and derision" (67). In the everyday lives of international students, the identity of 'international' itself turns into a negative stereotype that limits how international students are perceived and received, making it difficult for the students themselves to be anything else. The objectification of students as economic assets, and more recently, even "ideal immigrants" (Scott et al. 2015) sets up another tension between the students as desired and their reality of being treated as deficient (Stein and de Andreotti 2016).

Canadian Policies of Internationalization

Federal and provincial policies on international education and institutional strategic plans on internationalization are important sources of texts for this inquiry as they provide the sanction and the rules governing the recruitment of international students. For the purposes of this chapter, I will limit myself to examining the two main federal policies: *Canada's International Education Strategy: Harnessing our knowledge advantage to drive innovation and prosperity (2014–2019)* and *Building on Success: International Education Strategy (2019–2024)*.

The first Canadian strategy (Government of Canada 2014) unashamedly refers to international education as an economic enterprise: the opening message from the Minister of Trade states "international education is at the very heart of our current and future prosperity" (Government of Canada 2014, 4). The strategy was developed under Canada's Global Markets Action Plan and the commodity being marketed is education. The listed benefits of international education for Canadians are economic, with the primary benefit being the billions that international students spend in Canada. Other benefits include jobs created, addressing skilled labor shortages and ensuring the vitality of the labor force. The dominant tone of the document is that of "branding Canada to maximize success" (10) in order to realize those benefits in a competitive global marketplace. The main branding strategy was the *Edu-Canada* program, with its "Imagine Education au/in Canada" brand, which resulted in a 51% increase in the numbers of international students coming to Canada over the five-year period of the program. According to the document, the success of the program resulted in a resolve to 'refresh' the brand (10) and to set new targets: "Increasing the number of international students to more than 450,000 will create new sources of jobs, economic growth and prosperity in every region of the country" (11). The markets that are targeted are from developing and emerging economies, with three of the six countries identified being Asian (China, India, and Vietnam). The document also lists the key attraction for international students as recognizing "Canada's value proposition – a consistently high-quality education at an attractive price in a tolerant, diverse, safe and welcoming environment" (10).

This strategy can be critiqued at multiple levels, but one relevant to the present inquiry is that it casts international students as 'cash cows'. They "create at least 86,500 new jobs", spend "over $16.1 billion", "provide an annual boost to the Canadian economy of almost $10 billion", and "generate almost $910 million in new tax revenues" (Roslyn Kunin and Associates 2012 as cited in DFATD 2014, 11). The identity of "international student" locks students into a negative stereotype of the wealthy "foreigner", a perception that has been taken up by media as well. It is common to see stories about wealthy Asian international students: "Well-off foreign students are increasingly coming to Canada to obtain a variety of advantages, including for their families" (Todd 2016).

The second strategy, *Building on Success* (Government of Canada 2019), focuses more on encouraging Canadian students to go abroad, but the overall theme is still one of marketing Canadian education to international students in "key global markets" (7). The strategy is aligned with trade diversification ("New Markets, New Customers, New Jobs"), which leads to the objective of diversifying international student source countries, although China and India are still cited as important. The Student Direct

Stream service for fast-tracking visas offered previously only to students from Asian countries (China, India, Philippines, and Vietnam) will be expanded to other countries. An added emphasis is the access offered to international students for "pathways to permanent residency" (2) and "timely immigration services" (10).

The document is rife with the language of trade, markets, and competition, maintaining the idea that international education is primarily a matter of buying and selling. Global learning outcomes are tied to prosperity and success in the job market. Similar to the previous policy text, it authorizes the continued wooing of international students with "peaceful, welcoming and diverse communities; an enviable quality of life; opportunities to work and start careers; and pathways to permanent residency" (2). Students are simultaneously objectified as both talent and customers. Another noticeable addition to this document is the tone of national exceptionalism that carries on the neocolonial deficiency messaging that is imposed on students.

Multiculturalism

Canada's multiculturalism has been referred to in federal, provincial, and institutional policies as being one of the main reasons for Canada's popularity as a destination for international students (CBIE 2021; DFATD 2014; GAC 2019). Premised on the recognition of "the importance of preserving and enhancing the multicultural heritage of Canadians" (Government of Canada 1988), among other points, the Multiculturalism Act recognizes and promotes the understanding that multiculturalism reflects the cultural and racial diversities of Canadian society and acknowledges the freedom of all members of Canadian society to preserve, enhance, and share their cultural heritage (Government of Canada 1988).

Among others, the policy "ensure[s] that "all individuals receive equal treatment and equal protection under the law, while respecting and valuing their diversity" (Government of Canada 1988). This promise is used as a marketing tool to demonstrate how Canada is not just a safe space but a welcoming one to international students, no matter their country of origin.

Multiculturalism is seen as a Canadian success and part of Canadian identity (Simpson, James, and Mack 2011). It presents a way for Canadians and others to think of Canadian society in particular ways and projects multiculturalism as fact (Ng 1995; Simpson et al. 2011). The Multiculturalism policy promotes the 'fact' that by virtue of the policy, equal opportunities exist for everyone and that difference of varied kinds is welcomed. Multiculturalism is "so consistently and thoroughly asserted that most of those who take up its investments are unable to see its construction or even its existence" (Simpson et al. 2011, 287).

The Multicultural Act is, in my view, a key text that belongs in this discussion on ruling relations because of its emphasis on culture as the signifier of difference rather than race. Multiculturalism presumes and promotes the myth of cultural freedom, racial equity, and harmonious social relations in Canada (Simpson et al. 2011; Thobani 2007). Although multiculturalism purportedly invites diversity, that diversity is ranked against Whiteness that is equated to being Canadian. Multiculturalism is also seen as evidence of "the good nation" (Schick and St Denis 2005, 295), where tolerance of culturally different peoples is seen as the success of multiculturalism, but conceals relations of coloniality and race. Thus, minoritized and racialized people are often blamed for the rise in racism. As Henry and Tator (2006) argue, "it allows for the preservation of the cultural hegemony of the dominant cultural group ... [and fails] to deal with the problems of systemic racism in Canada" (Henry and Tator 2006, 49). Furthermore, the 'co-existence' of diverse groups as evidence of the success of multiculturalism makes it difficult for the reporting of discrimination and racism, which is deemed to be an individual problem.

Multiculturalism has resulted in the erasure of the history of anti-Asian racism. Coloma (2013) reviews these trends noting that the Chinese, Indians, and Japanese were welcomed into the country to work in mining, railway construction, fishing, agriculture, and lumber industries, but their immigration, citizenship, and rights were drastically limited when perceived to be a threat. He concludes: "Asians' economic usefulness was their key to enter Canada's racialized gates of labor, migration and eventual citizenship" (580). The parallels with the contemporary context of international students from Asia become apparent: their economic usefulness brings them to Canada, where they are then deemed to be a threat to local students, stereotyped, and racialized (see Sections 2 and 3). What becomes apparent is how the ideological frame of multiculturalism erases race by centering culture as its central concept. It validates international students from Asia and elsewhere as having cultural capital, and hence, invalidates and erases racism and multiple forms of discrimination they may face as individual problems.

Conclusion

I began this inquiry as an experimental exploration to apply IE thinking and textual analysis to understand how Asian international students are constructed and ruled by factors, discourses, and ideologies that shape their experiences in Canadian universities. What brought IE to my attention was the possibility of uncovering the hidden role of institutions in the cycle of international student life in a Canadian university. The notion of ruling relations resonated in accounting for how Asian students' lives can be coordinated by specific texts. It was, in Smith's terms, a way of seeing how the everyday experiences of students (the local reality) came to be and how various texts in internationalization are brought into action to coordinate and order the local through the translocal. I have illustrated the possibilities of this mode of inquiry by engaging in an introductory analysis of specific texts – definitions of internationalization and federal policies on international education and multiculturalism.

The implications of uncovering ruling relations of internationalization are that we can identify how texts and practices play into coordinating relations of the university. The identification of "textual technologies" (Smith and Turner 2014) turns our attention away from international students being the focus of their own problems and challenges to concealed power relations that influence their lives. Texts of internationalization are taken up in multiple ways by institutions, and although they are separate, often act in concert. For example, educational objectives of internationalization, such as educating for global citizenship (identified through the definitions and varied conceptualizations of internationalization), and practices such as recruiting students (established through federal and provincial strategies) involve fitting the students into the frames and discourses of internationalization. The discourses of multiculturalism are employed by federal policies to brand Canada as a welcoming destination and fit in well with the objectives of teaching for intercultural learning.

The uncovering of ruling relations in international higher education demonstrates how power continues to become reified through administrative practices. The relevance to this inquiry is in how the institutional identity of 'international student' is formed and constructed by discursive relations ordered by such texts as definitions and conceptualizations of internationalization, government and institutional policies, and multiculturalism. IE thinking can lead to identifying other texts, such as language policies and practices, language tests for admission, and institutional policies on equity, diversity, and inclusion and many others. IE thinking and a recognition of ruling relations lead to a greater understanding of how power is organized in internationalizing universities and focus attention on how forms of knowledge are objectified through texts and coordinate and order everyday lives.

References

Appia, Veronica. 2021. "Timeline: This Is Canada's History of Anti-Asian Racism that COVID-19 Has Amplified." Retrieved in June 15, 2022, from https://www.toronto.com/news-story/10349793-timeline-this-is-canada-s-history-of-anti-asian-racism-that-covid-19-has-amplified/
Bhabha, Homi. 1994. *The Location of Culture*. London: Routledge.

Campbell, Marie and Ann Manicom (Eds). 1995. *Knowledge, Experience and Ruling Relations: Stories in the Social Organization of Knowledge.* Buffalo, Toronto: University of Toronto Press.

Canada Bound Immigrant. n.d. "It's Challenging Being an International Student in Canada". Retrieved from https://www.canadaboundimmigrant.com/top-stories/its-challenging-being-an-international-student-in-canada

Carroll, William K. 2011. "'You Are Here': An Interview with Dorothy E. Smith." *Socialist Studies (St. Albert)* 6, no. 2.

CBIE. 2021. "The Student Voice: National Results of the 2021 International Student Survey." Canadian Bureau for International Education. Retrieved in January 2022, from https://cbie.ca/wp-content/uploads/2022/07/CBIE_2021_International_Student_Survey_National_Report.pdf

Coloma, Roland S. 2013. "'Too Asian?' On Racism, Paradox, and Ethno-Nationalism." *Discourse: Studies in the Cultural Politics of Education* 34, no. 4: 579–598. https://doi.org/10.1080/01596306.2013.822620

de Wit, Hans. 2002. *Internationalization of Higher Education in the United States of America and Europe: A Historical, Comparative, and Conceptual Analysis.* Westport, CT: Greenwood Publishing Group.

de Wit, Hans and Fiona Hunter. 2015. "The Future of Internationalization of Higher Education in Europe." *International Higher Education* 83: 2–3.

Dey, Sreyoshi and Erin Williams. 2021. "Anti-Asian Racism in Canada: Where Do We Go from Here?" *Asia Pacific Foundation of Canada.* Retrieved from https://www.asiapacific.ca/publication/anti-asian-racism-canada-where-do-we-go-here

Findlay, Stephanie and Nicholas Köhler. 2010. "The Enrolment Controversy" (originally titled "Too Asian?"). *Maclean's* (Nov 10, 2010). Retrieved in June 2022, from https://www.macleans.ca/news/canada/too-asian/

Firang, David. 2020. "The Impact of COVID-19 Pandemic on International Students in Canada." *International Social Work* 63, no. 6: 820–824. Retrieved in June 2022, from https://journals.sagepub.com/doi/full/10.1177/0020872820940030

Foreign Affairs, Trade and Development Canada (DFATD). 2014. "Canada's International Education Strategy (2014-2019): Harnessing Our Knowledge Advantage to Drive Innovation and Prosperity." Archived on *Government of Canada International Education.* Retrieved in June 2022, from https://www.international.gc.ca/education/report-rapport/strategy-strategie-2014/index.aspx?lang=eng

Gill, Robin. 2020. "Asian Communities across Canada Report Rising Racist Behaviour during COVID-19 Crisis." *Global News.* Retrieved in July 24, 2022, from https://globalnews.ca/news/7033253/coronavirus-asian-racism-crisis-canada/

Global Affairs Canada (GAC). 2019. *Building on Success: International Education Strategy 2019–2024.* Retrieved in June 2022, from https://www.international.gc.ca/education/strategy-2019-2024-strategie.aspx?lang=eng#:~:text=The%20Trade%20Commissioner%20Service%20of%20Global%20Affairs%20Canada,a%20large%20and%20growing%20contribution%20to%20Canada's%20prosperity

Government of Canada. 1988. Canadian Multiculturalism Act 1998. Retrieved from https://laws.justice.gc.ca/eng/acts/c-18.7/fulltext.html

Henry, Frances and Carol Tator. 2006. *The Colour of Democracy: Racism in Canadian Society* (3rd ed.). Toronto: Thomson Nelson.

Houshmand, Sara, Lisa B. Spanierman, and Romin W. Tafarodi. 2014. "Excluded and Avoided: Racial Microaggressions Targeting Asian International Students in Canada." *Cultural Diversity and Ethnic Minority Psychology* 20, no. 3: 377. https://doi.org/10.1037/a0035404

Hudzik, John K. 2011. *Comprehensive Internationalization: From Concept to Action*. Washington, DC: NAFSA.

Knight, Jane. 2004. "Internationalization Remodeled: Definition, Approaches, and Rationales." *Journal of Studies in International Education* 8, no. 1: 5–31.

Kurl, Sachi, Dave Korzinski, and Kimberly Noels. 2020. *Blame, Bullying and Disrespect: Chinese Canadians Reveal Their Experiences with Racism during COVID-19*. The Angus Reid Institute (June). Retrieved from https://angusreid. org/racism-chinese-canadians-covid19/

Ng, Roxana. 1995. "Multiculturalism as Ideology: A Textual Analysis." In Marie Campbell and Ann Manicom (Eds). *Knowledge, Experience and Ruling Relations: Stories in the Social Organization of Knowledge*. Buffalo, Toronto: University of Toronto Press.

Schick, Carol and Verna St. Denis. 2005. "Troubling National Discourses in Anti-Racist Curricular Planning." *Canadian Journal of Education* 28, no. 3: 295–317.

Scott, Colin, Saba Safdar, Roopa Desai Trilokekar, and Amira El Masri. 2015. "International Students as 'Ideal Immigrants' in Canada: A Disconnect between Policy Makers' Assumptions and the Lived Experiences of International Students." *Comparative and International Education* 43, no. 3: Article 5.

Simpson, Jennifer S., Carl E. James, and Johnny Mack. 2011. "Multiculturalism, Colonialism, and Racialization: Conceptual Starting Points." *Review of Education, Pedagogy, and Cultural Studies* 33, no. 4: 285–305.

Smith, Dorothy E. 1987. *The Everyday World as Problematic: A Feminist Sociology*. Boston: Northeastern University Press.

Smith, Dorothy E. 1990. *Texts, Facts and Femininity: Exploring the Relations of Ruling*. London: Routledge.

Smith, Dorothy E. 1996. "The Relations of Ruling: A Feminist Inquiry." *Studies in Cultures, Organizations and Societies* 2, no. 2: 171–190. https://doi. org/10.1080/10245289608523475

Smith, Dorothy E. 2005. *Institutional Ethnography: A Sociology for People*. Lanham, MD: AltaMira Press.

Smith, Dorothy E. and Alison I. Griffith. 2022. *Simply Institutional Ethnography: Creating a Sociology for People*. Toronto: University of Toronto Press.

Smith, Dorothy E. and Susan M. Turner. 2014. *Incorporating Texts Into Institutional Ethnographies*. Toronto: University of Toronto Press.

Stein, Sharon and Vanessa Oliveira de Andreotti. 2016. "Cash, Competition, or Charity: International Students and the Global Imaginary." *Higher Education* 72, no. 2: 225–239. https://doi.org/10.1007/s10734-015-9949-8

Thobani, Sunera. 2007. *Exalted Subjects: Studies in the Making of Race and Nation in Canada*. Toronto: University of Toronto Press.

Todd, Douglas. 2016. "Mixed Motives Fuel Rise of Foreign Students." *Vancouver Sun* (May 21). Retrieved in June 2022, from https://vancouversun.com/opinion/columnists/douglas-todd-mixed-motives-fuel-rise-of-foreign-students/

Trilokekar, Roopa Desai. 2010. "International Education as Soft Power? The Contributions and Challenges of Canadian Foreign Policy to the Internationalization of Higher Education." *Higher Education* 59, no. 2: 131–147.

Varughese, Anil and Saul Schwartz. 2022. "The Pandemic Exposed the Vulnerability of International Students." *The Conversation* (January 24). Retrieved in July 2022, from https://theconversation.com/the-pandemic-exposed-the-vulnerability-of-international-students-in-canada-174105

2 For Students, Look East; For Partners, Look West

How Canadian Internationalization Strategies Portray Asia and Europe

Elizabeth Buckner, Janine Knight-Grofe, and Cynthia Eden

Introduction

Over the past few decades, higher education institutions throughout Canada have declared internationalization a priority. As a strategic organizational activity, internationalization typically involves engagement outside one's national borders through international student recruitment, research collaborations, joint degrees and collaborative learning. Implicit in these definitions is the idea of engagement across national borders. Although many colleges and universities use the term "global engagement" as a synonym for internationalization, engagement is actually geographically localized: universities recruit students from particular high schools, cities and countries, and form partnerships with specific universities that are themselves embedded in local, national and regional contexts. Localized geographic targeting is an important aspect of how Canadian universities plan for internationalization. Studies have found that universities target specific countries and regions for strategic reasons, and tailor their activities and resources toward those locations (Buckner et al. 2020). However, the uneven geography of internationalization activities has received less attention in the literature on how institutions practice internationalization.

In this chapter we seek to build on important conversations about how internationalization is practiced at the institutional level by deconstructing how 'the world' is portrayed in official internationalization strategies from Canadian universities. Specifically, we conduct a content analysis and close reading of 32 internationalization strategies from English-speaking Canadian colleges and universities published between 2011 and 2020. We examine how discourses surrounding the world's major geographic regions vary and what this tells us about how internationalization is currently practiced in Canadian universities and colleges, with a more in-depth focus on how Asia and Europe are discussed.

DOI: 10.4324/b23160-4

We find that Canadian internationalization strategies explicitly name Asia, or countries in Asia, which includes East Asia, South Asia and Southeast Asia, more than any other world region, followed by Europe and then Latin America, suggesting that Asia is a particular focus of Canadian institutions. In line with prior studies, we find strategies are particularly likely to emphasize the importance of Asia as a source of international students. Relatedly, many strategic activities, such as building alumni networks and branding, are mentioned as geographically targeted at Asia for the purpose of recruitment. In contrast, strategies mention Europe or specific countries and institutions in Europe primarily as sources for potential research partnerships. We argue that even while colleges and universities are increasingly starting to view Asian universities as potential partners, current discussions still frame Asia primarily as a source of students and Europe as a source of knowledge in ways that reinforce long-standing academic hierarchies.

Literature Review

Asia is the world's most populous geographic region, with 60% of the world's total population (World Population Review, n.d.) and long-standing traditions of higher learning (Hayhoe 2001; Zha 2022). Partly due to this, Asia has been a priority region for internationalization activities among Canadian universities for decades. India, China, South Korea and Japan have been primary source countries for international students to Canada since 2000 (Statistics Canada 2021) and have contributed significantly to the 226% increase of Canadian higher education international students between 2001 and 2014 (Sá & Sabzalieva 2018). In particular, India and China represent 50% of the international students in Canada (Global Affairs Canada 2019). Additionally, many students also come to Canada from Southeast Asian countries, which had a cumulative total of 9,840 students come to study at a Canadian higher education institution in 2019 with Vietnam, the Philippines and Indonesia in the top three (Statistics Canada 2021).

Recruiting large numbers of international students has been typically framed as both necessary and beneficial practice for colleges and universities, and justified for economic, social, cultural, political and academic rationales (de Wit 2019; Knight 2012). International students in particular pay much higher tuition to Canadian institutions than domestic students, and help supplement the stagnant public funding (Buckner, Zhang & Blanco 2022; Galway 2000; Usher 2020). They are also thought to contribute to the quality of education that Canadian students receive, by helping prepare them for diverse labor markets (Altbach & Knight 2007; Buckner et al. 2021).

Yet, scholars criticize instrumentalized practices, including the extent to which the neoliberal logics that pervade internationalization treat students as fee-paying consumers and also the extent to which institutional partnerships reproduce global academic and racial hierarchies. A large literature has documented how broader geopolitical dynamics play out on Canadian campuses, with stereotypes of international students as wealthy but less-deserving students who are paying for access to Canadian universities, or competition for seats in prestigious universities (Stein & de Andreotti, 2016). In addition to these realities, widespread anti-Asian racism has increased globally since the onset of the COVID-19 pandemic (Tan, Lee & Ruppanner 2021), sparking incidents of hate and harassment (Times Higher Education 2020; Wu, Qian & Wilkes 2021). There is some concern that rising anti-Asian racism may make North American institutions a less-desirable study destination for international students.

The geopolitics of international higher education is also changing. Over the past decade, countries in Asia, including China and India, have become major economic and geopolitical powers on the world stage. Asian higher education institutions are gaining global prestige and reputation (Geerlings & Lundberg 2018). Studies document how China is now the world's largest spender on research and development funder and is now one of the top partners for scientific research collaborations with many G7 countries, including Canada (Johnson et al. 2022).

At the same time, China and other East Asian countries are increasingly viewed as competitors for international students within the globalized higher education market (Zha et al. 2019). For example, studies show that students from East Asian countries are increasingly likely to want to study in other Asian countries, which has only increased in the wake of COVID-19 lockdowns (Mok et al. 2021). Clearly, the region will play a significant role in the future of higher education and will be increasingly sought out by North American institutions for prestigious research partnerships. Yet it is not clear to what extent institutions in Canada have adapted their internationalization practices to these geopolitical shifts. Therefore, in this chapter, we explore how Canadian higher education institutions discursively frame different countries and world regions in their strategy documents to capture how dominant views of the world outside the national borders pervade internationalization projects.

Conceptual Framework

In this study, we draw on the concepts of *neocolonialism* and *Eurocentrism* to make sense of how regions are differentially portrayed in internationalization documents. Altbach and Kelly (1978) define neocolonialism as: "the deliberate policies of the industrialized countries to maintain their domination" (p. 30). Canto and Hannah (2001) find education to be a key component of a neocolonial structure, noting that education "helps to maintain and to some extent to perpetuate colonial links" (p. 29). Internationalization is implicated in neocolonial processes, as it is one way in which the power of Western knowledges and English language credentials becomes financially lucrative for countries in the Global North – as their tuition policies allow them to financially benefit from the desires of international students, many from countries in the Global South or formerly colonized countries, to study in their institutions (Anderson 2015, 176; Canto & Hannah 2001).

In addition to its neocolonial structure, the global academic system is also characterized by Eurocentrism, which frames Western knowledge and civilization as associated with modernity and science (Battiste 2002) and non-Western knowledges as largely outside the realm of science and the academy. Eurocentrism creates an "interpretative monopoly" (p. 10), which claims authority within the academy. The colonial politics of knowledge is "an imperial effort (always incomplete) to capture and contain the threat that other knowledges and ways of knowing pose to the modern Western episteme and its ordering of the world" (Stein 2017, S28) to understand how colonial hierarchies are being reproduced within Canadian higher education. In such a context, Western thought and knowledge systems' superior status creates an epistemological environment where cognitive imperialism devalues and maligns other knowledge systems (Battiste 2004) entrenching Eurocentric dominance.

Even when universities seek to build partnerships based on concepts such as mutual benefit, scholars have found that international partnerships are unequal in terms of resources and may reproduce unequal hierarchies in knowledge production (Canto & Hannah 2001). For example, Canto and Hannah's (2001) study found evidence of enduring coloniality in North–South partnerships that is relevant to our analysis. In our analysis, we use the conceptual tools of neocolonialism and Eurocentrism to make sense of how different world regions are portrayed in Canadian internationalization strategies.

Data and Methods

The data for this chapter comes from a larger project that used critical content analysis to examine 32 university and college internationalization strategies across Canada. This dataset elicited many themes that help to understand how Canadian institutions were discussing and what they were prioritizing in internationalization (for additional research from the project, see: Buckner et al., 2021; Buckner et al. 2020; Buckner, Zhang and Blanco 2022). The project focused on internationalization strategies specifically, not other types of publications, such as webpages, as strategies documents are best suited for conveying the institutional vision for internationalization. Internationalization strategies are high-level documents that articulate the institutional vision for internationalization, are typically supported by institutional leadership and play a role in allocating resources (Childress 2009; Taylor 2004). For this project, the strategies analyzed were those that were available in English in 2020 at Canadian universities and colleges.

To create the dataset, a team of researchers reviewed the membership list of Universities Canada and Colleges and Institutes Canada and searched the respective list of members' institutional websites for documents titled Internationalization Strategy, Internationalization Plan, Global Engagement Strategy or similar terms. The total sample included strategies, plans and white papers published from 2011 to 2020 from 23 Canadian universities and nine Canadian colleges. One important limitation to our study concerns the fact that some of the institutional strategies reviewed are more than a decade old and that in the past 10 years, societies, including universities and colleges, have changed.

Of the 32 strategies, 14 were from Ontario, 7 were from British Columbia, 3 were from Alberta, 2 were from Nova Scotia, 2 from Saskatchewan, and 1 from each of Manitoba, New Brunswick, Newfoundland and Labrador, and Quebec. The team used an iterative emergent process to code the documents; first, a team of ten graduate research assistants (RAs) individually did a close reading of a strategy document and identified overarching themes, and then, through multiple rounds, developed a detailed coding protocol with example codes, as well as the inclusion and exclusion criteria. All RAs were then rigorously trained on the coding protocol using Dedoose, a qualitative software developed for collaborative projects. The team developed three training modules in Dedoose and all RAs had to maintain consistency to ensure a high level of inter-rater reliability.

The finalized coding protocol had five overarching categories: (1) Priority Activities; (2) Rationales and Discourses; (3) Explicit Values; (4) Implementation Processes and (5) Geography and Geographic Priorities. Within the last category on geographic priorities, the team coded for mentions of specific geographic targets or priorities and identified these according to the larger world region identified in the target, including Europe (Eastern, Central and Western), Asia (Central, East, South and Southeast), Latin America and the Caribbean, the Middle East, and Africa, as well as other geographic priorities that emerged through coding, including mentions to Emerging Economies and the Global South, or related terms.

The findings of this chapter are based on a second stage of analysis conducted on those strategies that were coded as having some geographic

For Students, Look East; For Partners, Look West   35

priority. For this second stage analysis, we first examined the frequency of mentions and examined what other nodes were coded in conjunction with each geographic code (i.e. code co-occurrence). Although our focus was specifically on Asia and Europe, in our initial quantitative content analysis, we examined all regions to be able to make broader generalizations about frequency of representation. We then conducted a close reading of all the excerpts coded at the "Asia (Including China and India)" and "Europe" nodes to gain a more nuanced understanding of how the different regions are portrayed.

Findings

In this section, we provide a quantitative overview of how often major world regions are mentioned in Canadian internationalization strategies and then do a close reading of excerpts coded at both Asia and Europe regions to examine how regions are discussed within strategies and for what purposes. Table 2.1 shows the number of documents that specifically mentioned each geographic region or set of countries that we coded for. Not all institutions identified or listed specific geographic priorities for their internationalization activities, but of those that did, our quantitative coding shows that Asia was the only region mentioned as a priority region in more than half of Canadian strategies. As the table shows, 18 of the 32 strategies coded mention Asia as a geographic target or priority, followed by Latin America and the Caribbean (13), Africa (12) and Europe (12). We also coded mentions to broader terms such as "Global South" or "Emerging Economies", but these were much less frequent than naming specific world regions or countries. The important takeaway from this analysis is simply the extent to which Asia is viewed as a priority world region for Canadian internationalization, which, while unsurprising, reflects the uneven geography that is belied by the blanket calls to global engagement.

Table 2.1 Number of documents mentioning specific geographic priorities

Regional Grouping	# of Strategy Documents
Asia	18
Latin America and the Caribbean	13
Africa	12
Europe	12
Other Core Anglophone Countries (UK, etc.)	8
Middle East and North Africa	8
Emerging Economies (or related term)	3
Global South (or related term)	2

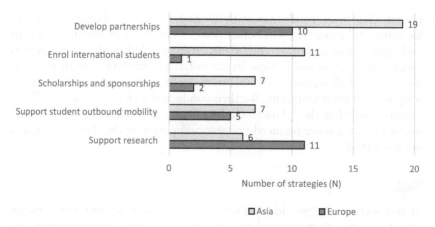

Figure 2.1 Regions mentioned as a target for priority activity – Asia versus Europe.

In a more detailed analysis, we examined what activities were associated with each geographic region, as shown in Figure 2.1. In terms of priority activities, we found that Asia is most often coded alongside developing partnerships, followed by recruiting and enrolling international students. Given the high number of international students from Asia in Canadian universities, the emphasis on recruitment is not surprising. A smaller number of strategies referenced supporting student outbound mobility, scholarships and sponsorships and supporting research. In contrast, as shown in Figure 2.1, supporting research is more frequently discussed as associated with Europe than Asia, in stark contrast to both international student recruitment and providing scholarships.

In fact, although Europe is mentioned less frequently than Asia (12 vs. 18), strategies that discuss Europe tend to do so in ways that would signify more robust forms of partnership. For example, in 11 instances from 5 universities, the most frequent instance of discussion of Europe, it is mentioned alongside supporting research. This is followed closely (ten instances) by developing partnerships, from 5 universities and 1 college. For example, one strategy noted that "Europe is a particularly important region for research collaboration, secondly only to the US, and we are now beginning to take advantage of these strong links to form strategic partnerships" (UBC, International Strategic Plan 2011, 16). A small number (5) mentioned supporting student outbound mobility in Europe.

Same Activities, Different Emphases

In addition to the different activities mapped onto Asia and Europe, our analysis identified more nuanced differences when we examined emphases of these activities. Specifically, we find that when strategies mention partnerships in Asia, activities appear largely numeric, superficial or opportunistic and are targeted primarily at recruitment. In contrast, supporting partnerships in Europe is primarily mapped onto research purposes.

In Asia, the most frequent partnership mentions are to take advantage of opportunities in a changing China. As one institution noted "The sheer scale and speed at which [China's] economy and higher-education system are developing make China both a tremendous opportunity and challenge to any Canadian university" (University of Calgary 2013, 21). Yet, in several cases, the discussion of partnerships with Asia emphasizes the number of partnerships as a quantitative achievement, leaving us to wonder about how substantive these partnerships are. For example, both the University of Windsor (2012) and Simon Fraser University (2013) emphasized the number of partnerships they had in Asia, without much detail on their purposes or benefits. In a notable exception, the University of Ottawa highlighted as an exemplar partnership in Asia its joint medical school with an institution in Shanghai, noting it as the first of its kind in the world. However, at the time of the strategy, this partnership was one-way, with students in China being able to study at the university's branch campus and be introduced to North American undergraduate education in medicine (University of Ottawa 2017).

Partnerships in Asia also occurred alongside student recruitment efforts. For example, UBC's 2011 Strategy exemplifies the institution's approach to targeting highly qualified students from China and India, stating: "Recruitment of Chinese graduate students is strong. This is supported by our links with the China Scholarship Council (CSC). UBC has signed special agreements with six leading Chinese universities as a preferred destination for their CSC winners" (The University of British Columbia 2011, 19). With respect to India, they state:

Student numbers are low … However UBC has a good number of faculty members with close ties to India. It is important to step up engagement in India now because India itself is in a rapid state of change. The Indian government is investing in education and there is a clear recognition that the post-secondary sector in India is simply not able to meet the needs of the emerging economy.

(The University of British Columbia 2011, 22)

Institutions are deliberate about their goals in attracting Asian students to Canadian campuses. For example, one institution noted that "India will remain our most important source of students; China is a high priority for growth" (Sheridan College 2018, 7). Another institution's strategic priority includes developing an office for sponsored students to "leverage external funding of talented graduate students from such countries as Brazil, Vietnam, China, Iraq, Libya etc. which provide funding to their top scholars abroad" (Memorial University of Newfoundland 2020, 14). Other institutions employ in-country partners to support recruitment of Asian students. For example, "DC has representative offices in India, Nigeria and China that work effectively with students through their recruitment, application and preparation for travel" (Durham College 2017, 11). Some institutions are specific about attracting the best and the brightest from Asia. For example, one strategy stated:

> Although student enrollment from China is healthy, we need to work to maintain our recruitment strengths especially as Chinese universities grow. At the undergraduate level, we need to continue to position [university] as a university of choice for outstanding students.
>
> (UBC, International Strategic Plan 2011, 19)

For those colleges and universities whose internationalization strategic plans include a listing of their top countries of origin for international students, Asian countries, specifically China and India, head the list.

Even partnerships with Asia are mentioned as grounded on principles of mutual benefits, strategies nonetheless also revealed deficit perspective. For example, even while UBC stated explicitly that it is "important to build our connections with a view to mutual benefits, rather than self-interest", (The University of British Columbia 2011, 20) following this statement, the language used perpetuates an unequal view. The quote continues with a deficit view of India, stating that "India is at a relatively early stage of development in its higher education and research" (The University of British Columbia 2011, 20). This is in keeping with Canto and Hannah's (2001) longitudinal study that found that attempts at balanced relationships are not always realized, and "constraints arising from historical and contemporary factors continue to pose barriers to genuine partnership" (Canto & Hannah 2001, 26).

Meanwhile, with respect to Europe, partnership is primarily in a context of existing research partnerships or research partnership opportunities and Europe is seen as an entrée into Europe for these purposes. In discussing their United Kingdom–based campus, one university highlighted its strategic geographic location that "could be leveraged to increase not only Memorial's presence in Europe, but the profile of the province as well" and that this campus "has acted as a gateway to Europe; in an informal, ad hoc manner for many years" and "its capacity could be harnessed to support ventures by researchers and industry to engage with European opportunities" (Memorial University of Newfoundland 2020, 21). One university strategy expressed concerns that current partnerships have not taken full advantage of the research opportunities in Europe, and that "as a result ... UBC is at risk of being excluded from the very significant research cooperation mechanisms that exist in Europe" (The University of British Columbia, 2011, 24). In contrast, international student recruitment is mentioned only once alongside Europe, and where this occurred, it was in relation to attending strategic recruitment events in Europe and not necessarily recruiting European students for programs on campus (Dalhousie University 2017).

Discussion and Conclusion

In this chapter, we examine the ways that Asia and Europe are differentially discussed in Canadian internationalization strategies. We find that Canadian internationalization strategies tend to map similar activities onto Asia and Europe but with important and nuanced differences. Asia most often appears alongside mentions of partnerships, participating in networks and enrolling and/or recruiting international students. In contrast, Europe is often cited alongside research and partnerships that support research. Indeed, our analysis suggests internationalization within the Canadian higher education context claims to be global, with a common set of activities, but actually maps particular activities onto particular world regions.

Moreover, when strategies mention partnerships in Asia, activities appear largely opportunistic. Particularly, in their discussions of Asia, Canadian colleges and universities continue to reflect drivers such as competition, financial rationales and rankings as anchors for internationalization strategies. The fact that mentions of Asia are largely discussed within the framework of international student recruitment and the high revenue it brings implicitly treats Asian countries as a source revenue for Canadian institutions, mapping onto past colonial relations in the world.

Meanwhile, Canadian institutions prioritize developing partnerships in both regions; however, the emphasis on partnerships in Asia is at times strategic, opportunistic or rooted in a deficit mentality. There is almost no mention of how Canadian institutions and students can learn from and with their Asian peers. For example, we noted that there were no discussions of the languages or cultural expertise of those who would engage in the partnerships from the Canadian perspective, leaving the assumption that the partnership activities would take place in English or in the case of a joint medical school, in Canada. This finding reflects Canto and Hannah (2001) finding that "the standard adoption of the language of the core partner is a manifestation of neocolonialism" (Canto & Hannah 2001, citing Altbach & Kelly 1978, 30). Moreover, in some instances, we noted a deficit orientation toward some Asian countries (for example, India). As a result, the tendency to view non-Western partners as objects rather than subjects of internationalization within Eurocentric paradigms (Buckner & Stein 2020) is perpetuated by our own institutions in strategy documents. Canadian institutions are also far less likely to seek out Asian partners for "supporting research", than their European partners, where "supporting research" is actually the most commonly mentioned reason for prioritizing Europe. It is clear that current approaches to internationalization strategies and dominant discourses reproduce existing hierarchies in the world that continues to position Europe as a center of knowledge, and other world regions, including Asia, as recipients of that knowledge. This finding also reflects a general ignorance, lack of appreciation and bias toward the immense scholarly history and knowledge traditions of Asian societies. This absence strikes us as somewhat ironic given that Asian knowledge traditions such as Confucianism frame education around personal cultivation and public good (Yang 2016; Zha 2022), which closely align with Canadian institutions' stated goals for their own institutions and internationalization projects. Particularly, given the rise of both China and India as geopolitical powers and the changing realities of internationalization in the wake of COVID, the failure to develop innovative research partnerships within Asia may even put Canadian institutions in a precarious position, unable to meet their own goals for internationalization.

In conclusion, we would like to recognize our own positionality, in that we are writing from English-speaking institutions in Canada and our institutions are engaging in internationalization in the ways illustrated in this chapter, and that we benefit directly from these dynamics. Nonetheless, we believe we all have a role to play in the process of reframing our institutions' global engagements and interrupting established academic hierarchies. One possibility for this might be to re-frame our relationship with Asian countries by asking, what can we learn from deeper conversations with other knowledge traditions?

References

Altbach, Philip G., and Gail Paradise Kelly. 1978. *Education and Colonialism.* New York: Longman.

Altbach, Philip G., and Jane Knight. 2007. "The Internationalization of Higher Education: Motivations and Realities." *Journal of Studies in International Education* 11, no. 3–4: 290–305.

Anderson, Tim. 2015. "Seeking Internationalization: The State of Canadian Higher Education." *Canadian Journal of Higher Education* 45, no. 4: 166–87.

Battiste, Marie. 2002. *Indigenous Knowledge and Pedagogy in First Nations Education: A Literature Review with Recommendation.* Ottawa, Canada: National Working Group on Education.

Battiste, Marie. 2004. "Animating Sites of Postcolonial Education: Indigenous Knowledge and the Humanities." *CSSE Plenary Address*. Manitoba, MB.

Buckner, Elizabeth, and Sharon Stein. 2020. "What Counts as Internationalization? Deconstructing the Internationalization Imperative." *Journal of Studies in International Education* 24, no. 2: 151–66. https://doi.org/10.1177/1028315319829878.

Buckner, Elizabeth, Scott Clerk, Adriana Marroquin, and You Zhang. 2020. "Strategic Benefits, Symbolic Commitments: How Canadian Colleges and Universities Frame Internationalization." *Canadian Journal of Higher Education* 50, no. 4: 20–36.

Buckner, Elizabeth, Punita Lumb, Zahra Jafarova, Phoebe Kang, Adriana Marroquin, and You Zhang. 2021. "Diversity without Race: How University Internationalization Strategies Discuss International Students." *Journal of International Students* 11, no. S1: 32–49. https://doi.org/10.32674/jis.v11iS1.3842.

Buckner, Elizabeth, You Zhang, and Gerardo L. Blanco. 2022. "The Impact of COVID-19 on International Student Enrolments in North America: Comparing Canada and the United States." *Higher Education Quarterly*, 76, no. 2: 328–42.

Canto, Isabel, and Janet Hannah. 2001. "A Partnership of Equals? Academic Collaboration between the United Kingdom and Brazil." *Journal of Studies in International Education* 5, no. 1: 26–41. https://doi.org/10.1177/102831530151003.

Childress, Lisa K. 2009. "Planning for Internationalization by Investing in Faculty." *Journal of International & Global Studies* 1, no. 1: 30–49.

"Coronavirus Sparks a Rising Tide of Xenophobia Worldwide." 2020. *Times Higher Education*, no. 2452.

Dalhousie University. 2017. *From a National University to an International University: Building on International Opportunity*. https://cdn.dal.ca/content/dam/dalhousie/pdf/dept/international-relations/DALHOUSIE%20INTERNATIONAL%20STRATEGY%202017-2020-June-2018.pdf.

de Wit, Hans. 2019. "Internationalization in Higher Education, a Critical Review." *SFU Educational Review* 12, no. 3: 9–17. https://doi.org/10.21810/sfuer.v12i3.1036.

Durham College. 2017. *Internationalization and Global Engagement Plan: Learn Locally, Engage Globally*. https://durhamcollege.ca/wp-content/uploads/dc-internationalization-and-global-engagement-plan-2017-final.pdf.

Galway, Adrienne Diane. 2000. "Going Global, Ontario Colleges of Applied Arts and Technology, International Student Recruitment and the Export of Education." PhD diss., University of Toronto. http://www.nlcbnc.ca/obj/s4/f2/dsk1/tape3/PQDD_0023/NQ50012.pdf.

Geerlings, Lennie R.C., and Anita Lundberg. 2018. "Global Discourses and Power/Knowledge: Theoretical Reflections on Futures of Higher Education during the Rise of Asia." *Asia Pacific Journal of Education* 38, no. 2: 229–40. https://doi.org/10.1080/02188791.2018.1460259.

Global Affairs Canada. 2019. *Building on Success: International Education Strategy 2019-2024*. Global Affairs Canada. https://doi.org/10.1002/smll.201390001.

Hayhoe, Ruth. 2001. "Lessons from the Chinese Academy." In *Knowledge across Cultures: A Contribution to the Dialogue among Civilizations*, edited by Ruth Hayhoe and Julia Pan, 334–70. Hong Kong: Comparative Education Research Centre.

42   *Elizabeth Buckner et al.*

Johnson, Jo, Jonathan Adams, Jonathan Grant, and Daniel Murphy. 2022. "Stumbling Bear, Soaring Dragon: Russia, China and the Geopolitics of Global Science." *Mossavar-Rahmani Center for Business and Government; Policy Institute at King's College London,* July 2022. https://nrs.harvard.edu/URN-3:HUL.INSTREPOS:37372501.

Knight, Jane. 2012. "Concepts, Rationales, and Interpretive Frameworks in the Internationalization of Higher Education." In *The SAGE Handbook of International Higher Education,* 27–42. Thousand Oaks: SAGE Publications, Inc. https://doi.org/10.4135/9781452218397.n2.

Marginson, Simon. 2011. "Higher Education in East Asia and Singapore: Rise of the Confucian Model." *Higher Education* 61, no. 5: 587–611. https://doi.org/10.1007/s10734-010-9384-9.

Memorial University of Newfoundland. 2020. *Strategic Internationalization Plan: Thinking Globally, Acting Globally.* https://www.mun.ca/vpacademic/media/production/memorial/administrative/office-of-the-provost-and-vice-president-academic/media-library/what-we-do/SIP_2020_Final.pdf.

Mok, Ka Ho, Weiyan Xiong, Guoguo Ke, and Joyce Oi Wun Cheung. 2021. "Impact of COVID-19 Pandemic on International Higher Education and Student Mobility: Student Perspectives from Mainland China and Hong Kong." *International Journal of Educational Research,* 105: 101718.

Sá, Creso M., and Emma Sabzalieva. 2018. "The Politics of the Great Brain Race: Public Policy and International Student Recruitment in Australia, Canada, England and the USA." *Higher Education* 75, no. 2: 231–53. https://doi.org/10.1007/s10734-017-0133-1.

Sheridan College. 2018. *The International Centre Plan.* https://www.sheridancollege.ca/-/media/files/www/about/administration-and-governance/priorities/the-international-centre-plan.ashx-?la=en&hash=FD2DAFBC5AA13C8A728FAC8AD5B69AA22BF0AF2D.

Simon Fraser University. 2013. *International Engagement Strategy: Relations Simon Fraser University 2013-2016.* http://www.sfu.ca/content/dam/sfu/international/documents/Int%20Engagement%20Strategy.pdf.

Statistics Canada. 2021. *The Changing Sociodemographic Characteristics of International Students.* https://www150.statcan.gc.ca/n1/daily-quotidien/210728/dq210728b-eng.htm.

Stein, Sharon. 2017. "The Persistent Challenges of Addressing Epistemic Dominance in Higher Education: Considering the Case of Curriculum Internationalization." *Comparative Education Review* 61, no. S1: S25–S50. https://doi.org/10.1086/690456.

Stein, Sharon, and Vanessa Oliveira de Andreotti. 2016. "Cash, Competition, or Charity: International Students and the Global Imaginary." *Higher Education* 72, no. 2: 225–39.

Tan, Xiao, Rennie Lee, and Leah Ruppanner. 2021. "Profiling Racial Prejudice during COVID-19: Who Exhibits Anti-Asian Sentiment in Australia and the United States?" *The Australian Journal of Social Issues* 56, no. 4: 464–84. https://doi.org/10.1002/ajs4.176.

Taylor, John. 2004. "Toward a Strategy for Internationalisation: Lessons and Practice from Four Universities." *Journal of Studies in International Education* 8, no. 2: 149–71. https://doi.org/10.1177/1028315303260827.

The University of British Columbia. 2011. *UBC International Strategic Plan.* https://research.ubc.ca/sites/research.ubc.ca/files/vpri/UBC-intl-strat-plan-2011.pdf.

University of Calgary. 2013. *Becoming a Global Intellectual Hub: Highlights of the University of Calgary International Strategy.* https://www.ucalgary.ca/research/files/research/becoming-a-global-intellectual-hub.pdf.

University of Ottawa. 2017. *University of Ottawa Internationalization Strategy.* https://www.uottawa.ca/president/sites/www.uottawa.ca.president/files/2017-12-04_-_full_report_final_accessible.pdf.

University of Windsor. 2012. *Moving toward Campus Internationalization.* http://web4.uwindsor.ca/international-development/sites/uwindsor.ca.international-development/files/internationalization_report_2011-12.pdf (No longer available).

Usher, Alex. 2020. The State of Postsecondary Education in Canada, 2020. https://higheredstrategy.com/the-state-of-postsecondary-education-in-canada-2020/.

World Population Review. n.d. *Asia Population 2022.*

Wu, Cary, Yue Qian, and Rima Wilkes. 2021. "Anti-Asian Discrimination and the Asian-White Mental Health Gap during COVID-19." *Ethnic and Racial Studies* 44, no. 5: 819–35. https://doi.org/10.1080/01419870.2020.1851739.

Yang, Rui. 2016. "The East-West Axis? Liberal Arts Education in East Asian Universities." In *Liberal Arts Education and Colleges in East Asia*, edited by I. Jung, M. Nishimura, and T. Sasao, 27–37. Springer.

Zha, Qiang. 2022. "Revisiting the Discourse of a Chinese Model of the University: A Confucian-Legalist Legacy Impact Perspective." In *Routledge Handbook of the Sociology of Higher Education*, edited by James Côté and Sarah Pickard, 333–46. London and New York: Routledge.

Zha, Qiang, Hantian Wu, and Ruth Hayhoe. 2019. "Why Chinese Universities Embrace Internationalization: An Exploration with Two Case Studies." *Higher Education* 78, no. 4: 669–86.

3 Framing International Students from Asia in Ontario Universities

Provincial Priorities, Deficit-focused Services, and Economic Benefits

Jean Michel Montsion and Daniela Caneo

Introduction

In its official 2018 Internationalization Strategy, the Ontario government strongly encourages universities to recruit international students (King 2021), as it aims to "lay the foundation for continued success in international education by strengthening international student recruitment and retention, supporting public priorities of economic growth, and meeting the evolving needs of 21st-century postsecondary learners" (Government of Ontario 2018, i). That year, universities in Toronto welcomed close to 170,000 international students, and the province was the venue of choice for about half of all international students coming to Canadian universities (CBIE 2018). In 2018, international students contributed C$7.8 billion to Ontario's economy and $1.8 billion in institutional revenues, with China, India, South Korea, Vietnam, Japan, Bangladesh, Taiwan, and Pakistan being the top source countries (CBIE 2018; Government of Ontario 2018; MAESD 2018).

In Canada, universities have different institutional realities based on the province where they are located, as each provincial government seeks "to align universities' activities or outcomes more closely with desired public policy goals" (Eastman et al. 2018, 72). The increased focus on recruiting international students, particularly from Asia, can be understood through a system-level policy lens, which brings to the forefront each institution's relationship with its provincial government (see Chan and Matsushita; Fanelli and Meades 2011; El Masri et al. 2015; Jones 2004; Rigas and Kuchapski 2016). In this chapter, we examine the interplay between the Ontario government and three universities – Toronto Metropolitan University (hereafter TMU), the University of Toronto (hereafter UofT), and York University (hereafter YorkU) – to assess the role of provincial priorities in the emphasis on, and related framing of, international students from Asia.

DOI: 10.4324/b23160-5

By documenting how the province conceives international students and how Ontario universities have responded to this framing, we show that the government–university relationship consolidates an understanding of this student group based mainly on its economic contribution to Canadian society and institutions, with little to no attention to the importance of student backgrounds, such as their country of origin. When the cultural and national profile of a student group is acknowledged, as it was in the case of students who graduated from high school in China, this interplay leads to an expansion of deficit-focused support services that not only play down students' cultural and social contributions but also play up their economic contributions. After briefly presenting the Ontario university context and how internationalization has emerged in recent years, we turn to how the three aforementioned universities in Toronto have adapted to provincial priorities in their reporting and in some of the services provided to international students from Asia. Finally, we discuss how deficit-focused support services are deployed in ways that optimize these students' economic contribution.

Methodologically, the findings in this chapter are based on an analysis of publicly available policy documents from the Government of Ontario and various strategic and university-wide documents from the three selected universities, notably their Strategic Mandate Agreements (SMA) with the province. We analyzed these documents around key themes of interest: internationalization, student recruitment and retention, and students' country of origin. While the Toronto region has the most postsecondary education institutions in Ontario, the three aforementioned universities were selected for their proximity to one another and their distinct relationship with the Ontario government.[1] This focus on only three universities from Toronto limits the generalization of our findings, but we believe they are valuable in shedding light on government–university relationships, which are often under-explored when it comes to the indirect consequences of these agreements for the lives of student groups, such as international students from Asia.

Ontario's University Sector and Internationalization

Ontario's higher education policy environment remained "relatively stable" from the early 1970s to the mid-1990s (Jones 2004, 40). While other jurisdictions were experiencing structural reforms during that time, Ontario universities did not experience much government interference and sectoral planning aside from some funding cuts (Fanelli and Meades 2011; Jones 2004). With the election of a Progressive Conservative government in 1995, then-Premier Mike Harris established a "Common Sense

Revolution" with direct, lasting impacts on the Ontario postsecondary education sector (Fanelli and Meades 2011). In this section, we argue that provincial priorities and policies regarding the neoliberalization of the Ontario higher education sector have set the stage for an understanding of international students from Asia through a narrow economic lens. In this framework, the country of origin for international students is only recorded to the extent that it reflects the ideals of internationalization and the business of international education.

Jones (2004) notes that, since 1995, Ontario universities have been strongly affected by provincial reforms, including the privatization and marketization of education, which led to increasing tuition fees; deregulating degree-granting institutions and related increases in competition; growing attention to institutional differentiation, which led to differential treatment of universities and programs; and expanding the province's entire higher education system. While these reforms were often advocated and realized by university actors themselves (Jones 2004), this "market fundamentalist" turn was sustained by subsequent governments, including during the 2008–2010 Great Recession, when the Liberal government of then-Premier Dalton McGuinty intensified province-wide austerity measures in the sector (Fanelli and Meades 2011). This resulted in Ontario becoming Canada's province with the highest costs for students to complete their undergraduate and graduate degrees (Chan 2015; Eastman et al. 2018; Fanelli and Meades 2011).

In this context, the Ontario university sector can now be understood as a "managed market," in which the provincial government steers institutions toward further marketization and privatization through incentives (Rigas and Kuchapski 2016, 54). The neoliberal restructuring of the sector did not result in a withdrawal of the province from university matters, but rather increased intervention in the plans and activities of university actors (Wellen 2011). Government measures for greater accountability from universities are meant to fortify a cultural and institutional shift in universities that portray students as consumers, oriented toward "economic self-interest, career skills and credential acquisition" (Rigas and Kuchapski 2016, 62). Part of these measures include the SMA process, through which each institution responds to provincial priorities and details their plans to meet them, including enrolment targets and financial stability. While the first round of SMA, known as SMA1, which was launched from 2014 to 2017, outlined the strengths of each institution, SMA2, covering the 2017–2020 period, focused on policy development in an attempt to attach provincial funding to each institution's performance in meeting these goals (MCU 2021).

The province has encouraged internationalization as a strategy for "branding [the] region for global investment, addressing gaps in shrinking domestic budgets, to enabling the evolution of a 21st century education for students" (MTCU 2016, 3). Accordingly, Ontario universities have embraced internationalization to increase revenue, expand market share, and compensate for the gradual reduction of provincial funding. Increasing the number of students who pay international fees is effective because these fees are not regulated like domestic fees (Cudmore 2005), hence helping institutions grow their tuition-based revenues (see Beck; Buckner, Kim and Vlahos; Trilokekar and El Masri 2016). Besides the "direct revenue benefit" they bring (MTCU 2016, 8), international students are also viewed as a human resource that can "fill Ontario's need for skilled and talented workers," and those who remain in the province after their studies to work can "contribute to the long-term economic prosperity of Ontario" (MTCU 2016, 6). As part of internationalization-at-home strategies, international students also "bring valuable diversity to the classroom, the campus, and the larger community, enhancing the academic experience for all students," along with providing global ties and international connections that can benefit Ontario in the future (Steenkamp 2008).

In their recruitment efforts, Ontario universities have increasingly focused on international students from Asia, so as to target the emerging economic and demographic source countries with the most economic promise for both the institutions and the economy. Most of the Ontario government's documents on international students do not provide a detailed portrayal of international students from Asia (see MAESD 2018; MTCU 2012; 2016), except when it comes to the evolving trends in international student demographics in Ontario, in which case international students from Asia are counted as part of a global profile of source countries (Williams et al. 2015). Mentions of countries of origin are not meant as a way to engage substantively with the diversity of experiences and backgrounds, but as a way to map international market shares. For instance, international students from China, and Asia more broadly, are only mentioned as follows, in a 2015 Higher Education Quality Council of Ontario report: "China, the second most common country of origin in 2012, was also important during 2000–2012. By 2012, international students were predominantly Asian, with the majority being of Indian or Chinese origin" (Williams et al. 2015, 25).

Portraying International Students (from Asia)

In line with neoliberal pressures from the Ontario government, representations of international students from Asia by Ontario universities are often reduced to their economic contribution, hence resulting in a cash cow mentality that does not serve the best interests of this student group (Zhou,

Liu, and Rideout 2017). In this section, we show that each of the selected institutions has a particular relationship with the provincial government. However, these relationships lead to a similar framing of international students from Asia based on deficit thinking, which conceives of support services from the standpoint that barriers to learning are individual shortcomings that students must work on themselves to meet institutional standards (Shields, Bishop, and Mazawi 2005). Interestingly, when the national or cultural profile of some international student groups from Asia is acknowledged, the deficit-focused approach to services is not limited but expanded in a way that increases these students' economic contribution to the institution.

University of Toronto

UofT represents international students at the intersection of internationalization, recruitment, and diversification of the student body. First, the institution's International Strategic Plan presents international students as the "best talent worldwide," and their recruitment is seen as a way to enhance the institution's "global competitiveness" (UofT 2018a, 1). By focusing on recruiting students from countries that are not the typical countries for recruitment (UofT 2018a), the institution is "continuing to attract the best and the brightest while further increasing diversity" (UofT 2019, 4). Nonetheless, it also points out that tuition fees are more favorable to students from "key international markets such as China, India, Pakistan, South Korea, Hong Kong and the United States" (UofT 2018b, 12), which are already some of the most common international student source countries for most Canadian institutions (see Buckner, Kim, and Vlahos; CBIE 2022).

In its second SMA with the province, UofT provides three representations of international students. First, international doctoral students are seen as contributing to the institution's research reputation, as they support "cutting-edge research by the world's best and brightest minds" (UofT 2017, 4). Second, international students are incorporated into a broader category of "international activities," which includes educational experiences, global competencies, research partnerships, and alumni networks (UofT 2017, 4). Finally, international students are presented as having some specific needs that will be met through an expansion of services, notably in terms of health and wellness, mobility, language, and transition to academic life (UofT 2017, 5). In sum, international students are conceived both as consumers of education and as a resource for all on campus, as bearers of "multiple, global points of view," but they are not portrayed beyond the opportunities they offer the institution and some of the needs they have ("UofT International Strategic Plan" 2018a, 1).

International students are supported by UofT's Centre for International Experience (CIE) to help them make a "smooth transition to academic life" (CIE 2022). The CIE helps international students with immigration, healthcare, and other integration services, and it hosts events, programs, and networking opportunities. However, one must turn to other branches of UofT to find targeted support for or attention to international students from Asia. UofT (2022) has an East Asia strategy, which focuses mostly on alumni networks in China "to build stronger academic, government and alumni collaborations and provide market intelligence to help further develop potential industry partnerships." For international students from Asia, particularly China, UofT created the elite Green Path Program – China (2022), located on the Scarborough campus, which is aimed at high school graduates looking for additional language, social, and research support in their academic and social transition. This initiative explicitly targets a specific group of international students from Asia and provides targeted services for additional fees.

Toronto Metropolitan University

Formerly known as Ryerson University, or X University, TMU (2019) considers the recruitment of international students as part of a broader strategy of global engagement that will strengthen global competencies for all on campus. Increased numbers of international students fit TMU's global brand as a diversified and internationalized learning environment, where students can "engage with the diversity of the world's cultures, knowledge systems, worldviews, perspectives, and nations" (TMU 2021). Aware of the limitations of framing this recruitment as part of a revenue-generating exercise, TMU warns that the economic benefits should not be the "focus of our efforts" (TMU 2019, 18).

This observation stands in contrast with TMU's reporting to the province. In its SMA2, the institution focuses on an economic rationale for "expanding programming to international students" and increasing international enrolments "to mitigate potential constraints on domestic enrolment increases" (TMU 2017, 23). TMU also frames international students as part of a larger ensemble of under-represented student groups, which includes "first-generation students, Indigenous peoples, persons with disabilities and internationally educated professionals" (TMU 2017, 12). As part of this group, international students are provided key support services to enhance their academic and social integration, especially English as a Second Language (ESL) courses and "academic advising services, cultural immersion activities and cultural competency training for students adapting to life in Canadian universities" (TMU 2017, 23).

TMU's International Student Support (ISS) "foster[s] a sense of belonging and community for all students who are new to Canada" by supporting international students "as they adjust to the new Canadian environment and culture" (TMU 2022a). It offers immigration advising, health, financial, and emergency support, as well as networking and cultural training opportunities. Academically, international students are offered various undergraduate pathway programs through TMU's International College, which provides additional academic training prior to obtaining preferential entry in one of TMU's undergraduate programs (TMU 2022b). This immersion and transition program is branded as providing "unparalleled access to diverse career opportunities and industry experts," while also allowing students to experience Toronto's "diversity and rich cultural landscape" (TMU 2022b). While the International College does not offer services that cater to particular national or cultural backgrounds, the Real Institute does. It offers English Language Pathway programs, and it markets them in Chinese on its website (Real Institute 2022). It is "for learners of different backgrounds and levels of proficiency," to "achieve academic and personal success" and to develop "a pathway to an undergraduate program" (Real Institute 2022).

York University

As of April 2022, YorkU had not released an official international strategy. Nonetheless, its motivations for internationalization, and increasing international enrolments, stem from heightened global competition, a community-based and social responsibility to solve global problems and training its student body with global skills (YorkU 2019). Over the last fifteen years, the institution has been more concerned with the value of its international students for the local labor market than their immediate contribution to the institution. The emphasis is on "programs considered relevant to career development, in areas such as applied sciences and engineering, health and medicine, and commerce and business" for international students, immigrants, and first-generation Canadians (Monahan 2010, 61).

YorkU's SMA2 reveals a strong alignment with provincial priorities, including recruiting more international students, facilitating mobility, and internationalizing the curriculum (YorkU 2017, 11). International students are framed as future "skilled and talented workers" who will be "driving economic growth and strengthening the post-secondary education system" (YorkU 2017, 31). With only a brief mention of "key international markets such as China, India and the United States" (YorkU 2017, 15), there is little to no information on how YorkU plans to support international students, including in the "student experience" section of the report. University-wide student services will assist international students, but their framing in the SMA2 mostly helps YorkU position its efforts within "Canada's global markets action plan and the six key markets identified within," the "Canadian brand of education," and "Ontario's international student strategy" (YorkU 2017, 31).

York International (2023) provides international students with immigration and financial advising and health and safety support services. Student services like the Learning Commons and the ESL Open Learning Centre are recommended to all international students in their transition to academic life (YorkU 2022a). As with UofT and TMU, YorkU has developed its own transition program so that international students can improve their language and academic skills before starting their undergraduate programs. The YU Bridge Program "is designed for high-achieving international high school graduates" (YorkU 2022b). For international students from China, YorkU advertises, in both Chinese and English, the Destination York program, which emphasizes language and academic skill development, while also offering "a core group of Chinese friends who helped [students] feel at home" (YorkU 2022a).

Economic and Deficit Benefits

While each institution has its own distinct SMA with the province, UofT, TMU, and YorkU have represented international students similarly in these reports. Despite the importance of this student demographic for all three institutions, they do not mention the cultural or national backgrounds of international students, not even in their section on student support services. When they do mention these services, they are the same for students of all national and cultural backgrounds (i.e., immigration, health coverage, and financial and academic advising). Rather than framing student services in ways that conceive of international students' diverse backgrounds as a key to success, all three institutions have designed two types of deficit-focused support services: blanket services for all international students and a targeted unit for international students from China. In this section, we assess the representations of international students based on economic considerations, and discuss the related deficit-focused approach to support services. We then focus on services targeting international students from China to show that they are expanding on the same deficit-focused support services in a way that practically dismisses these students' national and cultural backgrounds, even while they are increasing their economic contribution to the institution.

As Trilokekar and El Masri (2016, 554) observe, "current government policies focus mainly on internationalization's economic rationale." They are focused on human capital development and revenue considerations, and they lead to university measures that "give importance to academic and social/cultural rationales which are in synch with their missions and roles" (Trilokekar and El Masri 2016, 554). In this view, the cultural and diversity of backgrounds of international students are filtered through and reduced to an economic contribution that aligns with provincial priorities focused on the "economic and academic benefits of international education" (Steenkamp 2008). By centering these economic contributions, Ontario universities have de-emphasized, in their framing and support services, the social and cultural aspects of students' lives. Treated mostly outside of the SMA reporting process, the diverse cultural backgrounds of the students are reduced to implicit revenue generation and human capital considerations by Ontario universities, leading to a "static and homogenous" understanding of culture, which assumes that their contribution to campus life is providing domestic students with global and intercultural exposure (Buckner et al. 2021, 38).

Ontario universities have struggled to engage with international students' national and cultural diversity, in line with Ahmed's (2012) observation on the use of international students for their diversity and cultural labor by universities in ways that help change the perception of unspoken norms like whiteness, rather than being a transformative praxis. This has led to an uncritical continuance of a deficit-focused approach to fixing their perceived integration challenges, especially as they relate to language proficiency, cultural awareness, and academic adjustment (Pang and Smith and Zhou et al. 2017). International students from Asia are seen as global talents who require linguistic and cultural training to succeed in Canadian academia and society; hence, they are being asked to assimilate culturally and linguistically rather than integrating their cultural identities into their academic lives (Scott et al. 2015). While these universities have recently initiated structural shifts toward more equitable, accessible, and less Eurocentric institutional cultures (Tamtik and Guenter 2019), the inequities and challenges of succeeding in an academic setting through a default deficit-thinking framework remain intact. This approach focuses on what students lack in terms of their ability to succeed in a mainstream Canadian university context, and it creates measures to isolate, monitor, and test students until they meet the threshold of unspoken dominant norms (Page et al. 2021; Shield, Bishop, and Mazawi 2005).

With students from China accounting for a majority of the international students at Ontario universities, each of the three universities has country-specific support services for high school graduates from China. These students are framed as needing additional support prior to succeeding academically and socially in Ontario; hence the development of targeted programs in which they receive similar, expanded deficit-focused services but in a distinct environment. For students and families with enough wealth to cover at least one additional year of study at a higher tuition fee, UofT's Green Path Program (2022), TMU's Real Institute (2022), and YorkU's Destination York (2022a) are available, based on a model that isolates students from the main student population until they meet institutional standards before entering their undergraduate program of choice. In this case, matters of social class and economic wealth intersect with the students' international status to provide an experience distinct from that of other international students who are usually required to integrate quickly into mainstream academic and social life (Montsion 2018). Interestingly, the cultural or national profile of international students is used to target wealthy international students from China, but their cultural or national distinctiveness is practically put aside in their academic journey. A deficit-focused logic is still deployed to support them, which results mainly in increasing these international students' economic contributions to the institution, all of which remain in line with the goals of internationalization as established by provincial priorities.

Conclusion

The ways Ontario universities have incorporated the Ontario government's vision for international students into their operations are clear: these students are seen as consumers, workers, useful encounters for other students, and facilitators of potential partnerships, all to Ontario's benefit. Through the SMA process, provincial priorities are trickling down to universities, which have adapted their framing of this student group through their economic contribution. In this chapter, we have shown that the national or cultural origins of international students are usually excluded from official documentation, and that their integration is limited to a deficit-focused approach to support services. When national or cultural origins are acknowledged, this is mostly to target specific student groups like high school students from China, while universities continue to benefit economically from recruiting them by pushing deficit thinking further in the design of pre-degree transition models. For universities, deficit-focused pathway programs help increase their market share, secure undergraduate enrolment targets, and allow them to compete with training colleges for the recruitment of pre-university international students (Buckner, Brown, and Morales 2022). However, it is important to note that in recent years, Ontario universities have been over-reliant on international students to maintain and expand their operations. Revenue generated by international students, particularly from a small number of countries such as China, is a significant vulnerability of Ontario universities' financial planning, as "the loss of Chinese students would send many Ontario universities and colleges reeling" (Dehaas 2018, par. 1). In this context, deficit-focused pathway programs might help institutions meet provincial and institutional goals, but they also strengthen this over-reliance.

Note

1 UofT is considered the province's flagship university, while TMU and YorkU are "regional" or "in-between" universities, due to their balanced profiles in terms of teaching quality, research intensity, and accessibility. The former was a training college that consolidated its full university status in 2002 and the latter has been growing significantly since its creation in 1959 (Jonker and Hicks 2016).

Bibliography

Ahmed, Sara. 2012. *On Being Included: Racism and Diversity in Institutional Life.* Durham: Duke University Press.

Buckner, Elizabeth, Punita Lumb, Zahra Jafarova, Phoebe Kang, Adriana Marro-quin, and You Zhang. 2021. "Diversity without Race: How University Internationalization Strategies Discuss International Students." *Journal of International Students* 11, no. S1: 32–49.

Buckner, Elizabeth, Tayia Brown, and Sarah Morales. 2022. "Local Mandate, Global Market: How Canadian Colleges Discuss International Students." *Community College Journal of Research and Practice.* Advanced copy. https://doi.org/10.1080/10668926.2022.2045647.

Canadian Bureau for International Education (CBIE). 2018. "International Students in Canada." Accessed June 23, 2022. https://cbie.ca/wp-content/uploads/2018/09/International-Students-in-Canada-ENG.pdf.

Canadian Bureau for International Education (CBIE). 2022. "The Student Voice: National Results of the 2021 CBIE International Student Survey." Accessed May 5, 2023. https://cbie.ca/wp-content/uploads/2022/06/CBIE-2021-International-Student-Survey-National-Report-FINAL.pdf.

Centre for International Experience (CIE). 2022. "Begin Your Journey." University of Toronto. Accessed June 25y. https://internationalexperience.utoronto.ca/.

Chan, Vivian. 2015. "Implications of Key Performance Indicator Issues in Ontario Universities Explored." *Journal of Higher Education Policy and Management* 37, no. 1: 41–51.

Cudmore, Geoffrey. 2005. "Globalization, Internationalization, and the Recruitment of International Students in Higher Education, and in the Ontario College of Applied Arts and Technology." *Canadian Journal of Higher Education* 35, no. 1: 37–60.

Dehaas, Josh. 2018. "Why Ontario Universities Shouldn't Rely on International Students." *TVO Today*, August 15. https://www.tvo.org/article/why-ontario-universities-shouldnt-rely-on-international-students.

Eastman, Julia A., Glen A. Jones, Olivier Bégin-Caouette, Sharon X. Li, Christian Noumi, and Claude Trottier. 2018. "Provincial Oversight and University Autonomy in Canada: Findings of a Comparative Study of Canadian University Governance." *Canadian Journal of Higher Education* 48, no. 3: 65–81.

El Masri, Amira, Melisa Choubak, and Rashelle Litchmore. 2015. *The Global Competition for International Students as Future Immigrants: The Role of Ontario Universities in Translating Government Policy into Institutional Practice.* Toronto: Higher Education Quality Council of Ontario.

Fanelli, Carlo, and James Meades. 2011. "Austerity, Ontario and Post-Secondary Education: The Case of Canada's Capital University." *Journal for Critical Education Policy Studies* 9, no. 2: 216–240.

Green Path Program – China. 2022. "Welcome to the Green Path." University of Toronto. Accessed June 25, 2022. https://www.utsc.utoronto.ca/greenpath-china/welcome-green-path.

Government of Ontario. 2018. "Educating Global Citizens: Realizing the Benefits of International Postsecondary Education." Accessed May 5, 2023. https://www.tcu.gov.on.ca/pepg/consultations/maesd-international-pse-strategy-en-13f-spring2018.pdf.

Jones, Glen A. 2004. "Ontario Higher Education Reform, 1995-2003: From Modest Modifications to Policy Reform." *Canadian Journal of Higher Education* 34, no. 3: 39–54.

Jonker, Linda, and Martin Hicks. 2016. *The Differentiation of the Ontario University System: Where Are We Now and Where Should We Go?* Toronto: Higher Education Quality Council of Ontario.

King, Conrad. 2021. "Discursive Power and the Internationalization of Universities in British Columbia and Ontario." *Canadian Journal of Higher Education* 50, no. 4: 100–115.

Ministry of Advanced Education and Skills Development (MAESD). 2018. *Educating Global Citizens: Realizing the Benefits of International Postsecondary Education.* Toronto: Government of Ontario. Accessed June 25, 2022. http://www.tcu.gov.on.ca/pepg/consultations/maesd-international-pse-strategy-en-13f-spring2018.pdf.

Ministry of Colleges and Universities (MCU). 2021. *Archived – College and University Strategic Mandate Agreement, 2017-2020.* Toronto: Government of Ontario. Accessed June 25, 2022. https://www.ontario.ca/page/college-and-university-strategic-mandate-agreements-2017-2020.

Ministry of Training Colleges and Universities (MTCU). 2012. *Tuition and Ancillary Fees Reporting.* Toronto: Government of Ontario. Accessed June 25, 2022. http://www.tcu.gov.on.ca/pepg/documents/TuitionandAncillaryFeesReporting 2012.pdf.

MTCU. 2016. *Developing Global Opportunities: Creating a Postsecondary International Education Strategy for Ontario.* Toronto: Government of Ontario. Accessed June 25, 2022. https://www.tcu.gov.on.ca/pepg/consultations/international_education_strategy.html.

Monahan, Patrick. 2010. *Building a More Engaged University: Strategic Directions for York University 2010-2020.* Accessed June 25, 2022. http://vpacademic.yorku.ca/whitepaper/docs/White_Paper_Companion_April_15.pdf.

Montsion, Jean Michel. 2018. "Resource Centre or Experience Desk? Producing Spaces for Delivering Services to Indigenous and International Students at Universities in Ontario, Canada." *Canadian Journal of Higher Education* 48, no. 1: 132–147.

Page, Christina, Robin Leung, Neet Dhindsa, Tony Yuan, Rishab Sapra, Lovepreet Kaur Deol, and Gurmanpreet Kaur. 2021. *Getting to Know Your International Students*, 2nd edition. Surrey: Kwantlen Polytechnic University. Accessed June 25, 2022. https://kora.kpu.ca/islandora/object/kora%3A635/datastream/PDF/view.

Real Institute. 2022. "Brochures." Toronto Metropolitan University. Accessed June 25, 2022. https://www.torontomu.ca/realinstitute/brochures/.

Rigas, Bob, and Renée Kuchapski. 2016. "Strengthening' Ontario Universities: A Neoliberal Reconstruction of Higher Education." *Canadian Journal of Educational Administration and Policy* 180: 47–50.

Scott, Colin, Saba Safdar, Roopa Desai Trilokekar, and Amira El Masri. 2015. "International Students as 'Ideal Immigrants' in Canada: A Disconnect between Policy Makers' Assumptions and the Voices of International Students." *Comparative and International Education* 43, no. 3 (2015): article 5.

Shields, Carolyn, Russell Bishop, and Andre E. Mazawi. 2005. *Pathologizing Practices: The Impact of Deficit Thinking on Education*. Bern: Peter Lang Publishing.

Steenkamp, Philip. 2008. "The Development of Ontario's Internationalization Strategy." *Canadian EMagazine of International Education* 1, no. 3: September.

Tamtik, Merli, and Melissa Guenter. 2019. "Policy Analysis of Equity, Diversity and Inclusion Strategies in Canadian Universities – How Far Have We Come?" *Canadian Journal of Higher Education* 49, no. 3: 41–56.

Toronto Metropolitan University (TMU). 2017. "Strategic Mandate Agreement: Ryerson University Ministry of Advanced Education and Skills Development 2017-20." Accessed June 25, 2022. https://www.torontomu.ca/content/dam/university-planning/accountability-gateway/RU-SMA-2017-2020.pdf.

TMU. 2019. "International Strategy, Ryerson University 2019-2024." Accessed June 25, 2022. https://www.torontomu.ca/content/dam/international/Documents/RU_international_strategy_final_web_FINAL-s_1176627.pdf.

TMU. 2021. "Global Learning." Accessed June 25, 2022. https://www.torontomu.ca/global-learning/.

TMU. 2022a. "International Student Support." Accessed June 25, 2022. https://www.torontomu.ca/international/student-support/.

TMU. 2022b. "International College – About." Accessed June 25, 2022. https://www.torontomuic.ca/about/.

Trilokekar, Roopa Desai, and Amira El Masri. 2016. "Canada's International Education Strategy: Implications of a New Policy Landscape for Synergy between Government Policy and Institutional Strategy." *Higher Education Policy* 29: 539–563.

University of Toronto (UofT). 2017. "Strategic Mandate Agreement: University of Toronto Ministry of Advanced Education and Skills Development 2017-20." Accessed June 25, 2022. https://www.utoronto.ca/sites/default/files/University%20of%20Toronto%20SMA%202017-20%20%28for%20publication%29.pdf.

UofT. 2018a. "Global Engagement: UofT in the World. The 2017-18 Annual Report of the Office of the Vice-President, International." Accessed June 25, 2022. https://global.utoronto.ca/wp-content/uploads/2015/08/UofT-FinalAR-2018.pdf.

UofT. 2018b. "Budget Report 2018-2019." Accessed June 25, 2022. https://
planningandbudget.utoronto.ca/wp-content/uploads/2021/03/2018-19-Budget-
Report.pdf.

UofT. 2019. "A Global University: The 2018-19 Annual Report of the Office of the
Vice-President, International." Accessed June 25, 2022. https://global.utoronto.
ca/wp-content/uploads/2015/08/AR-2019_9.pdf.

UofT. 2022. "University of Toronto and East Asia." Accessed June 25, 2022.
https://global.utoronto.ca/global-engagement/east-asia/.

Wellen, Richard. 2011. "Grappling with Academic Capitalism in Canadian Universities." *Academic Matters: OCUFA's Journal of Higher Education*. Accessed
May 5, 2023. https://academicmatters.ca/grappling-with-academic-capitalism-
in-canadian-universities/

Williams, Keegan, Gabriel Williams, Amy Arbuckle, Margaret Walton-Roberts,
and Jenna Hennebry. 2015. *International Students in Ontario's Postsecondary
Education System, 2000-2012: An Evaluation of Changing Policies, Populations
and Labour Market Entry Processes*. Toronto: Higher Education Quality Council of Ontario.

York International. 2023. "International Students." Accessed May 5, 2023. https://
yorkinternational.yorku.ca/international-students/.

York University (YorkU). 2017. "Strategic Mandate Agreement: York University
Ministry of Advanced Education and Skills Development 2017-20." Accessed
June 25, 2022. https://oipa.info.yorku.ca/files/2014/04/York-University-SMA-
Final-November-22-2017-Published.pdf.

YorkU. 2019 "York University: Globally Minded and Globally Engaged: Towards
an Integrated Strategy and Framework for Internationalization and Global Engagement." Accessed June 25, 2022. https://pci.info.yorku.ca/files/2019/09/
Internationalization-Issue-Paper-v5-Sept-23-2019.pdf?x69140.

YorkU. 2022a. "China Brochure." Accessed June 25, 2022. https://futurestudents.
yorku.ca/sites/all/files/pdfs/intl-brochure-china-chinese-simp.pdf.

YorkU. 2022b. "YU Bridge Program." Accessed June 25, 2022. https://continue.
yorku.ca/programs/yubridge-program/.

Zhou, George, Tian Liu, and Glenn Rideout. 2017. "A Study of Chinese International Students Enrolled in a Master of Education Program at a Canadian University." *International Journal of Chinese Education* 6: 210–235.

4 International Education Pipeline

An Analysis of British Columbia's University Transfer System

Elic Chan and Brett Matsushita

Introduction

British Columbia (BC) is home to 25 public degree-granting post-secondary institutions and over 300 certified private colleges and institutes. These institutions are linked via a formal transfer system regulated by British Columbia Council on Admissions and Transfer (BCCAT). One unique feature of BC is the ability for students to transfer their courses and credits at the college level to degree-granting universities. In the past decade, about one-third of all post-secondary students in BC have used the transfer system to gain entry into their desired school (BCCAT 2020). International students (IS), who represent a sizable proportion in BC, are aware of and attracted to the flexibility of the system. Recent survey shows that over 70% of IS agree that the quality of the transfer system was important for their decision to study in BC (Adamoski 2015). Predictably, BC is one of the top provinces with the highest proportion of IS studying in colleges (ranked 2nd) and universities (ranked 3rd) in Canada (Statistics Canada 2021).

Although credit transfers and student mobility are tracked by the province, the overall pattern of flow between institutions is understudied and not well understood. Most reports focus on the total student population and limit the comparison between subgroups. Hence, the transfer pathways of domestic and international students are rarely discussed. Studies on internationalization often neglect the different pathways IS take to enter Canadian universities. As a result, the scale and direction of transfer for IS are largely unknown. As the number of international students continue to grow, their impact on the transfer system is increasingly transformative.

This chapter provides a detailed look at the transfer pathways of international students in BC. Through archival research of publicly available material such as university annual reports, BCCAT documents, and government statistics, we investigate how the transfer system has adapted to the neoliberal climate of post-secondary education and its relations to international students. We do this in three ways. First, we

DOI: 10.4324/b23160-6

compare the transfer pathways to key receiving universities, particularly the University of British Columbia (UBC). Second, we analyze the flow between private and public institutions and compare the differences between domestic and international students. Lastly, we highlight the challenges institutions face and evaluate the strengths and weaknesses of the transfer system. By doing so, we gain a better understanding of how institutions and the transfer system respond to the growing trend of internationalization.

International Students in BC

In the past decade, BC's IS population experienced accelerated growth. In 2010–2011, the international post-secondary student population was around 30,000 and in 2019–2020 doubled to 80,000 (Heslop 2021). International students from Asia aspire to study in BC for many reasons, one of which includes the quality of education offered by high-ranked institutions such as UBC. UBC is the largest post-secondary institution in the province. In the world university rankings, UBC consistently ranks in the top 50. In 2022, UBC ranks 37th in the Times Higher Education world rankings and 46th in the QS World University Rankings. Simon Fraser University (SFU) ranks second in the province and is rated within the 200–300th range according to both rankings. Since IS weigh school rankings to some degree in their decision to study abroad (see Kim, Abdulkarim, and Payne), the presence of a highly ranked school provides an attractive option for incoming students. Currently, UBC hosts over 19,000 international students, which make up more than 20% of the province's IS population (Mukherjee-Reed and Szeri 2022). From 2015 to 2020, the school increased their undergraduate enrolment by about 10% every year (Mukherjee-Reed and Szeri 2020). The growth is largely due to IS enrolment as this group increased by almost 40% in that period, whereas domestic student enrolment remained unchanged (34). Most IS at UBC are from Asia, as eight out of the top 10 source countries are from the region. China has consistently been the top source country as students from China makeup over one-third of the total IS population (Mukherjee-Reed and Szeri 2022). Students from India comprise the second largest group and have grown 170% since 2017. This trend mirrors IS trends across BC (Heslop 2021) as well as Canada (CBIE 2018) as India has outpaced China as the top source country in the past few years.

Students enter BC universities in a variety of ways. The most popular is direct entry, in which the university accepts the student directly from high school and into their first-year programs. However, in BC, many students are able to transfer from other institutions; particularly after two years of study at a college. A study of over 80,000 undergraduate students from 2013 to 2018 showed that over 30% of students in BC gain entry into university through the transfer system (BCCAT 2020). Although other provinces have similar systems in place, the proportion of students who pursue this pathway are few. For example, studies show that on average less than 15% of students in Ontario transfer to a university after studying in college (Acai and Newton 2015 and Lennon et al. 2016). Compared to Ontario, recent study shows that BC colleges themselves are found to focus more on academic pathways than labour market transitions (Buckner, Brown, and Morales 2022).

BC Transfer System: A Unique Feature

Although BC is not the only province with a college-to-university credit transfer system, it is a well-established one with a long history. Scholars generally attribute the Macdonald Report, written by the president of the UBC John Macdonald in 1962, as the catalyst for the development of the transfer system (Andres and Dawson 1998). To manage the antici-pated growth of post-secondary education, the report recommended a future system that would offer a diverse range of studies to respond to the needs of different communities (2). Specifically, Macdonald recom-mended the creation of two-year colleges which offer a range of pro-grams, including academic programs at the 1st- and 2nd-year level and technical programs as well as two four-year colleges in Victoria and Lower Mainland (3). Shortly after the publication of the report, the Uni-versity of Victoria (in 1963) and SFU (in 1965) become a full university with degree-granting status (Gaber 2005). Between 1965 to 1975, ten more community colleges were established that would be members of the transfer system. These include today's largest community colleges, namely Vancouver City College (later changed to Langara College), Douglas College, and Okanagan College. In 1966, students from Van-couver City College were among the first to be transferred to universities through informal agreements (2). Under BCCAT, a transfer describes the process when one post-secondary institution recognizes education com-pleted at another. It allows students to use the credits they have earned at one institution to meet some of the requirements for a credential at another institution. This college-to-university pathway model is utilized in many ways. Aside from the opportunity to experiment with post-secondary studies without too much commitment and financial burden, it is also designed for those who did not initially get into their desired university to start at a college and transfer. Since its inception, many students have employed this feature to obtain their undergraduate degrees.

A cohort study of BC's Bachelor's degree holders showed that over 40% enrolled in two or more schools to complete their undergraduate studies (Heslop 2015). Ultimately, the rationale for the system is to provide students with cost-effective and efficient access to higher education (BCCAT 2022).

Receiving and Sending Institutions

Although there are as many as 30 institutions that are part of the BC transfer system, the transfer pathway is dominated by a few institutions. Research universities such as UBC and SFU are among the largest receiving institutions. Their long history and global reputation make them an attractive destination for both domestic and international students.

Since UBC is considered the top school in the province and the destination of many transfer programs, courses and programs are designed to reference their transferability to UBC. There are primarily two types of transfers: external and internal. For example, a transfer student can enter a UBC degree program either after completing courses in a different UBC program (internal transfer) or after obtaining relevant post-secondary course credits from another recognized institutions (external transfer). Few IS enter UBC using the external transfer system. Table 4.1 examines the breakdown of new students by category of admissions. A large proportion (over 65%) of students are admitted through direct entry, of which one-third are IS. Although over 20% of UBC's total admission is from external transfer (including both domestic and international), few IS enter via this method. Less than 600 out of 11,000 students are international external transfer students. But the more pertinent question is: where do the transfer students come from?

Table 4.1 UBC admission categories, 2020–2021

Admission Categories	Percentage of students (%)	Number of students
Direct Entry Domestic	48.0	5,388
Direct Entry International	19.4	2,177
External Transfer Domestic	14.8	1,664
External Transfer International	5.2	586
Internal Transfer Domestic	9.3	1,043
Internal Transfer International	3.3	366
	100.0	11,224

Source: Table by author, adapted from Mukherjee-Reed and Szeri 2021.

Table 4.2 Top sending and receiving institutions in BC, between 2013–2014 and 2017–2018

	Province (BC)		UBC		SFU		UVic	
	%	n	%	n	%	n	%	n
Fraser International College	15.5	4,656	0.1	8	36.6	4,643	0.0	1
Langara College	13.8	4,145	24.3	2,373	11.3	1,430	4.9	257
Douglas College	10.1	3,047	6.4	624	17.1	2,170	3.3	174
Camosun College	10.7	3,230	2.3	222	0.8	99	51.1	2,693
Kwantlen University	7.4	2,226	6.9	674	10.8	1,371	1.9	99
Okanagan College	5	1,440	11.0	1,079	0.7	83	2.2	117
Coquitlam College	3.3	1,002	5.7	560	2.6	331	2.0	105
Other schools	34	10,358	43.4	4,244	20.2	2,557	34.7	1,828
	100.0	30,104	100.0	9,784	100.0	12,684	100.0	5,274

Source: Table by author, adapted from BCCAT, 2020.

Table 4.2 provides a descriptive profile of the sending and receiving institutions in BC. The data is adapted from BCCAT reports, which analyze students transferring to research universities between 2013–2014 and 2017–2018. In the 5-year period, over 30,000 students used the transfer system to gain entrance into other institutions. The analysis shows that there are several key schools that are responsible for transferring a large proportion of students into BC's universities. Some describe these as pathway colleges, and they vary by type of instruction and transfer mechanism (McCartney and Metcalfe 2018). For example, the top three institutions include Fraser International College (FIS), Langara College, and Douglas College which together transfer 40% of BC's students to the province's top three universities. If we include all schools that transfer over 1,000 students (there are seven of them), they constitute over 65% of all transfer students. Although there are over 25 other institutions in the provinces, they account for less than 35% of the transfer population. In sum, the transfer system is asymmetrical and primarily dominated by key sending and receiving schools.

Table 4.2 also provides a descriptive profile of the top receiving schools and their distribution from the key sending institutions. All three top receiving schools admit their transfer students through different pathways.

SFU receives about one-third of its students from Fraser International College (FIC), a private college that is affiliated with the university which caters specifically to IS. UVic provides another unique pattern. Due to its location on Vancouver Island, half of all transfer students are from Camosun College (also situated on the island). UBC presents a completely different picture. Although about 25% of all transfer students are from Langara College, their transfer students are not concentrated from any particular school. Rather, their entrance profile is more spread out over many schools, including smaller colleges.

Private Institutions and Pathway Programs

Under neoliberalist approach, education has shifted from state-centred to market-driven. As Fisher et al. (2009) observe, this trend is particularly strong in Ontario and BC as the provinces have introduced legislation that creates the conditions for the establishment of quasi-markets in post-secondary education. In BC, the number of private institutions registered with the province has grown from about 350 in 1993 to over 800 in 2005 (Fisher et al. 2009). As of 2022, the number of private institutions is over 1,700, with 300 of them certified to offer at least one program/certificate at the school. Within the privatized group, there are many types of schools and not all have an equal status. For example, there are vocational schools with no ties to university transfer courses or programs, while many other schools are in place to capitalize on the pre-transfer market. Private institutions in BC require to be registered with the Private Training Institutions Branch (PTIB). Since PTIB requires institutions to hold a designated permit to enrol IS, we can deduce the number of schools that cater to IS. Unsurprisingly, the information from the PTIB directory shows that over one-third have applied for designated status and can enrol IS in their programs. Still, institutions under PTIB are different in that not all of them are formally accredited and are not able to transfer students to degree-granting universities. As listed in BCCAT, there are only 12 that are formal members of BCCAT and have predestined credit transfer for their courses. This also means that over 90% of private institutions are not members of BCCAT. Although institutions outside of BCCAT do not have articulated programs, they are able to provide transfers through manual formal agreements and carve out specific institution-to-institution pathways for prospective students. For example, students from the Vancouver Film School's Advanced Production Programs are eligible to transfer into degree programs at the University of Fraser Valley (Vancouver Film School 2022). For smaller institutions that do not have such agreements, students may use informal block transfers to go from one school to another. However, the process relies heavily on the subjectivity of the admissions office and there is no guarantee for a successful transfer. Students from smaller schools may attempt to transfer their credits on an ad hoc basis, but many resort to transferring to other accredited institutions to increase their chances to be admitted into a university.

Private institutions often have lower tuition fees and admission requirements compared to larger public universities and position themselves competitively against public colleges. Columbia College is a good example. The school was founded in 1936 and has its own campus in downtown Vancouver. The current website celebrates "85 years of excellence" in serving BC. In 1991, Columbia College along with Coquitlam College became the first private institution to formally join the BC transfer system. Their tuition is considered one of the least expensive, currently charging $570 per credit excluding fees and taxes (Columbia College 2022a), lower compared to Langara College and Douglas College and which currently charge over $620 per credit (Douglas College 2022 and Langara College 2022). Per semester, the student would pay roughly $500 less compared to a public college with similar rules of entry and $10,000 less compared to UBC. As shown in Columbia College's promotional material, the price point of their tuition is one of the key selling features of the school. In particular, the school boasts that a student can save up to $16,950 in tuition costs if they attend their institution before going to university (Columbia College 2022a). Although an established institution, Columbia College contributes less than 3% of UBC transfer students and less than 2% for SFU (BCCAT 2020). For a college with a 2000 student enrolment, the annual rate of transfer is less than 8%. Private colleges use large universities like UBC as a selling point, but few students actually succeed in such transfers. This may be due to universities' strict monitoring of standards. BCCAT's performance research shows that the drop in grades at 15 credits at UBC and SFU is larger for students from private institutions compared to public ones (BCCAT 2020).

In addition to independent private institutions, a new type of private pathway program was developed in BC. In 2004, SFU partnered with Navitas Limited, an international provider of pathway programs, to form what would become North America's first international university pathway (for a complete history, see Rahilly and Hudson 2018). From 2008–20009 to 2012–2013, FIC transferred over 2,100 students exclusively to SFU. For the next four years, this number would more than double to 4,600. FIC students are able to experience SFU as university students, including the use of residence halls, libraries, gym, and other student services (Rahilly and Hudson 2018). The program has generated consistently positive student outcomes, with over 90% of students moving on to SFU's degree programs (268). In 2014, UBC followed suit with a similar setup with Vantage College. The enrolment for the first year was just over 150 students. In the 2021–2022 enrolment report, that number grew to almost

Table 4.3 Top sending institutions in BC by students' national status, between 2013–2014 and 2017–2018

	International		Domestic	
	%	n	%	n
Fraser International College	60.6	4,452	1.5	204
Columbia College	6.5	481	0.4	50
Coquitlam College	10.1	745	1.9	257
Other Private	8.3	612	3.8	509
Total Private	85.6	6,290	7.6	1,020
Langara College	7.3	537	26.8	3,608
Douglas College	3.6	267	20.7	2,780
Kwantlen University	1.0	76	16.0	2,150
Other Public	2.5	182	29.0	3,902
Total Public	14.4	1,062	92.4	12,440
Grand Total	100.0	7,352	100.0	13,460

Source: Table by author, adapted from BCCAT (2020)

300 (Mukherjee-Reed and Szeri 2022). Although the mechanism of a privatized pathway to degree programs exists at UBC, the scale is much smaller.

Private Colleges, even those outside of affiliated colleges, primarily target IS. Table 4.3 compares the number of domestic and international students from sending institutions by type. When looking at transfer students, over 90% of domestic students transfer from public institutions. In contrast, only 14% of international students utilize the same pathway and over 85% of them transfer from private institutions. Another noteworthy trend is that IS transfers are dominated by primarily a few schools, with FIC being the main institution. The proportion of students that transferred from other private and public schools that are not listed constitutes less than 12% of the provinces' total IS population. This pattern shows that the domestic and international have distinct pathways in the transfer system.

Challenges

Although the transfer system has been in place for some time, it is not without its challenges. To examine the discourse surrounding IS across post-secondary institutions, we examined the BCCAT Articulation meeting reports. Articulation committees are formed around specific disciplines, subjects, or programs. They meet annually to share information and review matters related to course curriculum. The meetings allow opportunities to foster a collaborative and collegial relationships among departments throughout the transfer system. Although formal articulation (i.e. course transfer equivalence) is not discussed at these meetings, the minutes provide a glimpse of the common issues that arise for the disciplines at different institutions. The advantage of examining articulation minutes is that it provides an insider perspective on each discipline and its institutional challenges. From the BCCAT website, we downloaded publicly available reports from the articulation meetings between 2017 and 2021. We examined over 40 articulation reports from 12 discipline committees for review. From these reports, key terms such as "international" and "transfer" were used to search for discourse surrounding relevant topics such as enrolment, staffing, and academic standards.

Theme 1 Student Representation

Although the inception of the transfer system is to provide domestic students with cost-effective and efficient access to post-secondary education, many institutions experienced substantial IS enrolment and experienced problems adapting to this growing group.

> This year will be the first time we will have second-year physics courses. The new courses are being funded through our international office, as IS wanting to complete an Associate of Science degree at NIC were asking for more options than just Biology ... Hopefully the additional offerings will also be attractive to domestic students, who may also decide to stay for two years and an Associate of Science degree before moving on.
> North Island College, Physics & Astronomy Articulation Meeting 2019 (Kirkey 2019, 49)

The increase in IS enrolment is experienced across all disciplines. One of the main concerns with the rise of IS is the lack of diversity among the student population. Historically, BC's international student enrolment is primarily from China, and more recently from India, many disciplines raised the issue of IS coming primarily from a few places. In addition, the concern for the lack of representation in regard to domestic population is also raised during the meetings.

> Selkirk College continues to offer only first year principle courses. However, over the past four years, our IS enrolments have quadrupled. The Business Administration program attracts the highest number of international students among other programs. The largest group of students are from India. Due to increased international enrolment, the number of sections offered have been increased.
> Economics Articulation Meeting 2017 (Denchev 2017, 29)

Enrolment in classes is split 50–50% in the courses: domestic vs. international. If they allow 100% for international, the domestic students get squeezed too much.
Langara College, Computer Science Articulation
Meeting, 2019 (Abdullah 2019, 8)

Some noted a lack of First Nations students and wondered whether international spots may be displacing them, Assumptions and narratives may lack numbers or evidence to support various claims about Indigenizing.
Political Science Articulation Meeting, 2020 (Hanlon 2020, 4)

Theme 2 Competency and Academic Integrity

The issue of competency of international students is frequently raised in articulation meetings. Many departments discuss students' lack of preparation and skills for university-level studies. This type of environment strains the quality of education, making any effort to upkeep academic standards counterproductive. Simultaneously, students become strained and frustrated and resorted to cheating and plagiarism while instructional departments negotiate ways to adapt and alter their curriculum to retain and transfer students.

International students tend to be under-prepared for college and university in terms of reading and writing skills. In many cases, students' IELTS scores do not match their actual abilities – i.e., some students' language competencies are at a Grade 10 level or less.
Sociology/Anthropology Articulation
Meeting, 2019 (Reynolds 2019, 6)

Not only does this issue relate to instruction but also organizational issues regarding attrition and trouble with transfers. From an organizational standpoint, student failure reflects poorly on the institution and its reputation. The issue with the academic competencies is further highlighted in the pressures which instructors feel to pass underachieving students.

Some students are "bargaining" with faculty for higher grades and in some cases this can shade over into "emotional blackmail". Faculty are feeling uncomfortable and reluctant to award failing grades, knowing the seriousness of the consequences for these students (e.g., being deported). This situation is enormously stressful for faculty and the fear is that it could potentially have a real impact on the security, safety and well-being of faculty.

Sociology/Anthropology Articulation Meeting,
2019 (Reynolds 2019, 7)

The issue of academic integrity is often raised in articulation meetings as well. Cheating by IS was a consistent issue discussed across multiple institutions. Many departments voiced out that international students are generally unprepared to do university-level studies.

The committee discussed the increase in academic dishonesty across institutions and other significant challenges with increased numbers of IS. Action: Add International students and plagiarism to agenda for next year and ensure that the committee collectively commits to speaking about race and international students respectfully.

Psychology Articulation Meeting, 2019 (Tonks 2019, 4)

Conclusion

From our analysis, BC relies on large universities such as UBC and SFU to attract IS to the province. Although top universities are directly recruiting students into their schools, the global demand for higher education exceeds the supply of spots in top-ranked institutions. The unanticipated growth of IS has led to the expansion of established colleges as well as the growth of private institutions. As a result, the privatization of post-secondary education has blossomed in the last two decades. Our data show that IS are more likely to study in private institutions and then transfer to universities. Although not all IS desire to transfer to top schools, private schools compete with each other through reputation and links to top-ranked institutions to secure enrolment. Affiliated schools such as FIC and Vantage College celebrate their direct connection with top universities to ensure IS a risk-free pathway. Others such as Columbia College and Coquitlam College boast their history, local experience, and affordable pricing to garner student confidence and value.

Although the BC transfer system has been in place for more than 50 years, it has dramatically evolved in the last decade. Our analysis reveals that domestic students are more likely to rely on public institutions whereas IS are more likely to transfer via private ones. Despite the countless options and flexibility, entrance to top receiving school is often dominated by a few pathways. For UBC, IS are more likely to be admitted via direct entry versus external transfer. Affiliated schools like Vantage College are also set up to safeguard student readiness when transferring into their second-year programs. For SFU, designated pathways from FIC can pipeline transfer the largest number of students than any other school. In this light, the transfer system amplifies the market-driven approach to internationalization via privatized pathways.

Analysis of articulation committee reports showed that post-secondary institutions face challenges with different waves of IS. The recent demographic shift of students from China to India create issues for many pathway colleges. The motivation and trajectory for the two groups seem to be different. Generally, Indian students are more likely to enrol in colleges and focus on Business & Management while students from China are more likely to enrol in research universities and focus on Arts & Science (Heslop 2018). Indian students are also more likely to acquire permanent residency after the completion of their study permit compared to other groups (Youjin, Crossman, and Hou 2021). As a result, smaller colleges face greater challenges as fluctuation in enrolment causes greater demand on instructional changes, hiring of qualified staff, bigger space, and different student support. Because smaller colleges rely on BCCAT membership to uphold their reputation and pipeline transfers, they constantly need to adapt to the changing programs and criteria of receiving institutions. Moreover, the pressure to help students to meet the academic standards of receiving institutions to garner a successful transfer puts a burden on both the student and the institutions. Owing to the fact that larger institutions have their own paths of recruiting international students, the utility of smaller private pathway colleges is becoming less relevant. Although it is beyond the scope of this study, future studies should focus on the changing role of sending institutions. If receiving institutions are relying less on external transfers and creating their own channels for student intake, the transfer system for IS becomes more emblematic than functional.

References

Abdullah, Mohd. 2019. *BCCEC Articulation Meeting*. Vancouver: BCCAT.

Acai, Anita, and Genevieve Newton. 2015. "A Comparison of Factors Related to University Students' Learning: College-Transfer and Direct-Entry from High School Students." *Canadian Journal of Higher Education* 45, no. 2: 168–192.

Adamoski, Robert. 2015. *BC International Student Survey*. Vancouver: British Columbia Council on Admissions and Transfer.

Andres, Lesley, and Jane Dawson. 1998. *Investigating Transfer Project, Phase III: A History of Transfer Policy and Practice in British Columbia*. Vancouver: British Columbia Council on Admissions and Transfer.

BCCAT. 2020. *2013/14-2017/18 Transfer Students: Profile and Performance*. Vancouver: British Columbia Council on Admissions & Transfer.

———. 2022. "Principles & Guidelines for Transfer." Accessed June 15 2022. https://www.bccat.ca/system/policies.

Buckner, Elizabeth, Taiya Brown, and Sarah Morales. 2022. "Local Mandate, Global Market: How Canadian Colleges Discuss International Students." *Community College Journal of Research and Practice*, 1-15. https://doi.org/10.1080/10668926.2022.2045647.

CBIE. 2018. *International Students in Canada*. Ottawa: Canadian Bureau for International Education.

Columbia College. 2022a. "Cost of Study." Accessed June 15, 2022. https://www.columbiacollege.ca/future-students/cost-of-study/.

———. 2022b. "University Transfer." Accessed June 15, 2022. https://www.columbiacollege.ca/programs/university-transfer/.

Denchev, Yolina. 2017. *Economics Articulation Business Meeting Minutes*. Vancouver: BCCAT.

Douglas College. 2022. "Tuition and Fees for International Students." Accessed June 15, 2022. https://www.douglascollege.ca/international-students/prospective-students/tuition-and-fees.

Fisher, Donald, Kjell Rubenson, Glen Jones, and Theresa Shanahan. 2009. "The Political Economy of Post-Secondary Education: A Comparison of British Columbia, Ontario and Quebec." *Higher Education* 57, no. 5: 549–566.

Gaber, Devron. 2005. *A Brief History of the Transfer System in British Columbia*. Vancouver: British Columbia Council on Admissions and Transfer.

Hanlon, Robert. 2020. *2020 BCPSA Articulation Meeting*. Vancouver: BCCAT.

Heslop, Joanne. 2015. *B.C. Bachelor's Degree Completers of 2013/2014*. Victoria: Ministry of Advanced Education and Skills Training.

Heslop, Joanne. 2018. *International Students in BC's Education System*. Student Transition Project.

Heslop, Joanne. 2021. *Student Transition Project (STP): Transition of B.C. High School Graduates into B.C. Public Post-Secondary Education*. Victoria: The Ministry of Advanced Education and Skills Training.

Kirkey, Jennifer. 2019. *Physics and Astronomy Articulation Minutes*. Vancouver: BCCAT.

Langara College. 2022. "International Student Fees." Accessed June 15, 2022. https://langara.ca/registration-and-records/tuition-and-service-fees/international-student-fees.html.

Lennon, Mary Catharine, Amanda Brijmohan, Eric Lavigne, Jinli Yang, Gavin Moodie, and Leesa Wheelahan. 2016. *Ontario Student Mobility: Carving Paths of Desire*. Toronto: Centre for the Study of Canadian and International Higher Education, OISE-University of Toronto.

McCartney, Dale M., and Amy Scott Metcalfe. 2018. "Corporatization of Higher Education through Internationalization: The Emergence of Pathway Colleges in Canada." *Tertiary Education and Management* 24, no. 3: 206–220.

Mukherjee-Reed, Ananya, and Andrew Szeri. 2020. *University of British Columbia Annual Enrolment Report 2019-2020*. University of British Columbia.

Mukherjee-Reed, Ananya, and Andrew Szeri. 2021. *University of British Columbia Annual Enrolment Report 2020/21*. University of British Columbia.

Mukherjee-Reed, Ananya, and Andrew Szeri. 2022. *University of British Columbia Annual Enrolment Report 2021/22*. University of British Columbia.

Rahilly, Timothy J., and Bev Hudson. 2018. "Canada's First International Partnership for a Pathway Program." In *University Pathway Programs: Local Responses within a Growing Global Trend*, edited by Cintia Ines Agosti and Eva Bernat, 267–285. Cham, Switzerland: Springer International Publishing.

Reynolds, Annette. 2019. *Sociology/Anthropology Articulation Meeting Minutes.* Vancouver: BCCAT.

Statistics Canada. 2021. *The Daily: Prior to COVID-19, International Students Accounted for the Growth in Post-Secondary Enrolments and Graduates.* Ottawa: Statistics Canada.

Tonks, Randal. 2019. *British Columbia Psychology Articulation Committee Meeting Minutes.* Vancouver: BCCAT.

Vancouver Film School. 2022. "VFS-University of the Fraser Valley Degree Pathway Program." Accessed June 15, 2022. https://vfs.edu/pathway/ufv.

Youjin, Choi, Eden Crossman, and Feng Hou. 2021. *International Students as a Source of Labour Supply: Transition to Permanent Residency.* Ottawa: Statistics Canada.

5 International Students and Equity, Diversity and Inclusivity (EDI) in Canadian Universities

A Critical Look

Tania Das Gupta and Bianca Gomez

Introduction

About 77% of Canadian universities report having Equity, Diversity and Inclusion (EDI) policies in their strategic plans and long-term planning documents (Charbonneau 2019). They have been part of the Canadian state's response to the burgeoning heterogeneity of its population in the context of post-1980s neo-liberal capitalist im(migration) priorities and social justice movements, managing these aspirations within existing frameworks of human rights and multiculturalism since the 1970s. EDI programs allow the Canadian state and state-funded institutions, such as universities, to recognize and manage racism and other cross-cutting issues.

In addition, these past decades have seen the entrenchment of neo-liberal policies, marked by state cutbacks in "welfare provisions and ... arenas such as healthcare, public education, and social services" (Harvey 2005, 76), the commodification of these basic services, partnerships with the private sector and the hegemony of individual responsibility. Government funding as a share of university revenues fell from 82.7% in 1982 to 24% in 2019, while tuition fees subsidized the shortfall, going from 13.8% of university revenues in 1982 to 37.5% in 2012 (Harden 2017; Valverde 2019; and also see Ajay et al.). One area that the Canadian state has not abandoned, however, is the regulation of migration and immigration policies, because as Harvey (2005) observes, one of the neo-liberal state's central contradictions is "to be activist in creating a good business climate and to behave as a competitive entity in global politics" (79), even while receding from social welfare programs.

Enter the international student, who subsidizes government cutbacks in the post-secondary sector (GOVision 2014; Usher 2018; and also see Kim, Buckner, and Montsion), and who is offered the possibility of permanent residency if they fulfil certain requirements. As neo-liberal restructuring deepened, one strategy deployed by the post-secondary sector is internationalization, understood at the "national, sector and institutional

DOI: 10.4324/b23160-7

levels" as the "process of integrating an international, intercultural, or global dimension into the purpose, functions or delivery of post-secondary education" (Knight 2003, 2). To such ends, a central component of internationalization has been the recruitment of thousands of international students, on the condition of having to pay up to four times the tuition fees that domestic students pay and abiding by the parameters of their study permit, including limited hours of work during the school year (Hassanein 2014; Government of Canada 2022b). The conditional pathway to permanent residency saw its accentuation and integration within the neo-liberal frameworks adopted by the state. As of June 2014, off-campus work authorization permits were issued by the state along with study permits to facilitate their entry through immigration programs, such as the federal Express Entry system or any Provincial Nominee Program. Interestingly, hours of work during the study period does not count towards permanent residency; only post-graduation work counts for that.

Recognizing the possibility of gaining permanent residency and Canadian citizenship in the near future, thousands of young individuals, particularly from China, India and Korea, enrol in Canadian colleges and universities hoping for a better future for themselves and their families. This is the context in which this chapter will explore the dynamics between EDI programs and discourses in Canadian post-secondary education and the international students they host. This chapter will (1) undertake a critical understanding of EDI programs in Canada from an anti-racist perspective; (2) determine if EDI programs in universities relate to international students at all; (3) explicate the conflation of the roles balanced by international students – as students, workers and migrants in Canada and (4) understand how international students and EDI programs in universities are part of a neo-liberal, racial capitalist framework.

An anti-racist view of EDI programs

EDI and related programs have been the efforts at addressing 'difference' and social inequalities in Canada, some more effective than others. Although "Equity, Diversity and Inclusion" are now enunciated in one breath, each of these terms has a different genealogy and discourse.

Equity programs arose in the mid-1980s with Judge Rosalie Abella's Report, *Equality Now*, as part of a movement of women, racialized folks, people with disabilities and Indigenous Peoples agitating around labour injustices and associated discrimination and poverty, involving trade unions, women's organizations, anti-racist organizations and disability and Indigenous justice organizations. A total of 274 written depositions were made, and hundreds of letters and documents received by the Commission, paving the way to the drafting of *Equality Now* (Abella 1984). The concept of 'equity', as an extension of the earlier notion of 'equality', emphasized substantive equality as opposed to formal equality of opportunity. Employment equity was passed into law first in 1986 and updated in 1996. In addition, the federal government established a contract compliance program, obligating organizations that received large contracts (currently over a million dollars) from the federal government (including universities) to demonstrate their commitment to employment equity in their own structures. The program was quite limited initially and still remains so. By 1998, 'diversity' had joined the discourse of equity (Almeida 2019).

EDI started out as an endorsement of 'EDI principles' by member institutions of Universities Canada, shifting in 2018 as a requirement by the Canada Research Chairs Program (CRCP) for all universities to submit "equity action plans to address the underrepresentation of chairholders in the four designated groups [as originally defined in the Abella report]" (Shen 2019). In 2019, an official initiation of equity coupled with diversity and inclusion, or EDI altogether, is seen, with the pilot launch of an EDI charter titled 'Dimensions.' This charter is government-backed, the result of nation-wide consultations with the Minister of Science and Sport as well as workshops organized by the Natural Sciences and Engineering Research Council in post-secondary institutions across Canada (Shen 2019). Today, while brief and pending an extended version, 'Dimensions' is formally endorsed by many Canadian universities (Shen 2019 and Wolbring and Lillywhite 2021). EDI efforts are also reportedly guided by the Canadian Multiculturalism Act, the Charter of Rights and Freedoms and the Canadian Human Rights Act (Wolbring and Lillywhite 2021).

At its inception, 'Dimensions' was not tied to research funding (Shen 2019), but the charter itself describes EDI as "essential for research" (Wolbring and Lillywhite 2021). Sources also establish a connection between EDI and research funding in recent years – as Beauline-Stuebing (2020) reports, CRC's equity targets, "which aim to increase representation of women, persons with disabilities, Indigenous people and visible minorities," have created some "political pressure for universities to do something about EDI."

From a critical perspective, the appending of 'diversity' to 'equity' flattens the notion of structural inequities based on racialization, gender, ability and Indigeneity that Abella had talked about, de-politicizing the notion of equity. Universities developed statements on equity and diversity which appeared at the bottom of job ads (Henry et al. 2017) and focused on collecting representational data of the targeted groups under the legislation. More recently, some organizations have added 2SLGBTQ+ to the list.

Thus, right from the first moment, employment equity was interpreted as a project of ensuring that target groups were represented rather than ensuring that deep-rooted discriminatory structures and hegemonic whiteness were dismantled (Leong 2013).

It is revealing that despite many decades of equity programs, certain groups remain under-represented, such as Black and Indigenous faculty. By the time equity programs became institutionalized within universities, they had become saturated within neo-liberal discourses on which Henry et al. (2017) comment that "diversity is experienced individually. It is located in the bodies of individuals rather than constitutive of institutions" (12). To fulfil their obligations under contract compliance programs, universities established offices, personnel and data collection infrastructures so that they would be able to demonstrate their commitment to equity, most notably through data collection. Indeed, based on their critical policy analysis of 15 research-intensive universities, Tamtik and Guenter (2019) explain how variances remain in the way EDI is understood and approached, highlighting how EDI may be less of a universal commitment than it is institutional discretion, i.e. institutions with established EDI offices are more proactive with initiatives as opposed to campuses without and the institutional jurisdiction to which EDI initiatives belong are different (staff and faculty versus physical spaces such as designated offices). From a critical anti-racist perspective, equity programs had become a marketable commodity along with the commodification of higher education, both of which have global markets.

EDI statements, policies and other representational forms have become ways of demonstrating that something was being done on equity. Regardless, hegemonic whiteness prevails; the colonial, anti-Black and racist genealogies of Canadian universities continue, simply re-positioning the deck-chairs as it were (Almeida 2019, 2023; Joseph et al. 2020 and Thobani 2022). Including diverse bodies within universities simply legitimizes continuing structures of white coloniality in universities, endangering racialized bodies able to conform to white norms of 'excellence' into complicity (Joseph et al. 2020) and rendering those who are unable to comply as less than excellent.

Internationalization, a policy direction mentioned earlier, ran parallel to EDI developments. It required universities and colleges to market themselves, their brands and their educational programs and degrees in the rising capitalist countries of China and India, among others, where a large middle-class could mobilize the capital needed to move to the West. The neo-liberal universities and colleges became unfettered in seeking global markets. Thobani (2022) observes that an "ideal faculty member as the "entrepreneurial globetrotter" and "the student who was newly turned into a consumer" (8) encountered each other in the neo-liberalizing university.

The aspirations of youth and their parents in these global marketplaces and their desire for Western education, whiteness and permanent residence in the West had been incubated in the bowels of colonial domination, mis-development and stunted opportunities and found their expression in neo-colonial histories of these regions. Increasing the numbers of international students not only increased the diversity of the student body, thereby increasing the marketability of Canadian universities in the global market-place, but also increased revenues for the post-secondary sector through dramatically high levels of international student tuition, which the govern-ment does not regulate, in line with the neo-liberal ethos and a kind of modern head tax which Chinese migrants had paid in the late 19th and early 20th centuries to land in Canada.

And so, EDI programs merely help as a marketing strategy in a competi-tive drive to increase student enrolments (Tamtik and Guenter 2019 and Beauline-Stuebing 2020). Tamtik and Guenter (2019) observe that most universities use broad and vague language around EDI and only a minority offer a more specific definition of the program (Beauline-Stuebing 2020). They comment that two of the features of the EDI policies have been the recruitment of equity-seeking students as well as the development of bur-saries, scholarships, services and curricular adaptations for presumably those same students. So, while racialized international student bodies increase diversity on campus, EDI programs remain non-performative or as Rinaldo Walcott observes '[performing] non-performativity' (quoted by Thobani 2022, xii).

By presenting this critical analysis of EDI programs, it is not suggested that there was no agency on the part of those who were in the margins of academia. Neither are we saying that there was no countervailing force on campuses which pushed the parameters within which EDI programs came into being. Indeed, working against the grain has been a constant feature of campus activists (Thobani 2022). Even the Dimensions Charter, men-tioned earlier, came out of a 2003 human rights complaint brought for-ward by eight women researchers against the Tri-Agency Institutional Program Secretariat for discrimination against equity groups in its award-ing of CRCP. New and higher targets based on representation of the four groups in the broader population based on the 2016 Census rather than their availability as researchers more narrowly in the population and strin-gent accountability measures for reaching targets were established (Halli-day 2019). Universities have until 2029 to reach their targets and risk losing research funding if they fail. In addition, the Truth and Reconcilia-tion Commission's (TRC) 'Call To Action' in 2015 catalyzed the state and the associated post-secondary education sector to respond to calls for truth, reconciliation and Indigenous justice. EDI has indeed been a con-tested area.

Be that as it may, the EDI programs remain limited in how much actual change and equality the state and universities can support. In the following sections, we discuss how these institutions abide by neo-liberal capitalist logics marked by markets, enrolments, revenues, brands and rankings and the resulting implications for international students.

International students and EDI programs in Canadian universities

Despite the concurrence of intensified international student recruitment and the proliferation of EDI language and programming on post-secondary campuses across Canada, international students are not commonly acknowledged, if included at all, within the latter as an equity-deserving group (Tamtik and Guenter 2019 and Tavares 2021). Instead, international students are positioned within the framework of internationalization (Tamtik and Guenter 2019 and Buckner et al. 2020).

While institutions justify internationalization as beneficial in terms of generating revenue, mainly through international student recruitment and tuition fees, as well as fulfilling 'reputational goals' such as world rankings and symbolic commitments of "increased intercultural understanding, global awareness, and global citizenship" (Buckner et al. 2020, 21–22), researchers have argued its marginalizing premises and outcomes. Operating behind internationalization's seemingly welcoming rhetoric towards international students is the instrumentalization of their enrolment and presence on campus for the purposes of revenue and the performance of multiculturalism and globality (Stein and Andreotti 2016 and Grantham 2018; Tavares 2021). De Wit (2019) has commented on the downfalls of internationalization as a "short-term neo-liberal approach," that give multiple 'pressures' to meet targets such as profits, talent recruitment, international research and prestige. There is little space to consider the merits of internationalization as a "long term comprehensive quality approach," that could focus on "global learning for all" and "the needs and opportunities of students and staff" (15). Indeed, Buckner et al. (2020) have observed that while there are symbolic commitments to values of diversity and intercultural awareness within internationalization, there is an absence of other values that implicate Canadian higher education and its communities, such as "equity, empathy, humility, and solidarity" (21). There is also no linkage to decolonization and Indigenization, which are likely to be mentioned in their respective institutional mandates, as well as to global environmental issues and geopolitical concerns. This compartmentalization of values is significant to note, relevant to the analysis of the neo-liberal university that encourages individualization rather than building solidarity among colonized and differently racialized communities and its implications on the construction of international students as neo-liberal objects.

The disregarding of international students in terms of equity issues translates into real-life harms of social exclusion, discrimination and racism experienced by international students in the classroom, in the campus life and in their interactions with domestic students, all "on the basis of their foreignized and othered status," on top of the tendency to view them as a homogenous group"[1] (Tavares 2021, 2). However, their primacy as strategic pillars for revenue generation and prestige building within the internationalization rhetoric, which remains void of anti-oppressive language, is quite in line with our earlier anti-racist interpretation of EDI programs. In the next few sections, we advance the idea of how the positioning of international students outside of the EDI framework and within that of internationalization may very well be an intended function of the neo-liberal ethos pervading Canadian post-secondary education, which also have implications for them as workers and temporary migrants.

International students and the conflation of roles

As mentioned before, international students are not only students but they are also workers and temporary migrants, all three positionalities intersecting to shape their precarious positions in Canada. In addition, many are racialized and subjected to gender differentiation. Their legal categorization as 'temporary' migrants on study permits, which come with certain stipulations and restrictions, render them as a captive group of workers and one of the largest groups of migrant workers in Canada. As such, they benefit the neo-liberal economy, providing cheap labour to small business owners such as grocery stores, restaurants, warehouses, cleaning companies, food services and delivery services. Newspaper reports have lately profiled international students who have been subjected to wage theft in these areas, as well as to long hours, working without breaks and often not paid their full wages (Nassar 2019; Hune-Brown 2021 and Keung 2022a).

Migrant Workers Alliance for Change (MWAC), a migrant justice group, refers to international students as "migrant student workers," an apt descriptor as most are compelled to work in order to save enough money for tuition, housing and living expenses. However, many are limited to working 20 hours per week while maintaining full-time status at school (Government of Canada 2022c) and are penalized if they violate that stipulation. This was seen in the case of Jobandeep Sandhu, a 22-year-old international student who was arrested and deported in 2019 for "working too hard" (or more than 20 hours per week as a truck driver). The Canadian government insisted that Jobandeep's primary focus should have been on his studies rather than on paid work and that he was also deemed inadmissible to Canada for breaking the terms of his study permit (Hill 2019). The status of being a 'worker' has become accentuated for international students during the pandemic as more and more of them are being utilized to fill the void left by domestic labour shortages. One measure is the temporary waiving of the 20-hour work limit, allowing certain international students to work full-time hours during their studies.[2] In addition, particularly for less-desirable labour sectors, the federal government has raised the proportion of temporary foreign workers allowed in the labour force, in sectors of manufacturing, retail, hotels, food services and long-term care, from 10% to 30% (and to 20% in other sectors) (Thanthong and Argitis 2022). The skilled labour provided by graduated students already here in Canada was recognized by the government as a part of its pandemic recovery strategy in the context of declining immigration intake during 2020 (Keung 2021). However, the pathway towards permanent residency has been unreliable during the pandemic amidst a huge backlog of over one million applications, precipitating the federal government to suspend any new applications for permanent residency through its skilled worker programs. Those international students with their post-graduate permits expiring and caught in the backlog were given an 18-month extension, which has since ceased (Keung 2022b, 2022c). Once their permit expires, they will have to return to their country of origin unless an employer decides to hire them. However, employers would be required to invest in an application for a Labour Market Impact Assessment (LMIA), likely to be a disincentive. In addition, if a post-graduate work permit-holder is compelled to leave Canada, they do not qualify for another work permit if they decide to return.

The above predicaments demonstrate how international students' precarity is constructed within the interstices of their status as students, as workers and as temporary migrants. In addition, the government's patronizing and punitive response to Jobandeep's situation indicates the lack of concern for the financial precarity of international students in light of the steep tuition fees they are required to pay. This coercive attitude also belies the fact international students have less access to educational funding than domestic students (OCASI 2022), which further makes them vulnerable to 'bad' employers who can subject them to 'illegal' work arrangements knowing their deportability. The state discourse that international students are not 'real' workers because they are primarily students allows employers to pay them less than their domestic counterparts (Crossman and Hou 2022), and yet they are arguably not considered as "real Canadian students," worthy of neither support nor recognition as equity-deserving members. We now turn to explore how their positionality and resulting exclusions are justified by the neo-liberal logic and racial capitalism.

International students, EDI and a neo-liberal racial capitalism

The competition for international students is unquestionable among post-secondary institutions across the globe. Canada, in particular, is a favourite destination for international students. Its "multicultural environment that is open, accepting, and conducive to growth" and "inclusive welcoming environments" (Arvind 2022 and EduCanada 2022) are strenuously marketed to reach international students. However, the disproportionate focus on them as recruitment targets, while being excluded from EDI frameworks, confirms that the desirability of international students lies primarily in their perceived market value, which erases their humanity and reduces them to commodities.

Leong (2013) defines racial capital as "economic and social value derived from an individual's racial identity, whether by that individual, by other individuals, or by institutions" (2190). While we have discussed here that the recruitment of international students is a strategy for revenue generation given the neo-liberal turn of the state, the racial diversification that it enables not only re-creates hegemonic whiteness as accessible and benevolent (Thobani 2022) but also creates opportunities for international engagements for Canadian faculty and students, elevates global profiles through partnerships and rankings and, at the same time, provides cheap labour to Canadian employers. EDI and internationalization imbricate and function as 'bait' for both international students and scholars, bolstering the marketing of both Canadian post-secondary education and the state as 'diverse', 'friendly' and 'welcoming.' The neo-liberal system of governments, employers and post-secondary institutions that welcome international students to Canadian campuses and life after graduation also continue to preserve their precarity through restrictions on their access to safe work, education and permanent residence.

Stein and Andreotti (2016) argue that the neo-liberal objectification of international students by western nations, including Canada, is in keeping with a 'global imaginary' forged by the history of colonialism and slavery. Buckner and Stein (2020) have similarly noted the dynamics of eurocentrism at play, in which international students and other international partners are objectified within internationalization "as objects of Western development by way of education" (163). We would extend their argument further in the case of Canada by tying it specifically to its racial settler–colonial capitalist logic, giving rise to a national imaginary that views international students as model minority settlers of the future. These imaginaries evolved from seeing them initially as short-term visitors to fulfil

Canada's post-war international development goals as a 'democratic' and 'multi-racial' nation-state to potential permanent residents and citizens today, considered 'ideal' due to their assumed self-sufficiency, 'local-made' credentials and labour market experience (Kelley and Trebilcock 2010; Gates-Gasse 2012; Cox 2014; McCartney 2016 and Trilokekar and El Masri 2019). These imaginaries also serve to reproduce 'brain drain', which arguably continues neo-colonial relations between the Global South and the Global North.

Global imaginaries also shape the attitudes and actions of Canadian citizens towards international students as well as nurture the self-perceptions of international students. The self-talk the second author of this chapter has encountered in previous works, and in her personal experience as an international student, suggests the tendency of some international students to oblige themselves to be self-reliant, or to "have to do things by themselves" (Gomez 2017), effectively fulfilling state constructions and policies. International students are falling through the cracks between institutional discourses when it comes to their social and emotional wellbeing and feelings of support and belonging – not acknowledged within EDI and instrumentalized within internationalization.

Conclusion

The marginalizing effects of international students' exclusion from EDI and their instrumentalization as "objects of internationalization", and the benefits reaped by the neo-liberal state continue even after their studies end. As post-graduate work permit holders, they are not eligible for settlement services, or for any social services. They are relegated to an 'outsider' status not seen to be deserving of Canadian state support.

While internationalization is considered a part (or becoming a part) of the EDI conversation (Beauline-Stuebing 2020 and Tavares 2021), it is unlikely that such a convergence will generate any meaningful outcomes for international students.

Notes

1 Tavares (2021) has also pointed out the harms of the label 'international student', suggesting that it 'obscures' the diversities of this particular populace, on the bases of gender, sex, race, ethnicity, age, language and culture (2).
2 As of November 15, 2022, those already in Canada studying or who have yet to arrive and/or begin their studies but have already applied for their permit on or before October 7, 2022, may work more than 20 hours in off-campus employment, a temporary change set to end on December 31, 2023 (Government of Canada 2022a). Nonetheless, MWAC argues that this change, as a temporary one, cannot shift the status quo for the better. It also excludes newer

international students, those who apply after October 7, 2023, and does not apply to those who study part-time (unless they were full-time students who switch to part-time in their final semester) (MWAC 2022; Government of Canada 2022a).

References

Abella, Rosalie Silberman. October 1984. *Report of the Commission on Equality in Employment*. Minister of Supply and Services Canada.
Almeida, Shana. 2019. "Mythical Encounters: Challenging Racism in the Diverse City." *International Journal of Sociology and Social Policy* 39, no. 11/12: 937–949.
Almeida, Shana. 2023. *Toronto the Good: Negotiating Race in the Diverse City*. Toronto: University of Toronto Press.
Arvind, Bharath. 2022. "How Much Does It Cost for International Students to Study in Canada?" *The Economic Times*, April 20, 2022. https://economictimes.indiatimes.com/nri/study/how-much-does-it-cost-for-international-students-to-study-in-canada/articleshow/90960631.cms.
Beauline-Stuebing, Laura. 2020. "Study Finds Equity, Diversity, Inclusion Off to a "Strong Start" in Research Intensive Universities." *University Affairs*, March 11, 2020. https://www.universityaffairs.ca/news/news-article/study-finds-equity-divers.
Buckner, Elizabeth and Sharon Stein. 2020. "What Counts as Internationalization? Deconstructing the Internationalization Imperative." *Journal of Studies in International Education* 24, no. 2: 152–166.
Buckner, Elizabeth, Scott Clerk, Adriana Marroquin, and You Zhang. 2020. "Strategic Benefits, Symbolic Commitments: How Canadian Colleges and Universities Frame Internationalization." *Canadian Journal of Higher Education* 50, no. 4 (December): 20–36.
Charbonneau, Leo. 2019. "Most Universities Report Having Equity, Diversity and Inclusion Plans, but Challenges Remain." *University Affairs*, November 5, 2019. https://www.universityaffairs.ca/news/news-article/most-universities-report-having-equity-diversity-and-inclusion-plans-but-challenges-remain.
Cox, Courtney Rae. 2014. "International Students in Canada: Policies and Practices for Social Inclusion." Master's thesis, Toronto Metropolitan University. https://doi.org/10.32920/ryerson.14656581.v1.
Crossman, Eden and Feng Hou. 2022. "International Students as a Source of Labour Supply: Pre-Immigration Study in Canada and Post-Immigration Earnings." Statistics Canada, Economic and Social Reports 36-28-0001. https://www150.statcan.gc.ca/n1/pub/36-28-0001/2022002/article/00004-eng.htm.
De Wit, Hans. 2019. "Internationalization in Higher Education, a Critical Review." *Simon Fraser University Educational Review* 12, no. 3 (December): 9–17.
EduCanada. 2022. "Top Reasons to Study in Canada." Last modified December 16, 2022. https://www.educanada.ca/why-canada-pourquoi/reasons-raisons.aspx?lang=eng.
Gates-Gasse, E. 2012. "International Students as Immigrants." In *Immigration and Settlement: Challenges, Experiences, and Opportunities*, edited by Harald Bauder, 271–296. Toronto: Canadian Scholars' Press.

Gomez, Bianca. 2017. "Pursuing Permanence: Former International Students' Trajectories to Permanent Residency in Canada." Master's thesis, Toronto Metropolitan University. https://doi.org/10.32920/ryerson.14645784.v1.

Government of Canada. 2022a. "International Students to Help Address Canada's Labour Shortage." *Immigration, Refugees and Citizenship Canada*, October 7, 2022. https://www.canada.ca/en/immigration-refugees-citizenship/news/2022/10/international-students-to-help-address-canadas-labour-shortage.html.

———. 2022b. "Work Off Campus as an International Student." Last modified October 24, 2022. https://www.canada.ca/en/immigration-refugees-citizenship/services/study-canada/work/work-off-campus.html.

———. 2022c. "Study Permits: Other Considerations." Last modified December 23, 2022. https://www.canada.ca/en/immigration-refugees-citizenship/corporate/publications-manuals/operational-bulletins-manuals/temporary-residents/study-permits/other-considerations.html.

GOVision. 2014. *The Impact of Changes to the CEC Program on International Students*. Toronto: Toronto Metropolitan University. https://doi.org/10.32920/ryerson.14639517.v1.

Grantham, Kate. 2018. "Assessing International Student Mobility in Canadian University Strategic Plans: Instrumentalist versus Transformational Approaches in Higher Education." *Journal of Global Citizenship & Equity Education* 6, no. 1 (November): 1–21.

Halliday, Matthew. 2019. "Canada Research Chairs Program Announces New, More Ambitious Targets." *University Affairs*, September 9, 2019. https://www.universityaffairs.ca/news/news-article/canada-research-chairs-program-announces-new-more-ambitious-equity-targets/.

Harden, Joel. 2017. *The Case for Renewal in Post-Secondary Education*. Ottawa: Canadian Centre for Policy Alternatives. https://policyalternatives.ca/sites/default/files/uploads/publications/National%20Office/2017/03/Case_for_Renewal_in_PSE.pdf.

Harvey, David. 2005. *A Brief History of Neoliberalism*. Oxford: Oxford University Press.

Hassanein, Salma. 2014. *Special Comment: Increased Policy Focus on International Students Credit Positive for Canadian Universities*. Toronto: University of Toronto Munk School of Global Affairs and Public Policy. https://munkschool.utoronto.ca/wp-content/uploads/2014/09/Salma-Hassanein-Moodys-Report.pdf.

Henry, Frances, Enakshi Dua, Carl E. James, Audrey Kobayashi, Peter Li, Howard Ramos, and Malinda S. Smith. 2017. *The Equity Myth: Racialization and Indigeneity at Canadian universities*. Vancouver: UBC Press.

Hill, Brian. 2019. "International Student Arrested, Facing Deportation for Working Too Many Hours." *Global News*, May 13, 2019. https://globalnews.ca/news/5269138/international-student-arrested-facing-deportation-work-permit/.

Hune-Brown, Nicholas. 2021. "The Shadowy Business of International Education." *The Walrus*, August 18, 2021. https://thewalrus.ca/the-shadowy-business-of-international-education/.

Joseph, Ameil J., Julia Janes, Harjeet Badwall, and Shana Almeida. 2020. "Preserving White Comfort and Safety: The Politics of Race Erasure in Academe." *Social Identities* 26, no. 2: 166–185.

Kelley, Ninette and Michael J. Trebilcock. 2010. *The Making of the Mosaic: A History of Canadian Immigration Policy.* Toronto: University of Toronto Press.

Keung, Nicholas. 2021. "Foreign Students Get Work Permit Reprieve." *Toronto Star*, January 8, 2021. https://www.pressreader.com/canada/toronto-star/20210108/281646782772028.

———. 2022a. "Work Rules Leave Students Vulnerable." *Toronto Star*, April 4, 2022. https://www.pressreader.com/canada/toronto-star/20220404/281509344706183.

———. 2022b "'I'm Terrified for My Own Future': Why Some of Canada's International Students Are Anxiously Eyeing Calendar as Post-Grad Work Permits Expire." *Toronto Star*, April 13, 2022. https://www.thestar.com/news/canada/2022/04/13/newcomers-on-expiring-work-permits-are-in-limbo-awaiting-a-reprieve-or-a-new-plan-from-ottawa.html.

———. 2022c. "Canada to Extend Expiring Work Permits". *Toronto Star*, April 23, 2022. https://www.pressreader.com/canada/toronto-star/20220423/281608128990861.

Knight, Jane. 2003. "Updating the Definition of Internationalization." *International Higher Education* 33: 2–3.

Leong, Nancy. 2013. "Racial Capitalism." *Harvard Law Review* 126, no. 8 (June): 2151–2226.

McCartney, Dale M. 2016. "Inventing International Students: Exploring Discourses in International Student Policy Talk, 1945–75." *Historical Studies in Education*, 28, no. 2: 1–27.

Migrant Workers Alliance for Change (MWAC). 2022. "BREAKING: More than 500,000 International Students Win Right to Work and Protect Themselves from Exploitation." October 7, 2022. https://migrantworkersalliance.org/press/20hrworklimitoct2022/.

Nassar, Shanifa. 2019. "Thousands Join Effort to Stop International Student from Being Deported for 'Working Too Hard,' He Says." *CBC News*, May 24, 2019. https://www.cbc.ca/news/canada/toronto/international-student-deportation-work-permit-1.5149434.

OCASI. 2022. "I Am an International (Foreign) Student. Can I Get Financial Assistance?" Last modified March 7, 2022. https://settlement.org/ontario/education/colleges-universities-and-institutes/financial-assistance-for-post-secondary-education/i-am-an-international-foreign-student-can-i-get-financial-assistance/.

Shen, Anqi. 2019. "Canada Launches Its Own Version of the Athena SWAN Charter." *University Affairs*, May 15, 2019. https://www.universityaffairs.ca/news/news-article/canada-launches-its-own-version-of-the-athena-swan-charter/.

Stein, Sharon and Vanessa Oliveira de Andreotti. 2016. "Cash, Competition or Charity: International Students and the Global Imaginary." *High Education* 2: 235–279.

Tamtik, Merli and Melissa Guenter. 2019. "Policy Analysis of Equity, Diversity and Inclusion Strategies in Canadian Universities – How Far Have We Come?" *Canadian Journal of Higher Education* 49, no. 3 (December): 41–56.

Tavares, Vander. 2021. "Feeling Excluded: International Students Experience Equity, Diversity and Inclusion." *International Journal of Inclusive Education* (December): 1–18.

Thanthong-Knight, Randy and Theophilos Argitis. 2022. "Canada Taps Migrants for Quick Fix to Labour Shortage." *Toronto Star*, April 30, 2022. https://www.pressreader.com/canada/toronto-star/20220430/281904481748276.

Thobani, Sunera. 2022. *Coloniality and Racial (In)justice in the University: Counting for Nothing?* Toronto: University of Toronto Press.

Trilokekar, Roopa Desai and Amira El Masri. 2019. "'International Students Are... Golden': Canada's Changing Policy Contexts, Approaches, and National Peculiarities in Attracting International Students as Future Immigrants." In *Outward and Upward Mobilities: International Students in Canada, Their Families, and Structuring Institutions*, edited by Ann H. Kim and Min Jang Kwak, 25–55. Toronto: University of Toronto Press.

Usher, Alex. 2018. *The State of Post-Secondary Education in Canada*. Toronto: Higher Education Strategy Associates. https://higheredstrategy.com/wp-content/uploads/2018/08/HESA_SPEC_2018_final.pdf.

Valverde, Mariana. 2019. "As Public Post-Secondary Funding Stagnates, the University of Toronto Explores 'Alternative Sources'". *Academic Matters*, Fall 2019. https://academicmatters.ca/the-university-of-toronto-explores-alternative-funding-sources/.

Wolbring, Gregor and Aspen Lillywhite. 2021. "Equity/Equality, Diversity, and Inclusion (EDI) in Universities: The Case of Disabled People." *Societies* 11, no. 2 (May): 1–34.

Inclusion and Exclusion in Universities

Section II

Inclusion and Exclusion in
Universities

6 Assessments of Universities by International Students from Asia

Institutional Resources, Adjustment, Inclusion, and Safety

Ann H. Kim, Firrisaa Abdulkarim, and Melissa Payne

Introduction

International students are reshaping the postsecondary landscape in Canada. Despite domestic student numbers remaining relatively stable, student enrollments in Canadian postsecondary institutions are rising due to international student numbers (see Kim, Buckner, and Montsion; Statistics Canada 2020). The growing importance of international students can be seen in university strategic plans and in regional and national policy statements as discussed in other parts of this book (see Kim, Buckner, and Montsion; Buckner, Knight-Grofe, and Eden; Montsion and Caneo), as well as in the surge of research studies on this population (Kim and Sondhi 2015). And yet, there is little published research on students' evaluation of institutional resources and services. This is the focus of this chapter.

There is an onus on institutions to improve and shift to meet students' needs and address larger issues around equity and inclusion. Jones (2017) argues there is a tendency to homogenize international students, which leads to institutions overlooking their diverse and distinctive needs. In this chapter, we examine how students from Asia evaluate institutions and their views on adjustment, inclusion, and safety, using the 2018 national survey conducted by the Canadian Bureau of International Education (CBIE). By country of citizenship, we explore what they felt was of essential importance in applying to their institution, the usefulness of institutional resources, areas of successful adjustment, and their feelings about inclusion and safety. We pay particular attention to and compare students from China, India, and South Korea (hereafter Korea), who comprise more than half of all international students studying in Canada (ICEF 2019). We also include students from Vietnam and the Philippines, two countries that have been playing a growing role in international education.

DOI: 10.4324/b23160-9

With a growing dependence on international students for enrolment and financial security, institutions face unique challenges. Postsecondary institutions must ensure that promises made to students are realistic and take seriously students' abilities to contribute to the development of the institution and wider student body. For one, support services and resources for international students, as part of more broadly-based services for all students, can positively influence student experiences (Ammigan and Jones 2018). The most important support services identified by international students included information and orientation, integration activities with local students and communities, language support, and immigration-related support (Kelo, Rogers, and Rumbley 2010). As Perez-Encinas and Ammigan (2016) argue in their review paper comparing international student satisfaction with university support services in Spain and the US, it is important that support services match the needs and expectations of students. International support services can play an important role in attracting and retaining international students by enhancing the student experience, not just at one point in time but throughout their time abroad.

Specific services tailored to international students by way of dedicated international student offices are often set up on campuses to support students in their academic and social transitions and these offices provide a wide range of services, which include support for housing, advising on immigration-related issues, and hosting social and cultural programs (Ammigan and Jones 2018). However, Choudaha and Hu (2016) argue that many support services are limited, focusing on immigration compliance and token gestures related to cultural festivals and events. When seeking support, international students often must interact with institutional silos (Choudaha and Hu 2016). This is in part due to the centralization of services through one isolated office or unit while international students have to navigate many parts of the institution and their retention depends on campus-wide experiences (Ammigan and Jones 2018; Buckner, Chan, and Kim 2022).

The significant increase in international students from Asia has generated scholarly interest in understanding the experiences of students and their levels of satisfaction with their overall experience (Slaten et al. 2016). In these studies, student satisfaction refers to the student's assessment of services provided by their chosen institution and relates to factors in the student's daily life such as quality of teaching, support facilities, social environment, and physical infrastructure (Wiers-Jenssen, Stensaker, and Grøgaard 2002). Students' satisfaction ratings give institutions a sense of what students are experiencing on campus and what really matters to them (Ammigan 2019). International student satisfaction has become a strategic priority at many postsecondary institutions as improving students' overall experiences is seen as a recruitment and retention strategy. In the national survey used in this chapter, 93% of international students were satisfied with their educational experience and 96% would recommend Canada as a study destination (CBIE 2018). It seems then that the overwhelming majority of international students are positive about their experience.

However, treating international students as a homogenous group runs the risk, as Jones (2017) argues, of overgeneralizing and failing to understand their diverse needs. International student experiences in the host country are influenced by their identities such as nationality, class, and gender (Arthur 2017), and levels of student satisfaction and integration have been found to differ between nationalities (Arambewela and Hall 2009; Merola, Coelen, and Hofman 2019). For instance, one study found differences in levels of integration among international students in the Netherlands, with less integration of students from non-Western backgrounds compared to others (Rienties et al. 2012). The integration issues among non-Western international students led to lower personal and emotional well-being, which potentially impacted students' overall satisfaction (Rienties et al. 2012). Another study found that international students from Asia in Australia tended to be more concerned with safety than other factors like cost (Arambewela and Hall 2007; see Zhang, Yuan, and Kang). As such, concerns about safety may play a larger role than other factors in potentially influencing decisions and satisfaction. Our data will allow us to itemize how students assessed some of these factors and compare them across origin groups.

Data and methods

To gauge student perceptions, we use 2018 survey data from the Canadian Bureau for International Education (CBIE), a national non-profit organization that conducts a survey of international students in member institutions across the ten provinces every few years. The survey questionnaire covers a wide range of topics, such as type of institution, program of study, country of citizenship, reasons for choosing Canada, factors affecting institutional choice, level of integration, life on campus, satisfaction with services and facilities, and post-study plans. Invitations are sent out to member institutions and participation is voluntary for both institutions and participants. Over time, an increasing number of institutions have been participating in the national survey.

We use the 2018 International Student Survey containing data from over 15,000 international students across 46 institutions out of more than 100 member institutions, including universities, colleges, and polytechnics. Data were collected from March to May, and the dataset includes roughly 4% of the international student population in Canada (CBIE 2018). Of the 46 participating institutions, 31 were universities, twelve were colleges, and three were polytechnics; as we are interested in international students in universities, we restricted our analysis to students who were attending a university at any level. We note that the survey sample is not representative of the international student population in universities. For one, several of the universities with the largest international student populations did not participate in the survey (e.g., the University of Toronto and the University of British Columbia) although others joined, such as McGill University, the University of Ottawa, the Université de Montréal, and Western University (CBIE 2018). Second, we cannot assume international student respondents within a given participating university were representative of the international student population in their university. We draw our conclusions in consideration of these limitations.

Our interest is in students from Asia and they were selected from the dataset according to country of citizenship. The sample was further restricted to student citizens from China, India, Korea, Vietnam, and the Philippines, as well as to those from the US and Western Europe[1] for comparison, bringing our total sample to 6,164 respondents in universities. Although the majority of students (80%) were enrolled in universities, there is a wide variation by origin (see Table 6.1); nearly all students in the sample from the US and Western Europe and 90% of students from China were enrolled in universities. However, roughly half of the students from India, Korea, and Vietnam were in universities and these students were almost as likely to enroll in community colleges. In our sample, students from the Philippines were the least likely group to be attending university with less than a third there and 55% in college.

In the sample, 31% were from China, 25% were from India, and 3% or less were from each of Korea, Vietnam, and the Philippines. Other groups from Asia were even smaller in sample size and were omitted from the analysis. In contrast, students from the US or Western Europe accounted

Table 6.1 CBIE 2018 survey by citizenship and university enrolment

Citizenship	Full survey sample	Percent of full sample (%)	Percent in university (%)	University sample (N)	Percent of university sample (%)
China	2,092	25.3	90.0	1,882	30.5
India	2,892	35.0	52.7	1,523	24.7
South Korea	284	3.4	50.7	144	2.3
Vietnam	361	4.4	50.7	183	3.0
Philippines	193	2.3	29.5	57	0.9
US and Western Europe	2,433	29.5	97.6	2,375	38.5
Total	8,255	100.0		6,164	99.9

for 39% of the sample. There were more female (53%) than male (47%) respondents and the mean age in the sample was 25.9 years of age (not shown). Nearly all students (98%) in the survey reported being full-time and more than one-third were in their first year. In terms of regional distribution, almost half of the university sample (48%) attended schools in Central Canada (Ontario and Quebec), a quarter attended schools in the Prairies (Alberta, Manitoba, and Saskatchewan), 20% attended schools in British Columbia, and 7% were in the Atlantic region. The majority of students (83%) were at a university located in the larger urban centers or a Census Metropolitan Area (CMA), and only two in every five students reported that they were working in Canada. With this profile, we examine how students rated their satisfaction level with various aspects of their institution, and their feelings related to adjustment, inclusion, and safety. As there are numerous items asked in the survey itself, in the interests of space, we focus our analysis on the most positive extreme or intense response category (as opposed to categories of less positivity) disaggregated by places of origin. While many studies group together response categories (i.e., very satisfied and satisfied), we felt it was more indicative of the perception of service quality to focus on the percentage of students who had stronger and more intense positive feelings.

Institutional appeal and resources

The survey asked respondents to rate the degree of importance of various reasons for applying to their current institution, the usefulness of various institutional resources in the decision, and the level of satisfaction with different institutional aspects when arriving in Canada and with institutional services and facilities. Each item was asked independently. Table 6.2 presents these items by place of origin and only for the most extreme positive response category. Overall, the three items strongly and independently rated for influencing decisions to apply to the institution were the quality of education, the prestige of a degree or diploma from the institution, and the cost. The availability of a particular program and the institution's position in ranking or league tables were less likely to be considered of essential importance in the decision to apply.

When examining the results by citizenship, we see differences in how each group rated the importance of these reasons. Although quality of education was the reason most likely to be of essential importance (versus very important, somewhat important, and not important, which are not shown) for the overall sample and for each group (except for those from the Philippines for whom cost was more likely to be of essential importance), rates varied across groups. The quality of education was more likely to be of essential importance for university students from India and the Philippines

Table 6.2 Student ratings of institutional factors and resources by country/region

	China	India	Korea	Vietnam	Philippines	US+WE	Total
Reasons for applying to current institution							
Percentage (%), essential importance							
The quality of education	34.9	45.7	26.4	27.3	42.1	33.9	36.8
The prestige of a degree/diploma	27.6	43.7	20.8	22.4	33.3	26.0	30.7
The cost of studying	20.2	38.7	26.4	27.3	50.9	29.9	29.1
The availability of a particular program	18.4	39.0	23.6	23.5	38.6	30.4	28.6
Position in ranking/league tables	16.2	27.9	12.5	11.5	10.5	10.1	16.5
Resources used in decision							
Percentage (%), very useful							
Institutional website	42.4	63.9	34.7	45.4	68.4	45.3	49.0
Websites/publications that rank	32.5	51.5	13.9	26.2	31.6	16.6	30.4
Online forums and blogs	20.5	39.5	9.7	13.7	29.8	11.8	21.4
Arriving in Canada							
Percentage (%), very satisfied							
Institutional orientation	27.8	41.2	14.7	29.3	36.0	22.1	28.6
International student orientation	27.4	41.4	14.8	23.1	35.1	22.2	28.5
International reception at airport/train or bus station	18.3	25.1	9.9	18.1	21.1	12.8	17.7
Moving into residence	18.8	16.6	12.7	11.5	12.3	15.7	16.6
Services and facilities							
Percentage (%), very satisfied							
Library services	34.0	51.6	24.0	42.7	63.0	45.4	43.0
Academic advisor	22.2	29.9	18.7	28.7	40.8	25.0	25.6
Recreational facilities	16.1	27.0	12.0	18.9	32.4	32.6	25.1
An IS Advisor	17.2	18.8	9.6	23.9	29.2	25.2	20.3
Registrar's office	18.4	26.3	10.8	25.3	37.0	16.5	19.6
Health services	16.1	26.8	18.0	12.9	37.0	17.5	19.4

compared to students from China, Korea, Vietnam, and the US/Western Europe, and this pattern holds for most of the other reasons as well, including the prestige of the degree or diploma from that institution, the cost of studying, and the availability of a program. The one exception is rankings: while 28% of the students from India stated that rankings were of essential importance in their decision to apply to their current institution, less than 17% of students in the total sample rated this of essential importance.

Students were also asked about the usefulness of various institutional resources when deciding on which institution to select. Overall, more international students rated university websites as very useful compared to ranking publications, online forums, and blogs. Across groups, institutional websites were very useful to roughly two-thirds of students from the Philippines and India and to fewer students from other places, although more than a third from the other places also found websites very useful. Fewer students, across all groups, found ranking publications and online forums and blogs as very useful but these resources were still rated highly by some groups. Students from Korea and the US/Western Europe were least likely of all groups to rate these latter resources as very useful.

Arrival in a new country is an exciting but also stressful experience. Students' first impressions of institutions through orientation sessions, reception upon arrival, and transitions to housing can be important for shaping their feelings toward and attachment to the institution. For example, providing airport pickup and assisting with transportation to their accommodation are important services that could have a positive influence on students' overall satisfaction (Perez-Encinas and Ammigan 2016). While these features are non-academic, they are nonetheless important aspects for institutional investment and attention (see de Oliviera Soares, Magnan, Liu, and Araneda). All the more so since less than half of the participants, across all groups, were very satisfied with these aspects. Although not all students responded to the items in this section, only 29% of students in the sample who responded were very satisfied with their institutional and international student orientations, but there were variations; over 40% of students from India were very satisfied while this applied to less than 15% of students from Korea. In terms of reception at the point of entry and moving into residence, these are specific areas in particular need of improvement.

High-quality facilities and services have been found to influence both decision-making about institution choice and overall satisfaction (Migin et al. 2015). Students in the sample were asked about their satisfaction with various services and facilities at their institution, and those used by most of the students are presented at the bottom of Table 6.2. While additional services and facilities were included in the survey, we excluded them from the table due to a large number of missing cases. Among services and facilities that were used by most students (approximately 70%), students were more likely to be very satisfied with the library and we see a similar pattern across countries here as well, with more students from India and the Philippines having stronger feelings than others. Again, fewer students from Korea compared to all other places were very satisfied with the library and this pattern holds for the academic advisor, recreational facilities, international student advisor, and the Registrar's office. The one exception is health services, which had the lowest level of students very satisfied with it, particularly students from Vietnam and China. Interestingly, with respect to advising services, students were more likely to say they were very satisfied with their academic advisor (26%) than the international student advisor (20%), and this was true for the disaggregated sample except for the US/Western Europe group.

Student adjustment to campus life and Canadian society, inclusion, and safety

Table 6.3 presents the results related to students' levels of adjustment, feelings of belonging, and safety on- and off-campus and we take caution in these results as there were a large number of missing cases in these questions. In terms of adjustment, we examine the degree to which students, after beginning their program, felt they succeeded along six items: understanding course content, performance on written assignments, finding help, meeting academic demands, living in Canadian culture and society, and becoming involved in campus activities.

Approximately 62% of students felt they had "a lot of success" in understanding information presented in their courses. Although more than half of the students across each group felt they had a lot of success in understanding information presented in class, less than half of the students from Korea felt the same. In contrast to students from Korea, among others, students from the Philippines felt they had a lot of success adjusting to the academic side of university (information in courses, performance in written assignments, and meeting academic demands) and living in Canadian culture and society, but fewer felt that way about involvement in campus activities. Students from Vietnam were low on this item as well, perhaps due to lower numbers of students from these countries in universities and fewer student associations and clubs. While still less than a third, students from India were the most likely to feel a lot of success in their involvement in campus activities, more than students from the US/Western Europe. The variation along the six items appears to be related to English language background as students in the Philippines, India, and US/Western Europe, in general, more highly rated these aspects compared to students from China, Korea, and Vietnam.

Table 6.3 Student adjustment, inclusion, and safety by country/region

	China	India	Korea	Vietnam	Philippines	US+WE	Total
Adjustment							
Percentage (%), a lot of success adjusting							
Understanding information presented in courses	51.4	63.2	42.4	59.0	64.9	70.5	61.8
Performing adequately in written assignments	35.9	56.5	27.1	41.0	64.9	61.1	50.9
Finding help with questions or problems	46.1	55.8	33.3	50.3	50.9	52.2	50.7
Meeting academic demands	40.5	48.3	34.0	41.5	63.2	59.8	49.9
Living in Canadian culture and society	31.5	51.6	43.1	44.8	63.2	58.1	47.7
Becoming involved in campus activities	20.7	31.7	23.6	19.1	17.5	24.2	24.8
Inclusion							
Percentage (%), strongly agree							
Canada is a welcoming and tolerant society	39.6	65.9	26.2	31.4	49.1	46.0	48.0
Canadian students are friendly when you get to know them	28.9	39.0	24.6	26.2	45.5	44.9	37.7
I would like more chances to experience Canadian culture	38.2	56.6	31.5	50.6	40.0	18.4	34.9
Faculty and teaching assistants help me to feel included in the classroom	23.1	42.1	20.0	28.5	45.5	28.2	30.0
Staff and students have shown an interest in my country and culture	12.1	29.2	10.8	17.4	16.4	19.2	19.2
It is difficult to meet Canadian people from outside the university	13.4	24.2	20.8	11.1	7.3	18.5	18.1
Canadian students are hard to get to know	5.0	8.7	10.0	9.9	0.0	11.1	8.5
I prefer to mix with people from my own culture	13.6	8.6	4.6	13.4	1.8	1.7	7.3
Safety							
Percentage (%), very safe							
On campus	74.5	86.5	60.6	74.7	74.1	83.5	80.7
Accommodations	65.6	74.2	54.3	69.1	69.1	81.1	73.8
Public transport	40.0	62.8	27.3	47.3	31.5	57.8	52.4
Public spaces (off campus)	28.6	49.1	21.3	28.7	20.0	55.9	44.2

Eight statements about studying in Canada, or what we refer to as inclusion, are also shown in Table 6.3. On average, less than half (48%) of the
students strongly agreed with the statement that Canada was a welcoming
and tolerant society. Students from India were the most likely to strongly
agree with this statement (66%) and all other groups, including the
US/Western Europe group, had less than half of their students in strong
agreement. Across all groups, less than half strongly agreed with the statement that Canadian students are friendly when you get to know them yet
very few agreed that Canadian students were hard to get to know. At the
same time, more of the students from Asia would like to experience Canadian culture and very few prefer to mix with people from their own culture. This suggests that international students have the desire for a closer
connection with Canadians but that this is not often warmly received by
Canadian students, although students feel they are not hard to get to know.
Interestingly, the US/Western Europe group had the fewest students who
strongly agreed with wanting more chances to experience Canadian culture, presumably as a result of having little interest, or more plausibly, a
result of already having gained access. They were also less likely to strongly
agree with the statement regarding mixing with people from their own
culture. Of the five groups from Asia, students from China and Vietnam
had the largest percentage of strongly agreeing with this statement although
the rates were less than 15%.

Strong feelings of inclusion in the institution, such as in the classroom
and among staff and students, were generally low. For most of the groups,
including the US/Western Europe group, about one in five students felt
strongly that faculty and teaching assistants helped them to feel included
(with the exception of students from India and the Philippines who had
over 40% in strong agreement) and even fewer students, less than one in
four, felt staff and students demonstrated an interest in their country and
culture (only the group from India had close to 30%). For diversity and
cross-cultural development to be one of the main goals of internationalization, these figures suggest that the people within our educational institutions have some distance to go to achieve a more inclusive environment.
When asked about their interactions outside the university, it seems students are not struggling to meet Canadians outside the university with
about 18% strongly agreeing with this statement. Students from India and
Korea felt the strongest about this, and those from Vietnam and the Philippines were the least likely to strongly agree.

Finally, we turn to questions about safety in various settings, which can
be an influential factor in student decisions (see Zhang et al.). The bottom
of Table 6.3 shares figures related to students feeling very safe on campus,
in their accommodations, on public transportation, and in off-campus
public spaces. In general, most students felt very safe on campus: more

than 80% of the students from India and US/Western European countries and about 75% of the students from China, Vietnam, and the Philippines. Students from Korea were the least likely to state that they felt very safe on campus even though it was still a majority (61%). Most also felt very safe in their accommodations, particularly students from US/Western Europe. In comparison to safety on campus or in their accommodation, there is a clear shift when students are off campus. Students were less likely to state that they felt very safe using public transportation or being in public spaces off campus. While most students from India and US/Western Europe felt very safe on public transportation and roughly half felt very safe in public spaces off campus, students from China, Korea, Vietnam, and the Philippines were less likely to feel very safe in public. In particular, students from Korea were the least likely to feel very safe in public, along with students from the Philippines, which is consistent with the experiences of hate that tend to be in public places (see Kim, Chung, Jeon, Klassen, Kwak, Shin, and Trudel).

Discussion

In this chapter, we examine the degree to which students from Asia had strong positive feelings about various factors related to their university and experiences in Canada. We find that there are a number of reasons for students' institutional choice, including the quality of education, prestige of a degree or diploma, and cost. It seems ranking is less of a driving force than these other factors, although several large and more highly ranked institutions were missing from the analysis. These data provide some suggestions on where institutions may want to focus their attention and resources – in educational quality, prestige but not necessarily in rankings, affordability, and particular programs. We also find that university websites are very useful to students, and ranking publications and online forums and blogs, less so.

In terms of services and facilities, universities can improve international student orientation and follow-up with students on the specific reasons for not being very satisfied with it. The data also speak to the need for more assistance at the point of entry and in moving students into residence. While libraries, overall, received good feedback, student interactions with advisors (both for academic and international students) and health services did not. However, there were differences in levels of positivity across groups. Generally, we find that students from India and the Philippines were comparatively more positive about institutional resources, services, and facilities than students from China, Korea, and Vietnam, and this may be related to the former groups' English-speaking backgrounds. However, a more in-depth analysis should be conducted to tease apart this pattern.

Interestingly, we find this pattern across countries holds strong, positive feelings around adjustment and inclusion. This suggests, as others have as well (see Montsion and Caneo; de Oliviera Soares et al.), the need for more targeted programs or services for different groups, particularly for students from Korea, who appear to have the least positive experiences of all the groups.

Having said this, an important finding in the data is that Canadian students, staff, and faculty have much work to do to help institutions meet the goal of diversity and inclusion. To be sure, *only half* of the students in the sample learned about Indigenous history and culture since arriving at the university (see Luo and Wilkinson about the University of Manitoba's efforts to promote Indigenous studies among international students). University leaders assume that the institution is capable of welcoming international students with open arms and that its people will know how to internationalize and Indigenize classrooms and interactions. But the data and past research make clear that Canadian students, staff, and faculty are not effective at making international students feel included. And while the value of international students, discursively, is about their contributions to diversity, in actuality, it places the onus on the shoulders of international students to execute this labor (see Das Gupta and Gomez; Chatterjee, Shahrokni, Gomez, and Poojary 2022).

Despite the institution's weakness in making students feel integrated, we do find students feel very safe on campus compared to public spaces, which suggests that institutions can continue to improve on student safety on campus but they can also orient students to the realities of the local environment and strategies for feeling and keeping safe off campus.

Although many institutions have dedicated international offices, the rising number of international students puts pressure on these offices to provide the necessary support. As Choudaha and Hu (2016) note, the majority of institutions continue to fall short in providing adequate resources and the expertise needed to meet the expectations of international students on their campuses. Not meeting the expectations of this growing and high-fee-paying population will likely lead to lower levels of satisfaction and, as a result, negatively affect institutions. The key question is whether we want to measure the success of internationalization in the numbers and revenue or whether success is measured by positive student experiences within those institutions.

Acknowledgments

We would like to thank the Canadian Bureau for International Education (CBIE) for access to their 2018 International Student Survey data and the

Social Sciences and Humanities Research Council (SSHRC) for funding support to the RAIS (Racialization of Asian International Students) Project. The content of the chapter is the responsibility of the authors and does not represent CBIE.

Note

1 Western Europe refers to the countries listed under the sub-region of Western Europe according to the UN Geoscheme. We have also included the United Kingdom and Ireland in Western Europe, which were not under the sub-region of Western Europe according to the UN Geoscheme.

References

Ammigan, Ravichandran. 2019. "Institutional Satisfaction and Recommendation: What Really Matters to International Students." *Journal of International Students* 9, no. 1: 262–281.

Ammigan, Ravichandran, and Elspeth Jones. 2018. "Improving the Student Experience: Learning from a Comparative Study of International Student Satisfaction." *Journal of Studies in International Education* 22, no. 4: 283–301.

Arambewela, Rodney, and John Hall. 2007. "A Model of Student Satisfaction: International Postgraduate Students from Asia." *ACR European Advances* 8: 129–135.

Arambewela, Rodney, and John Hall. 2009. "An Empirical Model of International Student Satisfaction." *Asia Pacific Journal of Marketing and Logistics* 21, no. 4: 555–569.

Arthur, Nancy. 2017. "Supporting International Students through Strengthening Their Social Resources." *Studies in Higher Education* 42, no. 5: 887–894.

Buckner, Elizabeth, Elic Chan, and Eun Gi Kim. 2022. "Equity, Diversity, and Inclusion on Canadian Universities: Where Do International Students Fit In?" *Comparative and International Education/Education compare et internationale* Special Issue 55, no. 1: 1–19.

Canadian Bureau for International Education (CBIE). 2018. "The Student's Voice: National Results of the 2018 CBIE International Student Survey." CBIE Research in Brief No. 9. August.

Chatterjee, Soma, Shirin Shahrokni, Bianca Gomez, and Monisha Poojary. 2022. "Another University Is Possible? A Study of Indigenizing and Internationalizing Initiatives in Two Canadian Postsecondary Institutions." *Comparative and International Education/Éducation comparée et internationale* Special Issue 55, no. 1: 39–56.

Choudaha, Rahul, and Di, Hu. 2016. "Higher Education Must Go Beyond Recruitment and Immigration Compliance of International Students." *Forbes Education*, March 5, 2016. https://www.forbes.com/sites/rahuldi/2016/03/05/international-student-recruitment-retention-success-higher-education-strategies/?sh=570082dd7f7e.

Government of Canada. 2014. "Canada's International Education Strategy. Harnessing Our Knowledge Advantage to Drive Innovation and Prosperity". https://www.international.gc.ca/education/assets/pdfs/overview-apercu-eng.pdf.

ICEF Monitor. 2019. "Canada's Foreign Student Enrolment Took aAnother Big Jump in 2018." February 20, 2019. https://monitor.icef.com/2019/02/canadas-foreign-student-enrolment-took-another-big-jump-2018/.

Jones, Elspeth. 2017. "Problematising and Reimagining the Notion of 'International Student Experience'." *Studies in Higher Education* 42, no. 5: 933–943.

Kelo, Maria, Timothy Rogers, and Laura E. Rumbley. 2010. *International Student Support in European Higher Education: Needs, Solutions, and Challenges.* Bonn: Lemmens Medien.

Kim, Ann H., and Gunjan Sondhi. 2015. "Bridging the Literature on Education Migration." *Population Change and Lifecourse Strategic Knowledge Cluster Discussion Paper Series* 3, no. 1.

Merola, Rachael H., Robert J. Coelen, and W.H.A. Hofman. 2019. "The Role of Integration in Understanding Differences in Satisfaction among Chinese, Indian, and South Korean International Students." *Journal of Studies in International Education* 23, no. 4: 535–553.

Migin, Melissa W., Mohammad Falahat, Mohd Shukri Ab Yajid, and Ali Khatibi. 2015. "Impacts of Institutional Characteristics on International Students' Choice of Private Higher Education Institutions in Malaysia." *Higher Education Studies* 5, no. 1: 31–42.

Perez-Encinas, Adriana, and Ravichandran Ammigan. 2016. "Support Services at Spanish and US Institutions: A Driver for International Student Satisfaction." *Journal of International Students* 6, no. 4: 984–998.

Rienties, Bart, Simon Beausaert, Therese Grohnert, Susan Niemantsverdriet, and Piet Kommers. 2012. "Understanding Academic Performance of International Students: The Role of Ethnicity, Academic and Social Integration." *Higher Education* 63, no. 6: 685–700.

Slaten, Christopher D., Zachary M. Elison, Ji-Yeon Lee, Mike Yough, and Dominick Scalise. 2016. "Belonging on Campus: A Qualitative Inquiry of Asian International Students." *The Counseling Psychologist* 44, no. 3: 383–410.

Statistics Canada. 2020. "International Students Accounted for All of the Growth in Postsecondary Enrolments in 2018/2019." November 25, 2020. https://www150.statcan.gc.ca/n1/daily-quotidien/201125/dq201125e-eng.htm.

Wiers-Jenssen, Jannecke, Bjørn Stensaker, and Jens B. Grøgaard. 2002. "Student Satisfaction: towards an Empirical Deconstruction of the Concept." *Quality in Higher Education* 8, no. 2: 183–195.

7 Between Intellectual Gateway and Intellectual Periphery

Chinese International Student Experiences

Min-Jung Kwak, Lucia Lo, Guanglong Pang, and Yun Wang

Introduction

For the last three decades, international student migration has gained an increasing level of policy and scholarly attention around the world. Following the Intellectual Migration (IM) framework developed by Li et al. (2021), our study borrows the concepts of 'Intellectual gateway' (IG) and 'Intellectual periphery' (IP) and pitches Toronto and Halifax, respectively, as such destinations for international students. In particular, we focus on analyzing the experiences of Chinese international students and their migration to Canada because China has been a top source country for international students to Canada, accounting for 20 percent to 30 percent of the new arrivals almost every year since 2000 (Crossman et al. 2021). Moving beyond investigating the simple push and pull factors of higher education migration, we examine the role of distinctive placeness in shaping the geography of intellectual migration. Specifically, we pay particular attention to the role of socio-cultural environment, economic opportunities, educational institutions, and government policies and programs in influencing the motivations and decision-making of Chinese international students. Drawing upon data from an original online survey (N = 554) and in-person interviews (N = 39) with Chinese international students in Toronto and Halifax, we examine and compare the ways in which different scales of institutional structure and different socio-economic environment shape the experiences of Chinese international students and how local institutions affect their intellectual migration plan.

Migration is a complex process and it would be hard to provide a clear and full explanation on different types and characteristics of migration (Castles et al. 2014; Li et al. 2021). Historically, various theories have been used to analyze the factors associated with migration decisions and the experiences of international migrants (Massey 2000). Adding to the literature, we aim to analyze the mobility of international students on a global scale as well as their lived experiences on a local scale.

DOI: 10.4324/b23160-10

Li et al. (2015) argue that migration of higher-education students should be considered as existing on a continuum with that of highly skilled professionals. They define *Intellectual Migration* (IM) as a continuum along which international students and highly skilled professionals acquire, improve, and utilize 'intellectual capital' for career advancement or upward social mobility through spatial mobility. Li et al. (2021) further argue that intellectual capital is not human capital in its simplest form of professional knowledge or competent labour skills. Instead, it represents an interconnected form of social, cultural, and symbolic capitals (Bourdieu 1986). While pursuing their educational and career goals, international students and highly skilled professionals obtain knowledge and skill sets but they also gain familiarity with local culture and expand their social network. Thus, the concept of intellectual capital highlights the importance of analyzing interconnection between various forms of capital. Furthermore, the pursuit of intellectual capital may affect mobility planning and the migration destination of international students and professional migrants.

While there has been a significant growth in international education on a global scale, not all places are equally popular or attractive as the choice destination of education migration. An intellectual gateway usually attracts a large number of international students and skilled migrants and becomes an important site of knowledge building and intellectual connection. An urban centre like Toronto has many intellectual nodes such as higher education institutions, research organizations, and innovative and high-tech employers. Higher education international students and highly skilled professionals are often drawn into the city for its high-quality education, research opportunities, and skilled and professional jobs. On the other hand, an intellectual periphery has few intellectual nodes and is not usually considered an attractive destination for higher education and skilled professionals. These cities are less able to provide a full range of supports and resources for intellectual migrants. With the noted differences between intellectual gateway and intellectual periphery, they may attract different types of students and career seekers. Nonetheless, with a set of right policies and programs in place, some argue that it is possible to transform an intellectual periphery into an intellectual gateway (e.g., Florida 2005; Li et al. 2021).

Utilizing the IM framework, we identify two Canadian cities, Toronto, Ontario and Halifax, Nova Scotia, as examples of an 'intellectual gateway' and an 'intellectual periphery'. Ontario has been the top destination province in Canada, attracting around 40–50 percent of new international student arrivals annually (CBIE 2018). The province of Nova Scotia has been the most popular destination among the provinces of the Atlantic region but only accounts for roughly 3 percent of international post-secondary students in Canada (ibid.).

As such, we aim to conduct a comparative analysis between Toronto and Halifax as cities of intellectual migration by analyzing the characteristics of students, their education and career goals, their motivations for studying abroad, and their post-graduation migration plans. In particular, we examine if the two cities have attracted distinct groups of Chinese international students with different backgrounds and migration plans. Our research findings will add to the body of scholarship on education migration and student mobility to explain the 'who moves where' and the 'why move there' of intellectual migration (Castles 2010; Li et al. 2021).

Methodology

The data for this study were collected from an online survey, first conducted in Toronto in 2018 among students from China who were enrolled in York University (Toronto) at the time. The survey yields 398 valid responses. In Halifax, the same survey was launched in February 2020, paused because of the COVID-19 pandemic, and resumed in January 2021. Survey participants attended Dalhousie University, Saint Mary's University, or Mount Saint Vincent University. The sample consists of 156 responses. The survey data collected in both cities come from non-probability sampling.

The survey questionnaire consisted of four sections: covering the demographic and socio-economic background of students, their academic background, their motivational factors for studying abroad and their experiences of studying in Canada, and their post-graduation migration plan. Participants were recruited by multiple means. In Toronto, recruitment included flyers posted on campus buildings and public spaces, invitation cards delivered in-person outside classrooms and at events hosted by Chinese international student associations and university offices for international students, and electronic mailing/broadcasting to relevant student lists and social media groups. In Halifax, we mainly used digital posters and social media platforms.

Following the online survey, semi-structured in-depth interviews were conducted with students who expressed their interest in participating in the second stage of the study. In Toronto, 12 undergraduate and 11 graduate students participated in the interviews. In Halifax, we talked to 9 undergraduate and 7 graduate students. These 39 interviews were conducted in Chinese and then translated, transcribed, and analyzed using a qualitative data analysis software Dedoose. We did not link the survey responses to the interview data to protect the confidentiality of the information shared by the research participants. Both sets of data collected in Toronto and Halifax were analyzed in a summary format and this chapter provides our findings from the aggregated data. Overall, our interview data supplement the descriptive nature of the survey data analysis.

Demographic Characteristics of Chinese Students in Toronto and Halifax

The demographic and socio-economic characteristics of our online survey participants reveal that there are slight differences among the students between the two cities (see Table 7.1). In both cities, female students were

Table 7.1. Demographic and socio-economic profile of the online survey participants

	Toronto (N=398)	Halifax (N=156)
Gender		
Female (%)	54	58
Male (%)	42	40
Other/Not to disclose (%)	4	2
Age (years)	18–44 (over 80% under 27)	19–49 (over 80% under 29)
Marital status (%)		
Single (%)	83	86
Married (%)	17	14
Spouse working/studying in Canada (%)	75	86
Transnational Childcare (%)	44 (among those married w/children)	25 (among those married w/children)
Family Background		
Only child to the parents (%)	56	70
At least one parent university educated (%)	46	56
Financial Support from Parents		
Full support (%)	46	64
Partial support (%)	45	30
No support (%)	10	6
Current Academic Level		
English as Second Language (%)	20	3
Undergraduate (%)	50	78
Graduate (%)	30	19
Current Major		
Business administration/ Economics (%)	50	47
Science/Engineering (%)	22	24
Social sciences/Humanities/ Arts (%)	18	20

the majority. A slightly higher proportion of students in Toronto identified themselves with other gender identity or did not wish to disclose. Between the two cities, the proportion of female students was slightly higher in Halifax. More than 80 percent of students in both cities were single and 29 years old and under. Of those married, 75 percent of married participants in Toronto and 86.4 percent in Halifax responded that their spouse was working, studying, or homemaking in Canada, and among those with children, 44 percent in Toronto and 25 percent in Halifax were maintaining transnational childcare between China and Canada.

Although most participants of our survey came from an upper-middle-class background, a higher proportion of the students in Halifax than in Toronto reported family background with the traits of higher socio-economic status. For example, while 46 percent of the participants in Toronto had at least one of their parents being university-educated with 56 percent of those in Halifax responding the same. On the other hand, a lower percentage of the participants in Halifax (3.2 percent of fathers and 1.9 percent of mothers) reported that their parents were peasants or urban migrant workers (5 percent each for Toronto participants). While their parents mostly (88 percent in Toronto and 90 percent in Halifax) reside in China, a lower percentage of the Toronto parents (75 percent versus Halifax's 81 percent) owned a family car there.[1] In terms of annual household income, about 50 percent of Toronto students and about 57 percent of Halifax students reported that their parents earned over 180,000 RMB (around $27,000 USD) when the average household income of China in 2018 was only 21,586 RMB (around $3,240 USD).

Most students in our sample relied financially on their parents, either fully or partially, to fund their education in Canada. However, the level of financial dependence on their parents was higher for the students in Halifax (64 percent with full support and about 30 percent with partial support) compared to those in Toronto (46 percent full support and 45 percent partial support). The difference can be somewhat explained by the higher proportion of undergraduate (around 78 percent) students in Halifax than those in Toronto (50 percent), as graduate students are more likely to receive graduate program fellowships or stipends from their school. In addition, a higher proportion of students in Toronto (19.4 percent versus 13.9 percent in Halifax) identified off-campus work as a main source of financial support for their education. The higher proportion of graduate students and more off-campus work opportunities in Toronto is a good indicator of an intellectual gateway city with many intellectual nodes. In terms of the field of the study, almost half of the students in both cities pursue a degree program in business administration or economics and another quarter of participants were studying science or engineering. The lowest enrolment areas were social sciences, humanities, or arts. Regarding academic background, an overwhelming majority (more than 90 percent for both cities) of our sample had attended high schools in China, with 66 percent in key high schools with better reputation and more resources from the state. A higher proportion of the students in Toronto reported being top performers in their high schools back in China, with 31 percent performing in the top 10 percent of their class and 42 percent being above average, compared to 20.3 percent in the top 10 percent and 32.3 percent above average among Halifax students.

Motivation Factors for Study Abroad and Choosing Study Destination

Student mobility is a complex process to analyze as different motivational factors affect the option of studying abroad or not as well as where to study. According to Pande and Yan (2018), some of main factors driving Chinese students to study abroad include: lack of quality education in China, the rise of middle-class Chinese families, the higher returns obtained from Western credentials, and the role of international education agency. The students in our sample also show generally similar motivations for their decision to study abroad. First, in terms of their level of study, most students came for universities, 54 percent (Toronto) and 73 percent (Halifax) at the undergraduate level and 27 percent (Toronto) and 12 percent (Halifax) at the graduate level. The rest (14 percent in Toronto and 6.3 percent in Halifax) came for secondary school first to avoid the extremely competitive university entrance examination (*gaokao*) in China. In both cities, the top three reasons among the answers rated as 'very important' or 'most important' for studying abroad were 'to experience the world', 'to obtain a foreign degree for better job opportunities', and 'to engage in more innovative and advanced research', respectively, at the rate of 57 percent, 41 percent, and 36 percent by Toronto respondents and at the rate of 57 percent, 33 percent, and 32.2 percent by Halifax students.

The importance of job opportunities and innovative and advanced research opportunities was a bit lower for Halifax respondents, reflecting the lower proportion of graduate students in the city. Interestingly, around 30 percent of participants from both cities rated 'to settle (permanently/temporarily) and develop their career abroad' as an important reason for studying abroad, indicating that Chinese students have shown a moderate level of interest in stay longer in Canada after graduation.

In terms of choosing their study destination, Canada was rated as the top choice by 62 percent of the Toronto participants and 72 percent of the Halifax participants. Those studying in Toronto chose Canada for its social and natural environments, its employment outlook, and the reputation of its higher education sector and the associated academic environment. Similar responses were provided by the participants in Halifax, but there was more emphasis on the socio-cultural environment, natural environment, and the academic environment. There seem to be a higher expectation about job opportunities in Toronto as an intellectual gateway city, and yet the participants in Halifax are more optimistic about obtaining permanent residency status after graduation. This is likely due to the favourable immigration policies (e.g., Atlantic Pilot Immigration program) in Nova Scotia. Two examples demonstrate student knowledge about the welcoming migration policies in Halifax.

The most important thing was that it is easier to get a work permit [in Nova Scotia, Canada]. I compared Canada to the UK, the US, and Australia. After comparison, Canada is the best (most accessible) one to get (the work permit).

(GR01, Halifax)

What I know is a so-called Atlantic policy. It seems that if you have a job within the range, you could apply for the PR [Permanent Residency] directly without the requirement of one year of working experience. This is a good signal as the policy is not strict as in the past, which you must have a job and work for one year. ... Its policy is directly related to whether I could stay here or not. Since this policy reduces the difficulty of [applying for] my immigration, it has substantial impacts.

(GR02, Halifax)

When asked about their opinion regarding the choices of 'studying at a Canadian university branch campus located in China', 'doing a joint degree by splitting their study time between China and Canada', and 'spending their entire study time in Canada', the choice seemed to be clear for the participants. Forty-seven percent in Toronto and 60.6 percent in Halifax preferred to physically study in Canada, about a third (39 percent in Toronto and 31 percent in Halifax) favoured a joint degree, and only a small percentage (14 percent in Toronto and 8.5 percent in Halifax) would like to study in a Canadian university branch campus housed in China. The majority said that full-time study in Canada provides the opportunity to experience its social and cultural environments and they believed Canada offers a better academic environment. To them, the 'real meaning of studying abroad' is to be physically present at a Canadian university for the duration of their degree.

The Experiences in Canada

As admitted by 67 percent of our Toronto participants and 92.8 percent of Halifax participants, their decision to study in Canada was not dependent upon financial aids or support provided by the Chinese government or the Canadian university they attended. This is another indicator that most of the participants came from relatively affluent families and Halifax had a higher proportion of undergraduate students than Toronto. While educational financing was not a major problem for our research participants, they encountered the usual adaptation challenges faced by many international students. While managing their academic programs and planning their future career, initial challenges faced by Chinese international students include limited social network, language barriers, and cultural differences (Arthur and Flynn 2011; Dyer and Lu 2010).

Before their departure, a majority had no or just a little knowledge about the lives of international students and about their post-graduation career experience in Canada. For those who had some understanding, it was primarily through families/relatives already in Canada (the top source of information for Toronto participants), through social media (the top source of information for Halifax participants), and from former classmates who had studied in Canada (for both groups). It is thus not surprising that they found life in Canada challenging. Pressure from their academic work, dealing with language barrier, difficulties integrating into Canadian campus life and Canadian socio-cultural norms were the major challenges. As noted by Ma (2020), Chinese international students are ambitious and motivated with their educational and career goals, and yet they are also anxious about fitting in Canadian/American educational system and culture. A lot of Chinese international students tend to maintain their own social network among Chinese students and are not able to reach out and make Canadian friends.

> Since I am new here, I know little about all aspects of Canada. Compared to my graduate classmates most of whom completed their undergraduate in Canada and know more about Canada, this is the biggest challenge for me. Then, the next significant challenge is that I have no idea how to communicate with people from various backgrounds/cultures. For example, if I want to chat with others on LinkedIn, I have no idea how to start the conversation naturally. Thus, I need to think of it and do some research online. ... I had no network.
>
> (GR02, Halifax)

Previous studies found that the biggest challenge international students of ethnic/racial minority background face is the process of labour market integration (Hasmath 2012; Zschirnt and Ruedin 2016). In our study, we also noticed that some students had experienced different forms of racial discrimination and microaggressions during their study in Canada.

In Canada, I faced a lot of prejudice against Chinese people. Once or twice a month, I'm generally called names, especially ones that are highly offensive to Chinese people. White people always bullied me.

(YU9, Toronto)

I actually heard about similar situations from others in other big cities and universities. One of my friends who studied at Dalhousie University is Vietnamese. Once applying for a job in the university, he was required to show a work permit because his name was not a typical name of white people, which was a serious discriminatory behaviour from my perspective.

(GR3, Halifax)

During my undergraduate, there were some cases on the campus. Once in the class, the professor divided students into different groups. Four students were in a group. Two students in the front row turned around, making the team with two students in the back row. Two students in the front were one female and one male. My friends, who were my current roommate [who is Chinese], and I sit at the back row. After turning around, the female student in the front row who saw my friend and me decided to turn back immediately and told the professor that she wanted to make a group with students in her left because she didn't want to make a group with us. The professor agreed with her. What made me mad was that the professor agreed with her.

(GR4, Halifax)

Prazeres et al. (2017) noted the reputation of higher education institutions tends to be over-emphasized when we consider international education and student mobility. They argued that the place of education offers much more than a good school and we need to pay attention to the importance of 'placeness' when we discuss geography of international education. Specifically, international students imagine and develop a notion of 'distinctive places' while constantly comparing different places of higher education and acquiring intellectual capital through the lived experiences in the place of their study (Beech 2014). This notion of 'distinctive and comparative places' continues to be developed even after graduation as the students engage with future mobility by seeking further education or career opportunities. In this study, we probe how geography matters for Chinese international students in Canada in selecting their destination of education, studying and living in the city, and planning their mobility for future career development.

To a certain extent, the notion of 'distinctive placeness' identified by international students (Prazeres et al. 2017) is in line with the geographical concepts of 'intellectual gateway' and 'intellectual periphery' in the IM framework. When asked about their motivation to study abroad and their future plans, our research participants often made direct and indirect connections with their experiences of living and studying in the city of their choice. The place of intellectual migration is constantly assessed by our participants if the place offers strategic social network and appropriate cultural capital for them to utilize for further socio-economic mobility.

I really love this city. In the past, I wanted to find a peaceful and not-developed city to live in. Halifax is suitable. This city is energetic without significant pressure, which is livable. It is inclusive and friendly enough.

(GR7, Halifax)

I want to be in Toronto if I stay in Canada. It's nice to be here. It is also Canada's largest city, whether in terms of population, economic strength, opportunity, or climate. I also have a greater understanding of the city.

(YU8, Toronto)

Toronto is a very Chinese city that is also extremely easy to live in.

(YU3, Toronto)

Halifax is a good place for living and retired life. However, it is not a good place for me to work for the long term, while it is a suitable place for studying. After completing studying, I will move to other big cities. But I really love it.

(UG4, Halifax)

Between Toronto and Halifax, our online survey reveals another interesting aspect of the two cities as cities of continuing education. Before attending York University, 9 participants in our Toronto sample reported that they studied in colleges in the Greater Toronto Area and 72 out of the 120 students had obtained a degree from other Canadian universities in Ontario (including York University), Alberta, Manitoba, Nova Scotia, and Newfoundland. However, most of the Halifax respondents had not studied in Nova Scotia or other provinces before they came to study in Halifax. Only four (2 undergraduate and 2 graduate students) out of 158 students had learning experiences in Southern Ontario. The finding indicates an important distinction between Toronto and Halifax: an intellectual gateway city like Toronto can provide more transitional and various types of education opportunities for Chinese international students.

Discussion: The Geography of Intellectual Migration

In this study, we examine the socio-demographic characteristics of Chinese international students and their motivations for studying in two Canadian cities, Toronto and Halifax. Drawing upon the conceptual framework of Intellectual Migration (IM)—which was developed to comprehend the migratory experience of highly skilled migrants for upward career and social mobility (Li et al. 2021)—we compare the experiences of Chinese students studying and living in Toronto as an intellectual gateway and Halifax as an intellectual periphery. While our research participants in both cities share many commonalities in dealing with the challenges of studying and living abroad, we found some notable differences between the two student groups. Examining their motivational factors for study abroad and their choice of study destination, we found that Chinese students develop the notion of distinctive placeness about Canada compared to other countries and about the city they study and live in. This unique sense of placeness is obtained through their own imagination as well as lived experiences. By analyzing the educational migration experiences and discourses of Chinese international students in both cities, we further investigate what make Toronto and Halifax, respectively, as an example site of intellectual gateway and intellectual periphery.

The IM framework allows for an examination of the two cities as sites for synergic capital acquisition, conversion, and upgrade between the different dimensions of intellectual capital; it also illuminates the geographical implications of being an intellectual gateway or periphery. Toronto attracts a large number of international students with many intellectual nodes and provides various transition opportunities within Canada. On the other hand, we learnt from our research that Halifax mainly welcomes those students who have never studied abroad or elsewhere in Canada. These findings suggest that intellectual gateways are attractive because of their different levels of degree programs and more employment opportunities, whereas intellectual peripheries can be easier entry points for international students but not places attracting further intellectual migration flows.

Li et al. (2021) emphasize that intellectual periphery cities may transform themselves into intellectual gateways when the local governments, higher educational institutions, and private sector work together to create an environment conducive to intellectual capital accumulation and thereby attractive to intellectual migrants. At the time of our study, we witness that the provincial government's efforts started to pay off in recruiting more intellectual migrants and potential immigrants into the province of Nova Scotia and the city of Halifax, albeit labour market opportunities still seeming to be lacking, at least in the minds of Chinese international students in Halifax. Between the two student groups, those in Toronto, linked their choice of permanent stay in Canada with 'employment opportunities and higher economic returns' as the top reason, whereas their Halifax counterparts considered 'less pressure living in Canada' as their primary reason for stay. We believe this is an interesting indicator of distinctive placeness development. Despite the commonalities in their migratory experiences, the unique sense of placeness associated with being in an intellectual gateway versus periphery is shaped by and reshapes students' current lived experiences (including strategies for intellectual capital accumulation and utilization) and their imaginations for future migratory plans.

Acknowledgements

This chapter draws on research supported by the Social Sciences and Humanities Research Council of Canada (grant number 435-2017-1168).

Note

1 Car ownership in China is an important aspect of social status.

References

Arthur, Nancy, and Sarah Flynn. 2011. "Career Development Influences of International Students Who Pursue Permanent Immigration to Canada." *International Journal for Educational and Vocational Guidance* 11, no. 3: 221–37.
Beech, Suzanne E. 2014. "Why Geography Matters: Imaginative Geography and International Student Mobility." *Area* 46, no. 2: 170–77.
Bourdieu, Pierre. 1986. "The Forms of Capital." In *Handbook of Theory and Research for the Sociology of Education*, edited by John G. Richardson, 241–60. New York: Greenwood Press.
Castles, Steven. 2010. "Understanding Global Migration: A Social Transformation Perspective." *Journal of Ethnicity and Migration* 36, no. 10: 1565–86.
Castles, Stephen, Hein de Haas, and M. J. Miller. 2014. *The Age of Migration: International Population Movements in the Modern World*. 5th ed. New York, NY: The Guilford Press.
CBIE (Canadian Bureau for International Education). 2018. *International Students in Canada*. CBIE Research in Brief. August 2018.
Crossman, Eden, Youjin Choi, and Feng Hou. 2021. "Insights: International Students as a Source of Labour Supply: The Growing Number of International

Students and Their Changing Sociodemographic Characteristics." *Economic and Social Reports* 1, no. 7: 1–11.

Dyer, Suzette, and Fen, Lu. 2010. "Chinese Born International Students' Transition Experiences from Study to Work in New Zealand." *Australian Journal of Career Development* 19, no. 2: 23–31.

Florida, Richard. 2005. *The Flight of the Creative Class. The New Global Competition for Talent*. New York: Harper Business, Harper Collins.

Hasmath, Reza. 2012. *The Ethnic Penalty: Immigration, Education and the Labour Market*. Routledge.

Li, Wei, Lucia Lo, Yixi Lu, Yining Tan, and Zheng Lu. 2021. "Intellectual Migration: Considering China." *Journal of Ethnic and Migration Studies* 47, no. 12: 2833–53.

Li, Wei, Wan Yu, Claudia Sadowski-Smith, and Hao Wang. 2015. "Intellectual Migration and Brain Circulation: Conceptual Framework and Empirical Evidence." *Journal of Overseas Chinese* 11: 43–58.

Ma, Yingyi. 2020. *Ambitious and Anxious: How Chinese College Students Succeed and Struggle in American Higher Education*. New York, NY: Columbia University Press.

Massey, Douglas. 2000. "Why Does Immigration Occur: A Theoretical Synthesis." In *The Handbook of International Migration: The American Experience*, edited by C. Hirschman, P. Kasinitz, and J. DeWind, 34–52. New York, NY: Russell Sage.

Pande, Amba, and Yuan Yan. 2018. "Migration of Students from India and China: A Comparative View." *South Asian Survey* 23, no. 1: 69–92.

Prazeres, Laura, Allan Findlay, David McCollum, Nikola Sander, Elizabeth Musil, Zaiga Krisjane, and Elina Apsite-Berina. 2017. "Distinctive and Comparative Places: Alternative Narratives of Distinction within International Student Mobility." *Geoforum* 80: 114–22.

Zschirnt, Eva, and Didier Ruedin. 2016. "Ethnic Discrimination in Hiring Decisions: A Meta-Analysis of Correspondence Tests 1990-2015." *Journal of Ethnic and Migration Studies* 42, no. 7: 1115–34.

8 Understanding Chinese Students' Manifold Transitions in a Canadian University

Eustacia Yu

Introduction

International students have become an important part of internationalization in higher education, simultaneously recruited to generate revenue to combat decreased government funding for Canadian universities and as ideal potential immigrants for an increasingly aging Canadian society (cf. Global Affairs Canada 2019). Chinese students have constituted the majority of enrolments in most broad university program areas in Canada (Statistics Canada 2020), thus playing a significant role in the internalization process of the Canadian higher education.

This study explores how Chinese international students navigate their manifold transitions from Chinese high schools to a Canadian university and how programs, structures, and environments of the Canadian institution shaped their experiences. The transition from high school to university is a major life change and is stressful for most students (Tinto 1993). However, undergraduate students in Canadian universities coming directly from Chinese high schools are a unique group. Coming to study in Canada, these students are also transitioning to a linguistically and culturally different country. Meanwhile, transitioning from adolescence to young adulthood is an important time in life for worldview and identity (re)formation (Arnett 2000 and Erikson 1985), when students are experiencing a dynamic transition of both physical and psychological development. These elements add more layers of transition to this group of students than those who do not have linguistic and cultural issues or new students in graduate programs who are more or less acculturated to the university life.

Chinese Undergraduate Students' Manifold Transitions

Previous studies have documented challenges international students encounter in Canadian universities, with frequently cited ones including cultural and linguistic barriers, feeling of isolation, and mental health issues

DOI: 10.4324/b23160-11

(Guo and Guo 2017 and Liu 2017). Besides, instead of viewing international students as a single monolithic group, more attention has been directed to distinctive groups shaped by various sociocultural factors (Marom 2022). Building on the extant literature, this study highlights Chinese undergraduate students' experience in navigating the three-fold transitions: from China to Canada, high schools to higher education, and adolescence to adulthood. Drawing on developmental perspectives, this study takes a holistic view to examine the manifold transitions these Chinese students navigate in their Canadian university life. The chapter will also discuss how these transitions tie into each other in the institutional context by analyzing key transition issues, such as schoolwork and social life balance, peer relationships, tension around independence, identity (re) formation, as well as systemic barriers and discrimination.

Transition from China to Canada

Discrepancies in cultural expectations in home and host countries may shape individual experiences along with other internal and external factors. Swidler (1986) conceptualized culture as a repertoire or "a toolkit of habits, skills and styles" that individuals draw on to manage everyday life and emerging situations (273). This toolkit metaphor serves well in the context of cross-cultural integration. The transition from China to Canada involves cross-cultural adaptations and adjustments of Chinese students' new campus life. Distinctions between Canadian cultural norms and those in China can be identified in many dimensions such as human relations, social structures, and interpersonal communication.

During the transitions to higher education, cultural factors may also impact students' learning experience. Different conceptions of learning rooted in cultures impact students' learning behaviors, as learning occurs within socially constructed environments (Greenholtz 2003). The multicultural context of teaching and learning shapes students' interaction with instructors and their classroom experience as cultural expectations may also come into play. To elaborate, scholars (Biggs 1996 and Tweed and Lehman 2002) have noted that Chinese students are taught to gain fundamental knowledge and skills before they are able to make judgments and question others. In contrast, teachers in Western society are perceived to view content as dynamic and the capacity to evaluate information critically as the goal of education (Greenholtz 2003 and Pratt 1992). Moreover, in Chinese culture, a high power distance exists between students and instructors (Hofstede 1986), which may prevent some Chinese students from communicating with their instructors in Canada pertaining to learning issues. This power distance indicates socialization not only to respect teachers and their authority but also to respect and expect their knowledgeability. Consequently, Chinese students usually have high expectations of their teachers in this relationship (Pratt 1992). Differences between the two education systems manifest in an emphasis on *the learning process* among Western educators and on *the product* (mastery of knowledge) among Chinese educators (Gardner 1989). In this case, some Chinese students may experience dissonance when they first arrive.

Transition from High School to University

For all students, the move to university is a significant social displacement as the university is a different environment from the high school even for students staying in their home country. In university, students no longer get intensive monitoring and supervision from teachers. Besides, course schedule, class duration, academic requirements and expectations, as well as campus life are all different. It is the students' own responsibility to access resources, get support, build their community, and keep up. Besides, many students move out of their parents' homes and live on their own, which may result in problems in the wake of the sudden independence for those with limited self-control. The existing literature has documented aspects of transition during students' initial university life, such as time management (Van der Meer, Jansen, and Torenbeek 2010), mental well-being and emotional needs for friendship (ACHA 2019), the need to develop academic literacy skills (Van der Meer, Jansen, and Torenbeek 2010), navigation of academic requirements (Blair 2017), and transient feelings of not belonging (Palmer, O'Kane and Owens 2009).

Another layer of transition is added to international students – the sociocultural transition. Briggs et al. (2012) argued that the challenges associated with the transition to university may be intensified when the individual is a first-generation university student or is from another culture or education system, as in the case of international students. Chinese students get significant scaffolding from teachers in high schools. Parental supervision and additional learning support also prove to be significant (Liu 2017). In China, teachers make parents aware of the student's learning situations at school, so parents can follow up and assist at home. In university, these Chinese students live away from their parents and they must keep up with their academic work on their own. Aside from learning university routines and study habits for a new academic environment and achieving the balance between academic activities and other aspects of university life, these students also need to function independently, manage finances, budget time, modify previous relationships with family and friends, and make new relationship (Briggs, Clark, and Hall 2012).

Transition from Adolescence to Adulthood

In addition to their academic and cultural transitions, undergraduate students are also in the process of moving from adolescence to young adulthood. Adolescence is a dynamic transitional period of both physical and psychological development, in which young individuals particularly need love, respect, and social acceptance, and have a desire for success, therefore, "a healthy way of passing this period will positively affect individuals' perspectives on life" (Özdemir, Utkualp and Palloş 2016, 717). Prior studies have demonstrated that, when transitioning to adulthood, individuals require holistic learning and preparation consisting of life skills for them to function independently, emotional skills, mental well-being, and life transitions (Bologna 2021).

While discussing the development in adolescence and young adulthood, Erikson (1968) observed a "prolonged adolescence", during which young adults engage in experimentation to determine their future roles in society. Building on this concept, Arnett (2000) proposed a new stage of development described as "emerging adulthood" to conceptualize the transitional period of profound change. Emerging adulthood covers the ages from late teens through twenties, a period distinct from both adolescence and young adulthood in which young people prepare for adulthood through exploration and experimentation. Since emerging adults have already left the dependence of childhood but not yet fully entered the responsibilities of adulthood, this is a period of frequent change and constant experimentation. During this stage, various life directions in love, work and worldviews remain possible (Arnett 2000). According to Arnett (2000), while this stage offers numerous opportunities for role exploration, it is also very demanding, as the most important events in life take place in this period. Exploration in emerging adulthood is also concomitant with risk taking and reckless behavior for many young people (Shifren, Furnham, and Bauserman 2003) since "emerging adults can pursue novel and intense experiences more freely than adolescents because they are less likely to be monitored by parents and can pursue more freely than adults because they are less constrained by roles" (Arnett 2000, 475).

Identity formation is another important topic for this period of development. Kramsch (2009) observed that identity formation is not only through intrapersonal reflection and changes, but also through interpersonal relationships in a given sociocultural context. Erikson (1968, 1985) specifically argued that, while identity formation is a lifelong process, a crucial period occurs at the end of adolescence when individuals encounter physical growth, sexual maturation, and imminent vocational choices.

Given the significant and complicated nature of this period in life, it is more beneficial to take a holistic view of these transitions by considering

120   *Eustacia Yu*

these students whole persons. Therefore, instead of reviewing isolate challenges they face, this study examines the holistic experiences during the Chinese international students' multiple transitions in their university life in Canada. The research questions guiding the study are as follows: (1) What are the diverse factors and forces Chinese international students encounter during their multiple transitions? (2) How do these factors and forces tie into each other in the institutional context to holistically shape these students' experiences in their university life in Canada?

Materials and Methods

This study adopts a qualitative methodology to explore how the diverse factors and forces interweave to shape the Chinese international students holistically. This approach is grounded in a philosophical position of constructivism in that it is applied to discover, understand, and interpret how people make meaning of their experiences embedded in the particular sociocultural setting and at a particular point in time (Bloomberg and Volpe 2016 and Creswell and Poth 2018). The developmental perspectives described above are used to understand the transitional processes of these international Chinese undergraduates and to review the key themes characteristic of their experience during their manifold transitions.

The Canadian institution where research participants were recruited is a research-intensive university located in Western Canada. It has around 33,000 students and 5,000 staff members, with 250 undergraduate and graduate programs. The university launched its international strategy in 2013, making internationalization a key institutional strategic priority. Support resources for international students available on campus include International Student Services, Student Wellness Services, and EDI Office. Seven Chinese students with dissimilar family backgrounds and personal histories were recruited from diverse faculties across campus in the Canadian university. They graduated from high schools all over China, across six different provinces or autonomous regions. At the time of the interviews, participants were all aged 19–22 (except one who spent more time in a language program), with three starting their second year of undergraduate study and four starting their third or fourth year. Their academic disciplines varied, spanning major faculties offering undergraduate programs at the university: Faculties of Arts, Science, Engineering, and Business. For all seven participants, this study experience was their first time visiting Canada.

Three rounds of hour-long semi-structured interviews were conducted one-on-one over four months. The interviews started in September and completed in December 2019 to get the second-year students' perspectives on their first year in a Canadian university. Upper-year participants were invited to focus on their first-year experience in university, a crucial year for transitions from high school to university (Tinto 1993), but experiences in other years were also included as transition is considered a process (Bridges 2009). Interview data were organized and analyzed in sequential steps: each participant's story was first collected and constructed and then all the stories were reorganized and analyzed by emerging thematic categories.

Analysis and Discussion of Key Themes During Manifold Transitions

The narratives of the seven participants revealed both collective and individual experiences of these Chinese students in their university life. The over-arching findings demonstrate that diverse factors and forces worked together shaping students' experiences in their campus life in Canada and impacting their holistic development during their transitions. The impact of these transitions can be either barriers or opportunities for learning and growth depending on how they are taken by these individuals (Schlossberg 1981). The process of the students' transition was unfolded and addressed through the capture of their rich experiences. The aspects of transitions they reported to face are demonstrated in Figure 8.1.

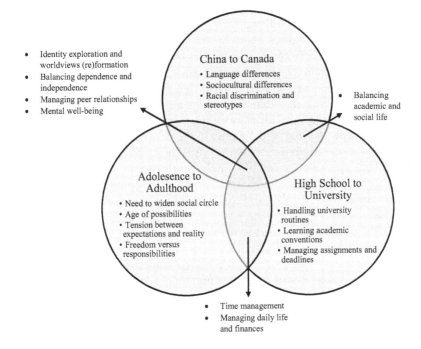

Figure 8.1 Aspects of transitions drawn from participant narratives

As demonstrated in Figure 8.1, some transitional aspects are unique for a specific transition, while others are overlapping in two or all three transitions. Different factors played out influencing a seemingly single area of transition. Consequently, from what they reported, when facing the same issue, these participants may often need to manage much more complicated multilayer situations than their peers going through only one or two transitions. Below are discussions of some key themes drawn from the table, many of which appear in more than one transition, impacting these participants' holistic experiences as they cross the three transitions.

Schoolwork and Social Life Balance

The findings demonstrate that an important area in the new life of these participants lies in their effort to balance their academic and social lives. This is a typical area for development during their transition to university as their major task in high schools was academic studies, especially in Chinese high schools. Meanwhile, the need for social networking in this emerging adulthood makes it overlap with the transition to adulthood. Most participants in this study reported to have viewed academic studies as their main goal of attending university abroad since traditional Chinese culture lays considerable emphasis on education (Pratt 1992) which put these students into a cultural transition as well.

Most participants agreed that, in an ideal world, students ought to maintain a balance between academic performance and social life, including extracurricular activities. However, they also reported encountering challenges in managing everything when they first arrived in the Canadian university. They indicated that they spent a great deal of time on social activities in their first year. First, away from family and established friendships, they needed a sense of belonging in the new surroundings. Secondly, social integration required more effort while they transitioned into the new culture. Time spent on "social life" included their effort in getting familiar with the new life such as food styles (ending up going out for meals or cooking their own meals) and local transportation (which could be time-consuming).

While they all made an effort to manage time more wisely to handle both academic requirements and social activities in their second semester or second year, some attached more importance to academic performance while others on social activities and networking. One participant put it this way, "As I was unable to balance between the two, I had to focus more on my courses and grades, because I have to meet my parents' expectations". Another participant added, "It's so expensive to engage in social and extracurricular activities". With the substantial amount of tuition, which was usually two to three times the amount of tuition for local students, most of these international students expressed they "don't feel comfortable adding more financial pressure" on their family. Participant narratives revealed that students' schoolwork and social life could be mutually affected (Tinto 1993), and the interwoven areas impacted individuals holistically, which require them to function independently (Briggs, Clark, and Hall 2012) to effectively manage both schoolwork and social life and keep the balance between the two.

Power Distance in Peer Relationship

A second key finding was about peer relationship which is overlapping in all three transitions. Friendships provided the students with a sense of belonging and that this was viewed as particularly important for them during their three-fold transitions. A need to widen their social circle is characteristic of this developmental period (Jensen 2011). However, participant narratives showed that friendship was not easily attainable for them in the new environment. Compared to situations at high schools in China where students were in classes with the same group for all courses, participants stated that relationship building needs special efforts in the Canadian university where students meet different individuals in each course they take. One participant recalled, "[When I wanted to connect with local students,] we only chatted a bit during class breaks or after class so deeper understanding was not possible". In this relationship, a power differential exists between Chinese international students and local students resulting from English being the dominant language in both daily communications and in the formal learning setting. As another participant put it "I find I cannot react quickly when communicating with local students .... Friendship with them is also high maintenance". Positioned disadvantageously, Chinese international students need to possess language proficiency to participate in authentic conversations, as the interaction is no longer solely for an academic purpose but also for generating interest in communications serving a social function, which requires proficiency in a different register from academic requirements, i.e. informal conversational English.

In participants' stories, the hierarchical relationship between them and local students lay in more than just the use of the English language as the same issues occur in the social aspect of interactions. Sometimes, it equally required these students to possess Canadian-specific cultural knowledge in order to generate meaningful conversation and lasting social connections. Out of a desire to get acquainted with local students, one participant reported taking the initiative to familiarize themselves with the common language for mutual understanding and meaningful interactions: "To make it easier to communicate with local students, I even watched the stuff they did when they were kids and tried to research on what they learned in high school".

Apparently, it's international students' responsibility to adopt Canadian social norms and cultural practices to integrate into the mainstream setting. The limited linguistic, cultural, and social capital (Bourdieu 1991), and even financial capital for some students, have made networking with Canadian peers more difficult as reflected in their narratives. Another factor prominent in the findings is the lack of structured opportunities in both the academic setting and the social setting for interaction and relationship building between the two groups.

Tension around Independence

Studying in Canadian universities was the first time most participants had lived so far away from home. Revealed in their narratives are participants' various sentiments and emotions. They reported mixed feelings as they left the protection of their parents, engaging in various explorations in this transitional period: homesick and loneliness at first, but the appreciation of independence dominated. One participant shared her feelings: "I had been protected by my parents.... I now feel the joy of being a real adult and can make my own decisions, though I sometimes felt lonely at the beginning and wasn't able to do everything perfectly".

In participants' experiences of transitioning into the Canadian university, a tension emerged in the interviews between the desire for independence and the need for relationships. While these students are eager to gain independence from their parents, they also simultaneously need to establish relationships with peers. In the new environment, one participant expressed her expectations: "I very much want to become an excellent student in people's eyes, so they like to work with me and become friends with me". This tension between the opposing desires was reflected in the works of Kegan (1982), who viewed the process of mental development as an effort to resolve the tension between people's longing for autonomy and their desire for relationships. By seeking friendship, these international students' goal of healthy development is relationships, as compared to their local peers whose goal of deployment at this age is more likely to be autonomy (Walsh et al. 2005).

Adolescence is also a time of reckless behavior for students with low self-regulation (Shifren, Furnham, and Bauserman 2003), resulting in some students reducing self-control in the wake of the sudden independence gained in the new environment. One participant chose a Chinese roommate in his first semester out of an expectation of a smoother transition and mutual support. This roommate indulged himself in regular whole-night game play, which negatively impacted this participant who worked around his roommate's schedule, leading to the suffering of his academic performance and morale. "I didn't want to undermine our relationship as he was the only friend I had then", he said, "but found it didn't work and had to leave him in the second semester". Most participants reported having similar experiences navigating the transition from parental supervision to independence, gradually gaining self-control and confidence in managing their own campus life.

Identity (Re)formation in Cross-cultural Context

As demonstrated in Figure 8.1, identity (re)formation also spans all identified transitions for these participants. As emerging adults, these students reported having engaged in a negotiation of identities on campus through how they were perceived and treated by others (Erikson 1968, 1985).

Some participants shared their experience that, when they first arrived in Canada, they distanced themselves from other Chinese students and Chinese language which they feared may inhibit their integration into the Canadian culture. Meanwhile, during this transitional period, some participants also strove to model practices and norms in Canadian society at the beginning by updating their own frame of reference. One participant reported that, though having more than a dozen former classmates from his Chinese high school on campus, he made great efforts to socialize with local students in his first year, including attending all events in the common room in residence and pubbing with dorm-mates every weekend while enduring embarrassment and psychological loneliness. In doing so, he shared he "wanted to adapt to the Canadian life more quickly and be accepted by local students round me". To a certain extent, avoiding their own culture may also imply a lack of confidence or denial of their own identity. In the ever-changing globalized context, identity is an important concept for understanding individuals in their interaction with the society from both psychological and sociological perspectives (Illeris 2014).

After everything they went through, participants later learned that renouncing their Chinese heritage may deny the essence of who they are and therefore deprive them of their identity and sense of belonging. One of them admitted, "I learned to slowly accept who I am.... and now really appreciate our Asian values.... this is just the way we are brought up ... with a different process of development". They started to understand that they did not have to choose between maintaining the Chinese ways of being and adopting the Canadian ways of thinking and doing. As reflected in one participant' perspective: "I would like to respect Canadian ways of doing things but feel the need to keep the Chinese ways as well.... I'm from China and would like to honour my Chinese heritage". Like him, many of these participants made effort to integrate into the Canadian society while taking pride in their Chinese identity. This may not be easy, especially in the current socio-political climate where anti-Asian racism, discrimination, hate crimes, and biases have become highly visible (APFC 2021). The disorientation, power differentials in peer relationship, and systemic barriers experienced by these emerging adults may make them more vulnerable and need more inner strength to achieve age-related tasks and identity formation than their local peers (Walsh et al. 2005).

Systemic Barriers and Discrimination

Based on the research findings, systemic barriers exist shaping the transition of these participants. One of the barriers is a curriculum that lacks cultural responsiveness. Participants in the faculties of science and engineering all found that the academic programs did not seem to make the transition from high school to university smooth for students from an Asian educational system. Some participants shared that, despite the promotion of internationalization of curriculum among Canadian higher institutions, ethnocentrism in the curriculum still prevails whereby Eurocentric perspectives and norms are privileged, making them "feel less related to their cultural background or lived experiences".

Findings also demonstrate a lack of academic support to these students from instructors and institutions. Many participants said they found support facilities and resources focus more on students' extracurricular activities than their academic performance. Some expressed dissatisfaction about the English writing support given its irrelevance to their disciplines, as suggested by other authors in this volume (see de Oliveira Soares et al.). In addition, most participants expressed challenges following their "fast-paced native English-speaking instructors". This aligns with literature which indicated that most instructors do not consider it their responsibility to assist international students therefore the responsibility of getting familiar with the academic system and instructional approach is entirely put onto the already overburdened international students (Guo and Guo 2017 and Liu 2017). One participant shared his experience in large classes, where he could not hear clearly, but thought "it was inappropriate to bring it up with the instructor, while not knowing where else to get help either". This confirmed that Chinese students are not used to seeking support since showing any signs of not being self-sufficient is viewed as weak (Xu et al. 2018). Another participant shared her experience interacting with peers in classroom. "In group discussions, I sometimes felt left out and ignored when I couldn't quickly follow the discussion". During class discussions, they reported sometimes experiencing what Mu et al. (2018) described as admiring native speakers, staying silent, and feeling embarrassed and marginalized due to the lack of linguistic and cultural capital (Bourdieu 1991) which is required for academic engagement. Because of the language barriers and the deficiency associated with international students, one participant ended up doing her "group work" alone. Same incidents also occurred outside of classrooms. As cited by several participants in this study, when some local students distanced themselves from these participants after class, these Chinese students felt isolated and marginalized. These systemic barriers reflected a lack of appropriate education to domestic faculty, staff, and students about international students and the importance of enlisting them to create an equitable, diverse, and inclusive campus as discussed in other parts of this book (see Kim, Abdulkarim, and Payne; Tavares).

Conclusion

While individual student experience in different institutions may vary, findings from this study reveal that these participants' transitional experience is not unidimensional; rather, diverse factors come into play and impact students holistically. These practical, social, emotional, psychological, and academic aspects of adaptation are intertwined and are all vital to their successful transition to university (Briggs, Clark, and Hall 2012). As such, efforts from institutions to facilitate a positive transition can be conducive to Chinese students' academic success and formation of a positive worldview.

As an important institution in this society, higher education has always confronted the tension between its duty for societal improvement and the reality of reproducing systemic inequalities (Patel 2021). By revealing and acknowledging the systemic barriers and structural challenges on campus for Chinese students, I hope this study offers insights for our teaching and learning praxis to support efforts in ensuring international students flourish on campus while building the capacity they need to thrive in the real world. Concomitantly, reflections on experiences of Chinese students can be an opportunity for Canadian universities to revisit their programs, structures, and internationalization strategies to include international students in the institutional planning, reorganize their compartmentalized support resources, and create a more culturally responsive curricula and services for students new to the culture.

References

American College Health Association (ACHA). 2019. *American College Health Association-National College Health Assessment II: Undergraduate Student Executive Summary Spring 2019.* Silver Spring, MD: American College Health Association.

Arnett, Jeffrey Jensen. 2000. "Emerging Adulthood: A Theory of Development from the Late Teens through the Twenties." *American Psychologist* 55, no. 5: 469.

128   *Eustacia Yu*

Asia Pacific Foundation of Canada (APFC). 2021. "Where Do We Go from Here? East Asian Young Adults Talk about Multiculturalism and Anti-Asian Racism in Canada, and Recommendations for Building an Inclusive Future." (May). https://www.asiapacific.ca/publication/anti-asian-racism-canada-where-do-we-go-here.

Biggs, John B. 1996. "Western Misconceptions of the Confucian-Heritage Learning Culture." In *The Chinese Learner: Cultural, Psychological and Contextual Influences*, edited by David A. Watkins and John B. Biggs, 45–67. Hong Kong: University of Hong Kong.

Blair, Alasdair. 2017. "Understanding First-Year Students' Transition to University: A Pilot Study with Implications for Student Engagement, Assessment, and Feedback." *Politics* 37, no. 2: 215–28.

Bloomberg, Linda Dale, and Marie Volpe. 2016. *Completing Your Qualitative Dissertation: A Road Map from Beginning to End*. Thousand Oaks, CA: Sage.

Bologna, Gabriella. 2021. ""Adulting": The Life Transition Program for the Typically Developed High School Population." Nova Southeastern University.

Bourdieu, Pierre. 1991. *Language and Symbolic Power*. Cambridge: Polity Press.

Bridges, William. 2009. *Managing Transitions: Making the Most of Change*. Philadelphia: Perseus Books.

Briggs, Ann R.J., Jill Clark, and Ian Hall. 2012. "Building Bridges: Understanding Student Transition to University." *Quality in Higher Education* 18, no. 1: 3–21.

Chen, Xinyin. 2011. "Culture, Peer Relationships, and Human Development." In *Bridging Cultural and Developmental Psychology: New Syntheses in Theory, Research and Policy*, edited by Lene A. Jensen, 92–112. New York, NY: Oxford University Press.

Creswell, John W., and Cheryl N. Poth. 2018. *Qualitative Inquiry and Research Design: Choosing among Five Approaches*. Thousand Oaks, CA: Sage.

Erikson, Erik H. 1968. *Identity: Youth and Crisis*. New York: Norton.

Erikson, Erik H. 1985. *Childhood and Society*. New York: Norton.

Gardner, Howard. 1989. *To Open Minds: Chinese Clues to the Dilemma of Contemporary Education*. New York: Basic Books.

Global Affairs Canada. 2019. "Building on Success: International Education Strategy (2019-2024)." https://www.international.gc.ca/education/strategy-2019-2024-strategie.aspx?lang=eng.

Greenholtz, Joe. 2003. "Socratic Teachers and Confucian Learners: Examining the Benefits and Pitfalls of a Year Abroad." *Language and Intercultural Communication* 3, no. 2: 122–30.

Guo, Yan, and Shibao Guo. 2017. "Internationalization of Canadian Higher Education: Discrepancies between Policies and International Student Experiences." *Studies in Higher Education* 42, no. 5: 851–68.

Hofstede, Geert. 1986. "Cultural Differences in Teaching and Learning." *International Journal of Intercultural Relations* 10, no. 3: 301–20.

Illeris, Knud. 2014. "Transformative Learning and Identity." *Journal of Transformative Education* 12, no. 2: 148–63.

Jensen, Lene Arnett, ed. 2011. *Bridging Cultural and Developmental Approaches to Psychology: New Syntheses in Theory, Research, and Policy*. New York: Oxford University Press.

Kegan, Robert. 1982. *The Evolving Self: Problem and Process in Human Development*. Cambridge, MA: Harvard University Press.

Kramsch, Claire J. 2009. *The Multilingual Subject: What Foreign Language Learners Say about Their Experience and Why It Matters*. New York: Oxford University Press.

Liu, Jingzhou. 2017. "Beyond the Cultural Approach: Understanding the Experience of Chinese International Students in Canada from an Intersectionality Perspective." *International Journal of Chinese Education* 6, no. 2: 236–58.

Marom, Lilach. 2022. "Outsiders-Insiders-in between: Punjabi International Students in Canada Navigating Identity amid Intraethnic Tensions." *Globalisation, Societies and Education* 20, no. 2: 221–35.

Mu, Guanglun Michael, Liwei Livia Liu, Wangqian Fu, Dongfang Hao, Ning Jia, Yimei Qin, Hongmei Sziegat, Xiaodong Wang, and Xueqin Wu. 2018. "Using English at an International Doctoral Workshop: A Three-Level Field Analysis." In *Bourdieu and Chinese Education*, edited by Guanglun Michael Mu, Karen Dooley, and Allan Luke, 192–213. New York: Routledge.

Özdemir, Aysel, Nevin Utkualp, and Aylin Palloş. 2016. "Physical and Psychosocial Effects of the Changes in Adolescence Period." *International Journal of Caring Sciences* 9, no. 2: 717.

Palmer, Mark, Paula O'Kane, and Martin Owens. 2009. "Betwixt Spaces: Student Accounts of Turning Point Experiences in the First-Year Transition." *Studies in Higher Education* 34, no. 1: 37–54.

Patel, Leigh. 2021. *No Study without Struggle: Confronting Settler Colonialism in Higher Education*. Boston, MA: Beacon Press.

Pratt, Daniel D. 1992. "Chinese Conceptions of Learning and Teaching: A Westerner's Attempt at Understanding." *International Journal of Lifelong Education* 11, no. 4: 301–19.

Schlossberg, N. K. (1981). "A Model for Analyzing Human Adaptation to Transition." *The Counseling Psychologist* 9, no. 2: 2–18. DOI:10.1177/001100008100900202.

Shifren, Kim, Adrian Furnham, and Robert L. Bauserman. 2003. "Emerging Adulthood in American and British Samples: Individuals' Personality and Health Risk Behaviors." *Journal of Adult Development* 10, no. 2: 75–88.

Statistics Canada. 2020. "International Student Enrolment in Postsecondary Education Programs Prior to COVID-19". https://www150.statcan.gc.ca/n1/pub/11-626-x/11-626-x2020003-eng.htm.

Swidler, Ann. 1986. "Culture in Action: Symbols and Strategies." *American Sociological Review* 51, no. 2: 273–86.

Tinto, Vincent. 1993. *Leaving College: Rethinking the Causes and Cures of Student Attrition*. Chicago: University of Chicago Press.

Tweed, Roger G., and Darrin R. Lehman. 2002. "Learning Considered within a Cultural Context: Confucian and Socratic Approaches." *American Psychologist* 57, no. 2: 89.

Van der Meer, Jacques, Ellen Jansen, and Marjolein Torenbeek. 2010. "'It's Almost a Mindset that Teachers Need to Change': First-Year Students' Need to Be Inducted into Time Management." *Studies in Higher Education* 35, no. 7: 777–91.

Walsh, Sophie, Shmuel Shulman, Benny Feldman, and Offer Maurer. 2005. "The Impact of Immigration on the Internal Processes and Developmental Tasks of Emerging Adulthood." *Journal of Youth and Adolescence* 34, no. 5: 413–26.

Xu, Xiuying, Xin-Min Li, Jinhui Zhang, and Wenqiang Wang. 2018. "Mental Health-Related Stigma in China." *Issues in Mental Health Nursing* 39, no. 2: 126–34.

9 Voices from Chinese International Students on Resources Offered by Montreal Universities

Roberta de Oliveira Soares, Marie-Odile Magnan, Yifan Liu, and Fabiola Melo Araneda

Introduction

International students encounter many challenges arising from cultural and academic differences as well as from racialization (Houshmand, Spanierman, and Tafarodi 2014; Sherry, Thomas, and Chui 2010 and Yeh and Inose 2003). In Canada, Chinese, Indian and Korean students represent the majority of international students (Canadian Bureau for International Education 2018). The principal challenges encountered during their time at university are mastery of the dominant language (French or English) (Dong and Aubin 2012 and Xing, Bolden, and Hogenkamp 2020), sociocultural adaptation (Dong and Aubin 2012 Zhang and Goodson 2011) and racism (Grayson 2014 and Houshmand, Spanierman, and Tafarodi 2014). Recognizing international students' needs, many universities provide student-facing services and resources. This chapter aims to give a picture of the resources offered in the Montreal universities, along with perspectives on these from Chinese international students. This cross-referenced view of these resources alongside the student point of view can lead to finding ways for improving the resources destined for Chinese international students.

Chinese International Students in Canada and in Quebec: Overview, Challenges and Stakes

In 2020, almost a quarter of all international students in Canada were from China (Canadian Bureau for International Education 2021). Studies consistently find that these students face challenges of linguistic (Xing, Bolden and Hogenkamp 2020) or academic nature (Ge, Brown and Durst 2019) or of sociocultural adjustment in the host country (Zhang and Goodson 2011); to these, one might add experiences of discrimination (Grayson 2014 and Houshmand, Spanierman and Tafarodi 2014), especially with respect to language (Ge, Brown and Durst 2019), in the

DOI: 10.4324/b23160-12

classroom, but also more generally in their experiences in the host country (Xing, Bolden and Hogenkamp 2020). These life experiences make socialization difficult, according to some researchers (Ma 2017 and Straker 2016). According to some qualitative studies, Chinese international students would feel they have insufficient linguistic and academic abilities during daily interaction with people from the host country (Ge, Brown and Durst 2019 and Lee and Rice 2007).

In Quebec, in 2019, and particularly in Montreal, Chinese international students represented the second-largest group of international students after those from France (Ministère de l'Enseignement supérieur 2021). These students, because of a lack of well-targeted support at the institutional level, admit to encountering challenges in terms of academic, sociocultural and linguistic adjustment, especially as regards the full mastery of the French or English language, making communication difficult, and thus generating a sense of isolation (Dong and Aubin 2012).

University resources prove to be important for international students experiencing these challenges (Banjong 2015; Cho and Yu 2015 and Andrade 2006). However, Chinese international students appear to be less active in searching for and using university resources (Cao, Zhu, and Meng 2021 and Liu and Winn 2009). In addition to the challenges discussed in studies concerning international students in general (especially linguistic hurdles and insufficient awareness of resources), studies focusing on Chinese students point to more specific reasons of a cultural nature (Liu and Winn 2009 and Yan 2017). According to some studies, Chinese culture prizes modesty, and Chinese parents have traditionally taught their children to be calm, studious and to refrain from drawing attention to themselves (Yan 2017). Therefore, Chinese students would have a tendency to be self-effacing, quiet and may appear to be lacking in self-confidence as compared to other students. Thus, studies have highlighted the fact that many students may tend to resolve problems themselves rather than seeking outside help (Cao, Zhu, and Meng 2021 and Liu and Winn 2009).

If prior studies outline the challenges experienced by Chinese students with respect to the use of resources made available by the universities, it is important to note that most of them adopt a position of deficit thinking, in which Chinese students may be less inclined to find and use these resources. Few studies focus on institutional roles and responsibilities concerning their own practices and resources. Therefore, this chapter wishes to go beyond deficit-oriented perspectives relating to Chinese students, in order to better address the institutional side. We might also add that the majority of studies that we have found examine "counselling services" (Ang and Liamputtong 2008; Misra and Castillo 2004; Olivas and Li 2006; Onabule and Boes 2013; Raunic and Xenos 2008 and Robertson, Holleran and Samuels 2015) or "library services" (Liu and Winn 2009; Mu 2007 and

Song 2004). However, this chapter will consider the point of view of Chinese students on the broad spectrum of resources offered in Montreal universities.

A Descriptive Overview of Resources in Montreal Universities

Montreal universities have large numbers of international students, with 11% at Université du Québec à Montréal, 15% at Université de Montréal, 20% at Concordia University and 31% at McGill University (Université de Montréal n.d.). These universities offer various resources to the entire student community as well as specific resources intended to welcome and integrate international students.[1] We will begin by presenting the resources offered to the general student community by the Montreal universities, as they pertain in part to international students, continuing with a focus on those resources specifically directed towards international students.

The four Montreal universities offer various activities to enhance student life, such as cultural, volunteer and humanitarian activities, along with those organized by student associations, among others. On top of that, the universities have set up offices and centers dedicated to meeting student needs, such as financial aid and scholarship offices, centers to support learning and promote student success, career counselling offices, etc. These resources are designed to welcome students and to help them with adjustment, support and involvement with student life. There are also specific resources intended to support students as they settle in and get about their daily life, such as assistance with housing, meals and transportation. All of the Montreal universities have resources in place to promote the physical and psychological well-being of the student community. For instance, a variety of athletic and recreational activities are organized along with counselling (Université de Montréal n.d.; Université du Québec à Montréal n.d.; Concordia University n.d. and McGill University n.d.). We also note that McGill University is the only one to have also established an office of spiritual and religious life to enhance spiritual well-being among the students (McGill University n.d.).

In addition to the above-mentioned supports, the universities offer specific resources aimed at certain groups of students, including those with disabilities, First Nations students, new students, racialized students, LGBTQ students, parents and international students. Specifically concerning international students, some resources are allocated to helping in welcoming and integrating international students into both the university and the city of Montreal. At the Université de Montréal, for instance, the office of international students offers general information on the procedures to follow prior to arriving in Canada and during their stay in Montreal, along with supporting activities throughout their entire journey (Université de Montréal n.d.). The Université du Québec à Montréal, Concordia University and McGill University also offer specific information regarding immigration procedures, medical insurance and life in the city of Montreal. Finally, the francophone universities offer linguistic and academic writing support services, as do their anglophone counterparts (Université de Montréal n.d.; Université du Québec à Montréal n.d.; Concordia University n.d. and McGill University n.d.). This overview of the Montreal universities corroborates the findings of Buckner et al. (2021) to the effect that the various resources or documents concerning international students in the Montreal universities do not address racism despite the fact that the majority of them are non-white. Also, in other Canadian universities, it was found that university services tend to focus more on initial integration than support throughout graduation and only recently have they started offering services taking into consideration students' "intersectional identities" (Buckner, Chan and Kim 2022).

The Voice of Chinese International Students on Resources Offered by Montreal Universities

In order to understand student perspectives on their university's resources, we conducted qualitative interviews with Chinese international students enrolled in the four Montreal universities (two francophone universities and two anglophone ones). The results we are presenting come from a qualitative study run as a series of semi-scripted in-depth interviews, approximately one hour in length, conducted over Zoom during the pandemic.[2] Despite the pandemic, recruitment proceeded without any major interruption, as students responded quickly and positively to the call for participants. The interviews were conducted in French or in English (according to the participant's choice) by doctoral and master's students being themselves international students or having themselves gone through the process of immigration to Canada.

The criteria for participation were as follows: one had to be a Chinese international student enrolled in a university program in a Montreal university. We used the Facebook platform via student groups and snowball sampling. A total of 15 respondents were interviewed, including 3 at the bachelor's level, 7 at the master's level and 5 at the doctoral level. These students began their studies in Montreal between the fall of 2016 and the winter of 2022. Nine students were enrolled in francophone universities in Montreal and six in anglophone ones. Seven participants identified as women, six as men, and two refrained from revealing their gender identity. In addition, one had at least one parent with a college degree, six had at least one parent with a bachelor's degree, four had at least one parent with a master's degree and four did not wish to disclose this information. The programs of study chosen by the students covered a diverse range. For reasons of confidentiality, and in accordance with the guidelines of the Multi-Faculty Research Ethics Board of the Université de Montréal, the participants are identified by pseudonyms.

Despite the fact that the students express satisfaction with some of the resources offered within their university, this chapter hones in on criticisms put forth by the students, with a view to uncovering pathways of thinking, action and change that might be put in place in the universities. Through inductive analysis, we have coded the following sub-themes: (1) Lack of awareness of available university resources; (2) Language barriers preventing access to resources; (3) Self-exclusion with respect to resources and (4) Lack of availability of resources or dissatisfaction with the resources offered.

Lack of Awareness of Available University Resources

Some of the students interviewed seem unaware of either the resources offered at the university or of the means to access them. For instance, Shan indicates that, at one point, he felt a need for mental health support. He goes on to say that he was unaware of how to locate such resources. He then decides to abandon the idea: "I kinda wanted to seek mental help, but it's just, I couldn't find it [...]. I just gave up finding those resources. So, I don't know how to seek for help, mental help at the university" (Shan, Université de Montréal).

Shan gets the impression that the university fails to provide proper guidance to students as to how to locate resources: "[I]t would be better if we got more instructions, like clear instructions about how, in this situation, what should we do?" He also feels that the university does not offer sufficient resources to international students: "I think there is like fewer resources paying attention to the international students. That's how I feel. I don't know if that's true, but I just think that I had a hard time asking anyone" (Shan, Université de Montréal).

Similarly, Tiange could not understand the procedures to use a resource in time:

> I chose to take French courses at the University of Montreal. But I didn't know that I needed to take a test at the beginning, so I didn't register for a test. And when I got to know I needed to register for a test, it was too late. I wasted half a year to figure out how I could get some language support.
> (Tiange, Université de Montréal)

After having acquired a better knowledge of the subject, she wishes to help new international students: "Now I figured out all the processes and

I can also help other foreigner students" (Tiange, Université de Montréal). Our findings corroborate those of others which have brought attention to the fact that Chinese international students may very well not have at their disposal the clues necessary for decoding ways of obtaining assistance within the universities, due to a lack of clear explanation at the structural and institutional levels (Liu and Winn 2009; Olivas and Li 2006 and Yan 2017). However, our findings highlight the tendency of Chinese international students, through their own agency, to make an effort to overcome this shortcoming by themselves and by helping other international students decode the system. Thus, they develop the feeling that they should help recently arrived students as they start to better understand the local system.

Language Barriers Holding Up Access to Resources

The students that we interviewed maintain that the university does not realize that some information transmitted by email is not always understood for reasons of language. In our interviews, this point was raised only by students enrolled in the francophone universities in Montreal. In fact, certain programs in these universities are offered in English with a view to attracting international students. Nevertheless, information is sometimes shared with the students in French, the dominant language of their university of enrollment. According to Shan, for instance, communication is not always carried on in the language of his program (English), which instils in him a sense of exclusion:

> I think the first difficulty is the French. Actually, I know [the] University of Montreal is a French-based school. So, I don't blame them for that, but there is a lot of emails facing international students written in French. So, I think it would be better to maybe write them in English, because it's like facing international students. [...] And another thing is that there's like, a few webinars before school, before the semester, facing international students. They will explain, try to explain something, but they are all in French. So, it can be a little bit difficult since I was expecting that they would be speaking English.
>
> (Shan, Université de Montréal)

This sense of exclusion is also felt on social networks: "There is a Facebook group, it's like a group for all the international students to seek help [...], but the problem is that [...] most of them are speaking and writing in French. So, I quit" (Shan, Université de Montréal). Our results corroborate findings elsewhere that have highlighted language as being a barrier to success and full access to available university resources for international students (Ang and Liamputtong 2008 and Banjong 2015). Nevertheless, we might add that we have noticed in our data the heightened degree of challenges for international students when undertaking a program in a language other than the official language of the university.

Self-Exclusion with Respect to Resources

Some students choose to exclude themselves, in fact, not availing themselves of available resources. For some, university resources are seen as a last resort which they do not really need: "I don't feel like I need it, but maybe I've kind of feel like I would like to join that or ask for that support to just improve my languages. But it's not an emergency" (Duanchen, McGill University). Ming also states that he has no need of these resources: "I never used that [mental health resources] because I could 'mental health' myself. I could adjust myself to have a happy mood" (Ming, McGill University). What Ming alludes to corroborates results from other research that highlight the fact that Chinese international students would prefer to solve their problems without seeking help from the university (Cao, Zhu, and Meng 2021 and Liu and Winn 2009).

Moreover, some students consider that certain resources are not meant for them, but rather are directed at other groups (e.g., student associations):

I didn't participate in many student activities, but I knew about them. [...] I know, like, there are maybe some happy hour events, things like that, but I didn't go [...]. I felt that I wasn't especially at ease with the university people, with the students. Because, as I told you, 99% of the students in my program are of Quebecois origin.
(Mengyi, Université du Québec à Montréal)

This excerpt from Mengyi's testimony, which attests to the feeling that resources, and by extension student activities, might be aimed at other groups (specially the majority group), does not appear to have emerged prominently in prior research conducted among international students; this sentiment might be explained by the barrier of "Them, the internationals" versus "Us, the nationals," which occurs in university spaces and thus within institutional activities.

Self-exclusion sometimes manifests itself in another way. In such a case, students feel that they lack the time to partake of the resources offered at the university because of work, family obligations, or even because of the heavy workload of university studies: "I wanted to discover the associations, things like that, but I was swamped by the demands of studying" (Mengyi, Université du Québec à Montréal). Along the same lines,

Duanchen affirms: "I think the university held a lot of like virtual activities on Zoom, but basically, I didn't participate or join any of them. Because, uh, I think I didn't have much spare time to join these activities" (Duanchen, McGill University). The lack of time as a justification for non-use of resources has been highlighted in prior research concerning international students (see Yu).

Lack of Availability of Resources or Dissatisfaction with the Resources Offered

The students also mentioned the lack of availability of resources. For instance, Jiang sought out help with language, both French and English, in his program at McGill (an anglophone university) as well as during his time in a program at the Université de Montréal (a francophone university). Regarding his experience at the Université de Montréal, he says: "[T]here is like a French course. But I never made it because it was just super popular, once they released the news [...] it's already gone" (Jiang, McGill University). Moreover, with regard to psychological counselling offered by the universities, some say that the wait time between submitting a request for help and receiving an appointment is very lengthy, and that not enough sessions are available to adequately meet their needs: "[T]he thing about the counselling is that whenever you book, it takes really long. I have to wait for like one or two months to get to see the therapist" (Fang, Université de Montréal). This finding corroborates those derived from prior studies of international students (from different countries) that have highlighted the perception of a lack of availability of resources (Ang and Liamputtong 2008).

Also, students sometimes wish to take advantage of resources, inquiring about and making an effort to use them. However, they find themselves dissatisfied with their quality and then cease to continue using them. For instance, Fang tried a resource for help with language only to find that the assistance offered did not turn out to be especially relevant:

> I went to the writing centre for help with my essays. I stopped using this resource because I feel like it's not really necessary. [...] I feel like it wasn't that helpful for me, I feel like it's a waste of time, so that's why I stopped going there.
>
> (Fang, Université de Montréal)

As for Mengyi, he finds that some activities are useful, but too short: "For instance, the workshop I sat in on to get help with taking notes in class, I think it lasted only 30 minutes, if I remember correctly" (Mengyi, Université du Québec à Montréal). This testimonial from Mengyi highlights the contradictions embedded in the statements from students. On the one hand, students say that they lack the time to properly benefit from the resources offered, while, on the other hand, complaining about the small amount of time offered in certain workshops and activities. Therefore, the students found the services irrelevant, or not targeted enough, and too general to be useful. Prior studies have also brought out similar dissatisfaction with resources; the study by Onabule and Boes (2013) highlights the fact that Chinese international students having had negative experiences with seeking help from the university stopped using these resources afterwards.

Limits to Resources and Possible Solutions

In this chapter, we focus on feedback received from Chinese international students regarding resources offered within the university environment. These students brought attention to the following limitations: (1) Lack of awareness of available university resources; (2) Language barriers holding up access to resources; (3) Self-exclusion with respect to resources and (4) Lack of availability of resources or dissatisfaction with the resources offered. The limitations identified by the students have allowed us to identify possible solutions aimed at improving the resources offered to Chinese international students:

1) Improve the quality of information detailing the existence and purpose of available resources, using a plurilingual approach to make documents accessible in the international students' mother tongue, if possible, or at least, in English and French. Moreover, students sometimes may not believe that they need a particular resource, but they are not always aware that these resources may be helpful to them. These possible solutions could be applied through university centers for supporting learning and promoting student success, language support centers, scientific writing services, psychological support services and services and centers mandated to welcome and assist international students, etc.
2) Ensure that resources are easier to find (online and on campus). In fact, international students can find it difficult to decode the local educational system, in other words, decoding the following implicit assumption: that they are expected to be able to locate resources, along with information pertaining to those resources on their own. In fact, some of them feel that the university and its staff are responsible for informing them of the resources they need. Therefore, a more inclusive, differentiated and even personalized approach could be put in place mainly through orientation services and even university centers for supporting

learning and promoting student success, language support centers, etc. Using mass emails should be avoided in favor of emails better targeted at certain groups of international students, based primarily on their native language or, at least, in English and French.

3) Create more heterogeneous spaces in university along racial, cultural and linguistic lines to truly welcome international students and allow a sense of belonging; therefore, preventing self-exclusion among certain groups, especially in activities organized by student associations or welcoming activities offered by universities, faculties or departments, also taking into consideration their intersectional identities. In several cases, students mention making the effort to avail themselves of a certain resource, after which, not having developed a sense of belonging after the initial experience, they choose not to return. In general, students speak of feeling out of place due to the presence of large numbers of students born in Quebec.

4) Ensure that the resources advertised (language support centers, academic writing services, university centers for supporting learning and promoting student success, psychological support and counselling services, services and centers mandated to welcome and assist international students, etc.) are made available in a timely manner to all students who choose to use them. Students complain about the fact that it is sometimes difficult for them to understand how resources function, due primarily to language barriers, but also because they do not fully understand the university system of the host country, hence the need to improve the quality of information about university resources. Even when they overcome these barriers, resources sometimes turn out to be unavailable. Having to wait to receive, for instance, language or mental health support, can complicate the university experience; in such a case, there are situations in which students need quick, punctual and effective assistance.

5) Continuously improve the quality of resources offered, frequently going back to students to receive their feedback on these resources, notably those furnished through services and centers mandated to welcome and assist international students, centers for supporting learning and centers for promoting student success or departments and faculties. Repeated canvassing of international students in order to obtain their point of view will allow universities to better adapt to their needs.

Notes

1 In creating this overview, we based our identification of the resources offered as found on the websites of the four Montreal universities.
2 These interviews have been recorded and transcribed in their entirety.

References

Andrade, Maureen Snow. 2006. "International Students in English-Speaking Universities: Adjustment Factors." *Journal of Research in International Education* 5, no. 2: 131–54. https://doi.org/10.1177/1475240906065589.

Ang, Pius L. D., and Pranee Liamputtong. 2008. "'Out of the Circle': International Students and the Use of University Counselling Services." *Australian Journal of Adult Learning* 48, no. 1: 108–30.

Banjong, Delphine N. 2015. "International Students' Enhanced Academic Performance: Effects of Campus Resources." *Journal of International Students* 5, no. 2: 132–42. https://doi.org/10.32674/jis.v5i2.430.

Buckner, Elizabeth, Punita Lumb, Zahra Jafarova, Phoebe Kang, Adriana Marroquin, and You Zhang. 2021. "Diversity without Race: How University Internationalization Strategies Discuss International Students." *Journal of International Students* 11, no. S1: 32–49. https://doi.org/10.32674/jis.v11iS1.3842.

Buckner, Elizabeth, Elic Chan, and Cathy Kim. 2022. "Equity, Diversity, and Inclusion on Canadian Universities: Where Do International Students Fit In?" *Comparative and International Education* 51, no. 1: 39–56.

Canadian Bureau for International Education. 2018. "Étudiants Internationaux Au Canada." Canadian Bureau for International Education. https://cbie.ca/wp-content/uploads/2021/08/2018-ISS-National-Report-FR.pdf.

———. 2021. "Infographique." Canadian Bureau for International Education. https://cbie.ca/fr/infographique/.

Cao, Chun, Chang Zhu, and Qian Meng. 2021. "Chinese International Students' Coping Strategies, Social Support Resources in Response to Academic Stressors: Does Heritage Culture or Host Context Matter?" *Current Psychology* 40, no. 1: 242–52. https://doi.org/10.1007/s12144-018-9929-0.

Cho, Jaehee, and Hongsik Yu. 2015. "Roles of University Support for International Students in the United States: Analysis of a Systematic Model of University Identification, University Support, and Psychological Well-Being." *Journal of Studies in International Education* 19, no. 1: 11–27. https://doi.org/10.1177/1028315314533606.

Concordia University. n.d. "Services & Resources. Students Hub." Accessed April 2, 2022. https://www.concordia.ca/content/concordia/en/students/services.html.

Dong, Lu, and Stéphane Aubin. 2012. "L'adaptation et l'intégration des étudiants chinois au Québec." *Revue Organisations & Territoires* 21, no. 1: 25–36. https://doi.org/10.1522/revueot.v21n1.288.

Ge, Lin, Douglas Brown, and Douglas Durst. 2019. "Chinese International Students' Experiences in a Canadian University: Ethnographic Inquiry with Gender Comparison." *Journal of International Students* 9, no. 2: 582–612. https://doi.org/10.32674/jis.v0i0.272.

Grayson, J. Paul. 2014. "Negative Racial Encounters and Academic Outcomes of International and Domestic Students in Four Canadian Universities." *Journal of International Students* 4, no. 3: 262–78.

Houshmand, Sara, Lisa B. Spanierman, and Romin W. Tafarodi. 2014. "Excluded and Avoided: Racial Microaggressions Targeting Asian International Students in Canada." *Cultural Diversity & Ethnic Minority Psychology* 20, no. 3: 377–88. https://doi.org/10.1037/a0035404.

Lee, Jenny J., and Charles Rice. 2007. "Welcome to America? International Student Perceptions of Discrimination." *Higher Education* 53, no. 3: 381–409. https://doi.org/10.1007/s10734-005-4508-3.

Liu, Guoying, and Danielle Winn. 2009. "Chinese Graduate Students and the Canadian Academic Library: A User Study at the University of Windsor." *Journal of Academic Librarianship* 35, no. 6: 565–73. https://doi.org/10.1016/j.acalib.2009.08.001.

Ma, Junqian. 2017. "Cooperative Activity as Mediation in the Social Adjustment of Chinese International Students." *Journal of International Students* 7, no. 3: 856–75. https://doi.org/10.32674/jis.v7i3.305.

McGill University. n.d. "Student Services." Student Services. Accessed April 2, 2022. https://www.mcgill.ca/studentservices/.

Ministère de l'Enseignement supérieur. 2021. *Les Étudiants Internationaux à l'enseignement Supérieur: Portrait Statistique.* Québec, QC: Gouvernement du Québec.

Misra, Ranjita, and Linda G. Castillo. 2004. "Academic Stress among College Students: Comparison of American and International Students." *International Journal of Stress Management* 11, no. 2: 132–48. https://doi.org/10.1037/1072-5245.11.2.132.

Mu, Cuiying. 2007. "Marketing Academic Library Resources and Information Services to International Students from Asia." *Reference Services Review* 35, no. 4: 571–83. https://doi.org/10.1108/00907320710838390.

Olivas, Monique, and Chi-Sing Li. 2006. "Understanding Stressors of International Students in Higher Education: What College Counselors and Personnel Need to Know." *Journal of Instructional Psychology* 33, no. 3: 217–22.

Onabule, Adebayo I., and Susan R. Boes. 2013. "International Students' Likelihood to Seek Counseling while Studying Abroad." *Journal of International Students* 3, no. 1: 52–59.

Raunic, Adam, and Sophia Xenos. 2008. "University Counselling Service Utilisation by Local and International Students and User Characteristics: A Review." *International Journal for the Advancement of Counselling* 30, no. 4: 262–67. https://doi.org/10.1007/s10447-008-9062-0.

Robertson, Lloyd Hawkeye, Kathryn Holleran, and Marilyn Samuels. 2015. "Tailoring University Counselling Services to Aboriginal and International Students: Lessons from Native and International Student Centres at a Canadian University." *Canadian Journal of Higher Education* 45, no. 1: 122–35.

Sherry, Mark, Peter Thomas, and Wing Hong Chui. 2010. "International Students: A Vulnerable Student Population." *Higher Education* 60, no. 1: 33–46. https://doi.org/10.1007/s10734-009-9284-z.

Song, Yoo-Seong. 2004. "International Business Students: A Study on Their Use of Electronic Library Services." *Reference Services Review* 32, no. 4: 367–73. https://doi.org/10.1108/00907320410569716.

Straker, John. 2016. "International Student Participation in Higher Education: Changing the Focus from 'International Students' to 'Participation'." *Journal of Studies in International Education* 20, no. 4: 299–318. https://doi.org/10.1177/1028315316628992.

Université de Montréal. n.d.-a "Services aux Étudiants de l'Université de Montréal." Services aux étudiants. Accessed February 12, 2022. http://www.sae. umontreal.ca/.

———. n.d.-b "Université de Montréal en chiffres." Université de Montréal. Accessed February 12, 2022. https://www.umontreal.ca/l-udem/en-chiffres/.

Université du Québec à Montréal. n.d. "Services à la vie étudiante." Services à la vie étudiante (SVE). Accessed April 2, 2022. https://vie-etudiante.uqam.ca/.

Xing, Deyu, Benjamin Bolden, and Sawyer Hogenkamp. 2020. "The Sound of Silence: A Musically Enhanced Narrative Inquiry into the Academic Acculturation Stories of Chinese International Students with Low Spoken English Proficiency." *Journal of Curriculum and Pedagogy* 17, no. 1: 25–47. https://doi.org/10.1080/15505170.2019.1627616.

Yan, Kun. 2017. *Chinese international students' stressors and coping strategies in the United States.* Singapore: Springer.

Yeh, Christine J., and Mayuko Inose. 2003. "International Students' Reported English Fluency, Social Support Satisfaction, and Social Connectedness as Predictors of Acculturative Stress." *Counselling Psychology Quarterly* 16, no. 1: 15–28. https://doi.org/10.1080/0951507031000114058.

Zhang, Jing, and Patricia Goodson. 2011. "Acculturation and Psychosocial Adjustment of Chinese International Students: Examining Mediation and Moderation Effects." *International Journal of Intercultural Relations* 35, no. 5: 614–27. https://doi.org/10.1016/j.ijintrel.2010.11.004.

10 Pushed to the Periphery

Understanding the Multiple Forms of Exclusion Experienced by International Students from Asia

Vander Tavares

Introduction

This chapter examines the lived experiences of three students from Hong Kong, Macau, and Taiwan through a narrative inquiry approach. It draws attention to the exclusion the students experienced at their host university in Ontario, despite the "international" profile of the university. This chapter foregrounds the experiences of students of an under-represented national profile within the imagined monolithic Chinese demographic, where students of a Chinese background are generally presumed to be from the mainland. In discussing the students' experiences, exclusion is presented within three areas of concern: academic, social, and linguistic. Considering the impact that such experiences of exclusion had for the students, this chapter focuses on the timely importance of inclusive internationalization, particularly for students from Asia, who presently account for the majority of international students in Canada.

Internationalization of Higher Education: Who Benefits?

The "internationalization of higher education" (IHE) has become a common phrase in the vocabulary of academic institutions around the world. IHE has been informed primarily by the need to develop and foster intercultural knowledge and engagement across all dimensions of higher education in light of globalization, particularly in teaching and learning (Leask 2008). IHE is traditionally understood to include the movement of students and staff between institutions abroad, although initiatives geared toward internationalization "at home" have also grown since the early 2000s (Harrison 2015). In addition to potentially meeting intercultural needs, IHE is now important for reputation and branding in an increasingly competitive market (Eggins, Smolentseva, and de Wit 2021). However, critical perspectives on IHE point to the dominance of neoliberal frameworks which have obscured "the values of learning and teaching in

DOI: 10.4324/b23160-13

international and intercultural contexts" through the growing economic impetus (Ilieva, Beck, and Waterstone 2014, 877).

Questions about who benefits from internationalization have also emerged in the domain of the internationalization of the curriculum. Leask (2015) proposed that an internationalized curriculum should "engage students with internationally informed research and cultural and linguistic diversity," and also "purposefully develop their international and intercultural perspectives as global professionals and citizens" (10). However, international students in Canada are known to encounter stereotyped, static, and even discriminatory representations of their cultures within the curriculum and sometimes no representation at all, despite the multicultural profile of their universities (Guo and Guo 2017; Tavares 2021b). Internationalization of the curriculum is not only about the content delivered, but whether and how teaching and learning the content includes international and intercultural approaches. When Western forms of engagement are the only ones recognized or valued, international students may experience exclusion as a result.

On the surface, many institutions promise an international experience to incoming international students. Yet, research has demonstrated that the lack of an inclusive internationalization framework continues to perpetuate the hierarchy of cultures and languages in academia (Tavares 2022). Lee and Rice (2007) have used the term neo-racism to refer to discrimination, exclusion, and marginalization that are justified on the basis of preserving the "good" or "better" cultures, which are those already in place in Western academia. International students of a multilingual and racialized background have their behaviors, accents, and traditions looked at with suspicion, but more explicit discrimination has also been reported (Tavares 2021a). Neo-racism in academia stands in stark contradiction to a more ethical internationalization, which at the most basic level should take contextualized forms of cultural and linguistic diversity into consideration, especially the positioning of different social groups in academia, for the development of pedagogical and administrative initiatives that aim to promote student success based on social justice (Tavares 2021b).

Internationalization focused on revenue and superficial diversity leaves Asian students vulnerable to experience discrimination, exclusion, and marginalization. To begin with, an environment defined by neoliberal multiculturalism – which acknowledges diversity as long as it does not disrupt the Western cultural foundation of academia and the use of "standard" English (Jiang, 2020) – sustains a hierarchy through which stereotypes of others can flourish. Teaching and learning styles that only value an "active," vocal, and dominating style of participation results in a dichotomy of active–passive learner stereotypes – the latter which is often and uncritically assigned to Asian students (Huang and Cowden, 2009; Xiao, 2021).

Because dominating and competitive engagement is considered good or normal, those who learn differently may be viewed inferiorly as less intelligent, critical, and withdrawn (Fell and Lukianova 2015), and even feel penalized for it (Li and Campbell 2008).

Feelings of exclusion can also be experienced outside the classroom. Some multilingual international students of an Asian background report feeling as though their Canadian peers have little or no interest in getting to know them and their cultures (Tavares 2021b). Li et al. (2017) found that the lack of meaningful social connections, generally due to linguistic and cultural differences, can lead Chinese students to experience ongoing feelings of loneliness and frustration. Xing and Bolden (2021) documented the experiences of Chinese students in being "on the margins" of their communities at a Canadian university. One student commented: "I still felt that I did not belong to the place where I was at, a Canadian university. [...] That image I envisioned for my Canadian university life now only feels like a dream that will never come true" (52–53). As this quote suggests, multilingual international students of an Asian background may find an incongruence between their lived experiences and their perceptions of Canadian students as welcoming and interculturally oriented.

Marginalization is also sustained by ideologies of native-speakerism tied to the English language. Native-speakerism can manifest in the belief that the native speaker of English is, by proxy of their language status, more intelligent and the model whom non-native speakers should work to resemble (Slavkov, Melo-Pfeifer, and Kerschhofer-Puhalo 2021). Yet, ideologies of language cannot be detached from race for it is not simply any native speaker of English who is positioned superiorly (Kubota and Lin 2006). Racialized native speakers who do not enact the "standard" English spoken by the majority of White speakers in Canada face structural challenges in areas such as education and employment (Creese 2010). In their study, Houshmand, Spanierman, and Tafarodi (2014) found that racialized, multilingual international students in Canada felt ridiculed by native-speaker students and instructors for speaking English with an accent. In the next section, these issues will be examined in the experiences of three students at a Canadian university.

Research Design: Narrative Inquiry

Narrative inquiry is a qualitative approach to research that seeks to understand lived experience through stories. When working with narrative inquiry, researchers critically position participant stories within and against dominant discourses that influence cultural, social, and institutional experiences (Clandinin 2006). In other words, stories can replicate or confront larger narratives. Stories are based on field texts, traditionally termed "data" in qualitative research. Field texts originate from different sources, including interviews, observations, and a range of artifacts, such as documents, photographs, and objects that hold personal meaning to the participant. The composition of field texts adheres to three important aspects of narrative inquiry research: temporality, sociality, and place (Schaefer and Clandinin 2011). "Temporality" is tied to the subjective (a participant's reflection on their own experiences) and co-constructed (between researcher and participant) nature of field texts. "Sociality" is about the participant's individual and social responses to the events experienced. Finally, "place" has to do with the location where the events (within both the narrative and the research) took place.

Participants, Setting, and Field Texts

In this chapter, the stories of three participants are presented: Gina, Wang, and Lee. All names are pseudonyms. Gina was 33 years old and originally from Taiwan. She was in her fifth and final year of a bachelor's degree in psychology. The final year of her program consisted of conducting research and writing a thesis. Wang was 22 years old and an exchange student from Hong Kong. He was in his third year of a five-year-long teacher education program with a focus on English at his sending university. At Star University for one semester, he was taking three courses in English language and literature whose credits would be transferred over to his teacher education program. Lee was 24 years old and a transfer student from a college on the west coast of the United States, where he had completed an associate degree in computer science. He was originally from Macao and enrolled in a Bachelor of Arts with a major in linguistics at Star University.

Star University is the pseudonym for a large, research-oriented university in southern Ontario. In the year when this study was conducted, statistics on the university's web page indicated that the institution enrolled more than 6,000 international students through which about 150 countries could be represented. Star University is known for having an ethnically and racially diverse student body, which reflects the diversity of Star's surrounding communities, though such diversity is not exclusive to students. In terms of social experience, Star had more than 300 student clubs and associations available at the time of this study. The international office managed programming that sought to facilitate cultural and social experiences for international students. Additionally, a peer mentorship program was also available to support international students in their transition to the university.

Recruitment and interviewing began following ethics approval by Star University. For a period of five months, I recorded six semi-structured interviews: four with Lee, one with Gina, and one Wang. Interviews were recorded within the last five years, but the exact year has been masked in order to help maintain the anonymity of the students. The quantitative variance in interviews is due to Gina and Wang joining the study in its last month, which limited the scheduling availability of both researcher and participants. Through the interviews, I sought to learn about the students' lived experiences by exploring topics related to adjustment, academics, language learning, social life, and cross-cultural learning. Each interview lasted about 60 minutes and was subsequently transcribed.

The analysis of interviews consisted of writing a personal summary for each participant (Murray 2003). The summaries followed a story format that included a beginning, middle, and end. Since narrative inquiry considers human experience a situated phenomenon (Clandinin and Caine 2008), a personal summary helps to establish the interrelationship between the individual and the context in which they are embedded. Savin-Baden and Niekerk (2007) noted that "this process demands that we locate the person in a context and community, describe what she/he does and how she/he sees her/himself" (466). I read the personal summaries multiple times, highlighted key findings, and re-wrote them into stories that include the participants' quotes. In designing the stories, it is important to acknowledge that stories will always be incomplete and unable to answer every question due to a number of reasons, such as space and scope.

As the researcher, I play a key role in the interpretation and construction of the stories. When tending to the concept of justification in narrative inquiry, which accounts for "the reasons why the study is important" (Clandinin, Pushor, and Orr 2007, 24), the researcher provides a *personal justification*. This entails "situating yourself in the study" (25). For over a decade, I have held different teaching positions in higher education in which I have worked primarily with multilingual international students who speak English as an additional language. Moreover, I have been involved in research focused on international students' experiences in which I have attempted to draw attention to the students' experiences by discussing the gaps and issues sustained by a neoliberal approach to internationalization. In this sense, I bring these concerns, experiences, and knowledge into this study.

Narratives

Gina: There is Only One Language to Success

Prior to joining Star University, Gina had completed a teacher education program at a university in Taiwan. Her program focused on the teaching of biology to grade 7 students. However, Gina had never intended to work as a teacher. Becoming a psychologist had always been her career dream. Her journey took a turn to teacher education as a result of her score on the university entrance exam, which was not high enough to gain admission into the psychology program. Gina was passionate about helping others. It was the opportunity to learn from and about people that inspired her to desire a career in psychology. Despite the diversion into teaching, she continued to cogitate about how to materialize her long-held career dream. The prospect of studying psychology re-emerged on the horizon following her graduation from the teacher education program. The prospect of studying in Canada, in particular, was sustained by family ties, since her other siblings lived in Canada at the time.

Gina's academic journey in Canada began with a long and intensive experiment with the English language. She came to understand the importance of English through conversations with her siblings. Yet, it was not simply "speaking English well" that weighed on her mind, but rather, speaking like a "native-speaker Canadian." Language was used to differentiate her from her siblings, especially her younger brother: "my brother came here when he was 13, so he speaks like a native speaker." Accordingly, the image of the native speaker became the compass to her linguistic development, instead of the development of English for academic study. For 12 months after her arrival, Gina studied English at an English as a second language (ESL) school. She enjoyed the small classes at the school, but felt unsatisfied with her oral progress. Therefore, she began taking classes at the same ESL school precisely on how to change her accent. Still, the new classes were seemingly not enough. In the end, Gina decided to repeat one year of high school in Canada so that she could learn how native speakers learn and use the language.

Gina imagined that admission into the psychology program at Star would change the pressure she put upon herself to speak like a native speaker. After all, in her view, the linguistic and cultural diversity of Star, and especially the large multilingual international student population, would contribute to a more international take on English. Put differently, she expected that diverse ways of speaking English would be valued or perhaps not even noticed in such a multicultural environment. A few weeks into her program, Gina experienced the opposite. Only *one* English was recognized in the classroom. Most of her peers and professors had a "native Canadian" accent. In conversations with her professors, they confirmed her perception: there is no middle ground. Gina felt lost and further pressured to not only succeed academically, but also, or perhaps more, linguistically. Now in her final year, she could not dispel the image of the native speaker from her dream, although at such point it was no longer about language, but also an identity with its own ways of knowing and thinking: "I try to know how native speakers know it." She explained:

> I want to be a psychologist, to be honest, but I don't have the confidence that I can do that because the language demand is very high. I have to admit that to myself. I wanted to do a PhD and become a psychotherapist because most of my interests are focused on therapy and on how to understand people. But like, for writing, I am trying to get rid of the ESL structure, the "ESL bubble," and I'm trying to improve my flow. I want to write from English to English, not from ESL to English.

Despite the five years spent at Star University, Gina did not feel encouraged to confront her own perceptions of the English language. Instead, though Star was an international community, her academic and social experiences only solidified the notion of success as something dependent on native-speakerism. Zacharias (2019) termed this feeling as "the ghost of native-speakerism." This "ghost" follows multilingual speakers of English and evokes feelings of inferiority and insecurity because of their non-native status. A consequence of "the ghost of native-speakerism" is that "non-native speakers" must constantly prove their abilities to others, most notably by speaking English like a "native speaker." They need to work harder and, at times, even make different career choices. In here, Gina's dreams and skills were devalued due to her non-native status, which she worked to erase through varied language training. In a multicultural environment that privileged native-speakerism, Gina always saw herself as the other: *the ESL speaker.*

Lee: The Local Student in Mind

As a student completing a major in linguistics, Lee was expected to take several introductory courses in the social sciences. A feeling of comfort emerged when, in these classes, he could see and feel cultural diversity embodied through his peers. Everyone looked different and, at first, he felt like he belonged. This early experience suggested that the class would therefore be an equal playing field for everyone. However, Lee began questioning the international ethos of Star once he experienced a very monocultural orientation to instruction. For him, the instructors in his linguistics courses conceptualized teaching and learning with the local, native-speaker student in mind. This meant that teaching and assessment did not consider students' multilingual and multicultural profiles. In teaching phonetics, for instance, his instructor attempted to convey the sounds of English vowels and consonants to students by providing examples whose phonemic nuances were completely unknown to Lee as a multilingual speaker of English as an additional language.

On a test, he could not identify the correct names of the phonemes of certain English words because he had never heard those words previously. While native-speaker students would have been able to know what sound the phoneme /g/ in *gibberish* had simply on the basis of speaking English as a first language, this was not the case for Lee, despite having diligently prepared himself for the test. He was confused as to whether that /g/ sound was the same one in *get, genre,* or *gel.* "She [the instructor] should teach in a way that doesn't have to be... [that] it's not sided to the local students—then it will be more fair," he identified in frustration. The continuity of this pattern in his courses left him feeling disadvantaged, in addition to increasingly anxious about the low grades he was receiving. In the introductory social sciences courses, Lee also felt left out when the concepts explained by the instructors relied on Canadian-based content that was familiar to local students. Consequently, he could not offer insight into the issues discussed because he had never lived in Canada prior to university. Coupled with other challenges, Lee nearly failed his first semester.

Wang: Why Am I Here?

The desire to improve his English and to experience Canadian culture shaped Wang's decision to study in Canada. However, despite fluency from years of education in the English language, Wang was quickly impacted by ideologies of language within and outside the classroom at Star University. "I'm an introvert, so I don't talk much. But when English is your second language, people think you don't talk because you don't know English," was his reflection following weeks of in-class learning. Nevertheless, Wang's experiences were not affected by ideologies of language alone, but also by those of academic engagement. He felt disadvantaged by the preference of his instructors for more active, competitive, and vocal engagement in class and group discussions. Wang felt hesitant to replicate his peers' behavior because, to him, speaking for the sake of speaking did not necessarily stem out of a meaningful or valuable place from which all students could benefit.

For all of his time at Star, Wang felt conflicted about respecting his own identity while meeting the expectations of his instructors. After all, participation was assessed through oral participation in his courses, but he preferred a more reflexive style of engagement which was mechanically equated to the absence of participation. Yet, it was not a coincidence that his "active" peers were also native-speaker students. He felt as though he experienced a double kind of deficit because language also positioned him as an outsider: "It doesn't help when I'm both quiet and a non-native speaker. They both come across as negative in the seminars where the teacher expects us to talk." Wang never experienced an openness within the classroom toward other forms of engagement. He felt differentiated from his peers, despite having something to contribute, but not in the manner in which local students did.

Socialization with local students was another important dimension of Wang's hoped-for experience at Star. He attended several activities and events organized by the international student office that were intended to bring local and international students together. However, as the semester progressed, fewer local students continued to participate in such events and, as a result, Wang ended up meeting other international students, who like him, hoped to gain first-hand experience in matters related to Canadian culture in interaction with local students. More importantly, he had always believed that studying at a Canadian university would lead to developing friendships with Canadian students. His exchange was not motivated only by the desire to grow academically, but also socially by expanding his circle of friends. By the time we met, Wang was feeling dissatisfied with his overall experience. He explained carefully that:

> There isn't much interaction with Canadian students. I don't want to blame the international student office, but I don't think they give us much opportunity to interact with local students, there aren't many social and cultural events where I can meet them. In terms of the use of English, the experience does not meet my expectations because I don't have a chance to meet and talk in English with Canadian students and this is the biggest thing I wanted to accomplish when I first started planning my exchange.

The inviting image Wang held of studying at Star University changed drastically in response to his experiences. He befriended a Chinese student whom he came to spend much of his time with. They cooked, studied, and explored the city together, identifying with each other on the fact that they both felt neglected by the university. Furthermore, the lack of continuous and meaningful social interaction with English-speaking local students outside the classroom demotivated Wang to continue to enhance his proficiency in English. Contrary to his expectation, he and his friend resorted to Mandarin and Cantonese for communication. The feeling of aloneness Wang experienced whenever he was at Star, even with many other students around, changed his views on being an international student at the university. He felt unsupported in his need to socialize and othered in his ways of learning. As the end of his exchange neared, he began to rethink the role his experience at Star played in supporting him to be a culturally and linguistically well-versed, soon-to-be, English teacher.

Discussion and Conclusion

This chapter presented an account of the experiences of three international students in light of the IHE. Based on the narratives presented, a few points are worth revisiting. First, the experiences of the students highlight the diversity and variance when it comes to the experiences of Chinese students, who are generally discussed as a single and static group in the literature. The narratives presented illustrate the different trajectories, desires, and goals that characterized each student's journey to and within their Canadian university. The label "Chinese student" can often obscure the individual path taken and shaped by each student. Additionally, this chapter provided insight into the experiences of Chinese students who are not from the mainland, whose national groups[1] tend to receive less attention in scholarship.

Despite the diversity, all three students encountered challenges at Star University that were not intrinsic to being a Chinese student. These challenges were located in the domains of language, academics, and socialization, sometimes simultaneously, and are implicated in the potentially neoliberal orientation to internationalization in the context of Star University. Internationalization focused on diversity from a monolingual-monocultural perspective contributed to creating dichotomies in which the differences stemming from not being a local and native-speaker student were positioned inferiorly. As a result, Gina attempted to adopt an identity based on native-speakerism in order to attain and experience feelings of success. Rather than empowering Gina to confront the status quo of her university, the internationalization framework whose influence she was under served to displace non-dominant ways of speaking through the attitudes of peers and instructors. Even after multiple attempts to reconstruct herself, Gina still felt othered by being an ESL student, which was exclusive in itself as she believed some careers were available only to native speakers.

The narratives also demonstrate the ways in which the students approached their challenges, primarily through critical reflection. An internationalization framework that did not consider international students' lived experiences in context led to Wang and Lee feeling socially and academically neglected, respectively. The students experienced little to no support by Star University in meeting their needs and goals as international students. The impact was such that Wang questioned his own international experience, while Lee nearly failed an entire semester due to insufficient linguistic and academic support. While international students exercise agency over their own trajectories, it is important to highlight that not all international students will be impacted in the same manner as the three Asian students were in the study. Asian students, when compared to students from Europe, are more likely to experience exclusion due to stereotypes that have to do with race and accent (Houshmand et al. 2014).

The findings reinforce the need for reform of dominant IHE frameworks so that international students, Asian students in particular, may be better supported. As the experiences of the students reveal, the mere inclusion of Asian students into Star University through neoliberal multiculturalism is insufficient to help adequately identify and confront the mechanisms of exclusion the students faced. Jones (2022) has called on academic communities to think interculturally, rather than only internationally, and to transform internationalization "through purposeful and constructive engagement with perceived cultural 'otherness' of any kind" (3). Departing from this stance, it is essential that Canadian universities move beyond internationalization for reputation, revenue, and surface diversity that can engage the local community into self- and critical reflection with respect to their roles in sustaining inequality, both locally and globally. One possible way in which this work can begin to happen is by recognizing international students as an equity-seeking group or, as Jones (2022) put it, as an othered group. By doing so, institutions of higher education may be able to move from reflection to both policy and action that can improve the experiences of Asian students.

Note

1 It is beyond the scope of this chapter to discuss the political relationships of mainland China to the other regions and the sense of national or ethnic identity characteristic of each region.

References

Clandinin, D. Jean, ed. 2006. *Handbook of Narrative Inquiry: Mapping a Methodology*. Thousand Oaks: Sage Publications.

Clandinin, D. Jean, and Vera Caine. 2008. "Narrative Inquiry." In *The Sage Encyclopedia of Qualitative Research Methods*, edited by Lisa Given, 542–45. Thousand Oaks: Sage.

Clandinin, D. Jean, Debbie Pushor, and Anne Murray Orr. 2007. "Navigating Sites for Narrative Inquiry." *Journal of Teacher Education* 58, no. 1: 21–35.

Creese, Gillian. 2010. "Erasing English Language Competency: African Migrants in Vancouver, Canada." *Journal of International Migration and Integration* 11, no. 3: 295–313.

Eggins, Heather, Anna Smolentseva, and Hans de Wit, eds. 2021. *Higher Education in the Next Decade: Global Challenges, Future Prospects*. Leiden: Brill Sense.

Fell, Elena V., and Natalia A. Lukianova. 2015. "British Universities: International Students' Alleged Lack of Critical Thinking." *Procedia-Social and Behavioral Sciences* 215: 2–8.

Guo, Yan, and Shibao Guo. 2017 "Internationalization of Canadian Higher Education: Discrepancies between Policies and International Student Experiences." *Studies in Higher Education* 42, no. 5 : 851–68.

Harrison, Neil. 2015. "Practice, Problems and Power in 'Internationalisation at Home': Critical Reflections on Recent Research Evidence." *Teaching in Higher Education* 20, no. 4: 412–30.

Houshmand, Sara, Lisa B. Spanierman, and Romin W. Tafarodi. 2014. "Excluded and Avoided: Racial Microaggressions Targeting Asian International Students in Canada." *Cultural Diversity and Ethnic Minority Psychology* 20, no. 3: 377.

Huang, Jinyan, and Peter Cowden. 2009. "Are Chinese Students Really Quiet, Passive and Surface Learners? – A Cultural Studies Perspective." *Comparative and International Education* 38, no. 2: 75–88.

Ilieva, Roumiana, Kumari Beck, and Bonnie Waterstone. 2014. "Towards Sustainable Internationalisation of Higher Education." *Higher Education* 68, no. 6: 875–89.

Jiang, Shanshan. 2020. "Diversity without Integration? Racialization and Spaces of Exclusion in International Higher Education." *British Journal of Sociology of Education* 42, no. 1: 32–47.

Jones, Elspeth. 2022. "Problematizing the Idea of Curriculum 'Internationalization'." *Journal of International Students* 12, no. 1: 1–5.

Kubota, Ryuko, and Angel Lin. 2006. "Race and TESOL: Introduction to Concepts and Theories." *TESOL Quarterly* 40, no. 3: 471–93.

Leask, Betty. 2008. "Internationalisation, Globalisation and Curriculum Innovation." In *Researching International Pedagogies*, edited by Meeri Hellstén and Anna Reid, 9–26. Dordrecht: Springer.

Leask, B. 2015. *Internationalizing the Curriculum*. London, UK: Routledge.

Lee, Jenny J., and Charles Rice. 2007. "Welcome to America? International Student Perceptions of Discrimination." *Higher Education* 53, no. 3: 381–409.

Li, Mingsheng, and Jacqui Campbell. 2008. "Asian Students' Perceptions of Group Work and Group Assignments in a New Zealand Tertiary Institution." *Intercultural Education* 19, no. 3: 203–16.

Li, Zhen, Melissa A. Heath, Aaron P. Jackson, G. E. Allen, Lane Fischer, and Peter Chan. 2017. "Acculturation Experiences of Chinese International Students Who Attend American universities." *Professional Psychology: Research and Practice* 48, no. 1: 11.

Murray, Michael. 2003. "Narrative Psychology." In *Qualitative Psychology: A Practical Guide to Research Methods*, edited by Jonathan Smith, 111–31. Thousand Oaks: Sage.

Savin-Baden, Maggi, and Lana Van Niekerk. 2007. "Narrative Inquiry: Theory and Practice." *Journal of Geography in Higher Education* 31, no. 3: 459–72.

Schaefer, Lee, and D. Jean Clandinin. 2011. "Stories of Sustaining: A Narrative Inquiry into the Experiences of Two Beginning Teachers." *Learning Landscapes* 4, no. 2: 275–95.

Slavkov, Nikolay, Sílvia Melo-Pfeifer, and Nadja Kerschhofer-Puhalo, eds. 2021. *The Changing Face of the "Native Speaker": Perspectives from Multilingualism and Globalization* 31. Berlin: Walter de Gruyter GmbH & Co KG.

Tavares, Vander. 2021a. *International Students in Higher Education: Language, Identity, and Experience from a Holistic Perspective*. Lanham, MD: Rowman & Littlefield.

Tavares, Vander. 2021b. "Feeling Excluded: International Students Experience Equity, Diversity and Inclusion." *International Journal of Inclusive Education*: 1–18. https://doi.org/10.1080/13603116.2021.2008536.

Tavares, Vander. 2022. "Neoliberalism, Native-Speakerism and the Displacement of International Students' Languages and Cultures." *Journal of Multilingual and Multicultural Development*: 1–14. https://doi.org/10.1080/01434632.2022.208 4547.

Xiao, Meng. 2021. "Chinese International Graduate Students at Canadian Universities: Language Barriers, Cultural Identities and Perceived Problems of Engagement." *International Journal of Inclusive Education* 26: 1–18.

Xing, Deyu Cindy, and Benjamin Bolden. 2021. "Learning at Half Capacity: The Academic Acculturation Reality Experienced by Chinese International Students." In *Multidisciplinary Perspectives on International Student Experience in Canadian Higher Education*, edited by Vander Tavares, 41–61. Hershey: IGI Global.

Zacharias, N. T. 2019. "The Ghost of Nativespeakerism: The Case of Teacher Classroom Introductions in Transnational Contexts." *TESOL Journal* 10, no. 4: e499.

11 International Students from Asia Studying in Canada
A Review of Barriers to the Learning Experience by Revisioning Astin's I-E-O Model

Guanglong Pang and Brandon R. G. Smith

Introduction

International students from Asia who are studying in Canada have shared characteristics such as being a foreigner and typically a racial minority. Those characteristics often entail navigating extra layers of challenges, including speaking a new language for some, when adapting to new socio-cultural and academic norms. How campuses address those characteristics and the associated challenges affect students' overall experience and level of integration into campus life. In Canada, international students from Asia face similar challenges from being excluded and rendered invisible on campus, mocked for their accent, and disregarded for their values and needs; additionally, they also experience microaggressions based on their country of origin (Houshmand et al. 2014). We argue student characteristics and campus navigation co-constitutively shape the educational outcomes for international students from Asia. This responsive relationship is particularly important when considering how many institutions today commit to enhancing the student experience on campus (Bowden et al. 2021).

Although the literature on international student experience in Canada is rich, there are few pieces focusing specifically on those from Asia. This chapter establishes a conceptual linkage to understand how components in the model are responsive with one another for international students from Asia by reconceptualizing Astin's *Inputs-Environment-Outcomes* (I-E-O) model (1988, 1993) in a Canadian context. While Astin's model is useful for universities and colleges to understand how student characteristics interact with campus environment, its development focuses on White domestic students; moreover, the literature examining international students from Asia predominantly comes from the United States (US).

DOI: 10.4324/b23160-14

Therefore, contextualizing the model from the perspective of Asian international students offers perspectives about how this vast population experiences higher education in Canada. Our reimagining allows an integrative view of student inputs and their navigation in the campus environment. Applying the revised model allows for a more nuanced understanding of the experiences of international students from Asia, specifically their campus integration *outcomes*, which cannot be fully understood without considering the interaction between *inputs* and *environments*. We argue that inputs and environments are responsive and inductive to one another.

We begin with a broad definition of international students from Asia and their access to Canadian higher education. Next, we introduce the I-E-O Model before offering critiques and revisions for this population. Then we use two sections to explain the interaction between inputs and the environments before discussing their implications for campus integration as outcomes. Finally, we offer concluding remarks and implications for future research and practices.

Asian International Students and Their Access to Canadian Higher Education

We broadly define international students from Asia studying in Canada as degree-seeking individuals with a student visa who possess citizenship from any Asian country. Historically, this population dominated the larger percentages of international student populations in Canada; in 2021, countries with top numbers of students attending higher education in Canada are India, China, South Korea, the Philippines, and Vietnam (CBIE 2022). In Canadian universities, China continues to represent the greatest international enrolments in most university offerings, and India represents the greatest international student population in Canadian colleges (Frenette et al. 2020). While we acknowledge diverse geographical regions in Asia, the existing literature heavily focuses on Eastern Asian international students.

I-E-O Model

We critique and revise Astin's I-E-O Model (1988, 1993) to address the problematic experiences of international students from Asia. This model was developed to understand college student experiences in the US (Renn and Reason 2021). Astin's work suggests that better student experience and engagement on campus can improve the student's potential to be retained and graduate (Astin 1993). According to Renn and Reason

(2021, viii) "in the most basic formulation, the framework lays out a longitudinal model that incorporates inputs (I), the college environment (E), and outcomes (O)" to understand college student experiences in the US. *Inputs* represent any student characteristics when entering college, such as identity, location, socioeconomic status, and academic grades; those inputs often intersect. *Environments* are physical, academic, and sociocultural sectors on campus, which have their own existing values and atmospheres. *Outcomes* represent a broad sense of student experiences, including engagement, integration, persistence, retention, and graduation. Since its initial development, the model has been adapted to different contexts and demographics of American college students, refurbishing the model as inclusive of nontraditional student populations (Astin and Antonio 2012).

Although the literature on international students in Canada is rich, few pieces focus on international students from Asia and even less utilize the I-E-O model. Grayson (2008) was an exception that used inputs like being an English language learner to predict international students' sense of coherence and academic performance on Canadian campuses. Recently, Pang and Montsion (2022) used the model to explore the interactions between the pre-migration expectations of international students from Asia and their experiences on a Canadian campus to highlight that their feelings before arriving in Canada and their postgraduate plans are active parts of their present studies. Our contribution is exploring the potential of this model for the diverse experiences of international students from Asia in Canada.

Critiques

A major concern with the I-E-O model is its insufficient attention to international and minoritized student populations. The model was mainly used to study the college impact and student experience for "traditional" White students who graduate from high school and continue at a four-year institution, particularly considering American postsecondary education in the 1980s and 1990s (Renn and Reason 2021). While literature since then has used the I-E-O model for minority student populations—for example, Black students (Palmer et al. 2010; Young et al. 2014) and Indigenous students (Pidgeon 2008; Waterman 2012)—few studies explore *international students*. Moreover, international students should not be viewed as one group because they "actually have more differences between them than any commonalities" other than the fact that they all chose to study internationally (Lee and Castiello-Gutiérrez 2019, 109). International students come from diverse sociocultural, religious, ethnic, linguistic, and national backgrounds, revealing the literature gap.

The model is also limited in terms of its conceptual representation of inputs and environments. Although the model highlights the direction between inputs and environments, it fails to account that certain inputs emerge as the result of being in a specific environment. We demonstrate that campus is key for constructing and imposing the new meanings of certain inputs carried by international students from Asia. We will also highlight that certain inputs mediate the type and extent of environments available to this population for integration. Based on those findings, we argue that inputs and environments should not be represented as two separate entities as the model indicates. For international students from Asia, we must acknowledge a co-constitutive relationship, specifically how inputs and environments induce one another to shape this population's integration on campus. This is a crucial consideration from the lenses of student engagement and success (Bowden et al. 2021).

Revision

Our model focuses on the interaction between inputs and environments to understand how it translates into problematic experiences for integration (outcomes) among international students from Asia. We argue that inputs and environments in the I-E-O model are mutually responsive to each other, and they highlight a bi-directional interaction. The direction from environments to inputs demonstrates an environment-induced interaction, meaning that campuses construct and impose new input meanings for being Asian and international. In contrast, the direction from inputs to environments represents an input-initiated interaction to expose certain challenges when the environments respond to inputs from the population.

The interaction between inputs and environments affects the experiences of integration for international students from Asia, which are framed in this study as outcomes. Specifically, academic, social, and cultural integrations are three key outcomes in the I-E-O model that are evaluated by students for making decisions on persistence or departure (Renn and Reason 2021). Although we acknowledge international students could have individually different ideas about educational outcomes—from learning a new language, acquiring technical knowledge, getting a foreign diploma, to obtaining immigration status—we emphasize on select integrations because they are among the most studied topics for international students from Asia (Figure 11.1).

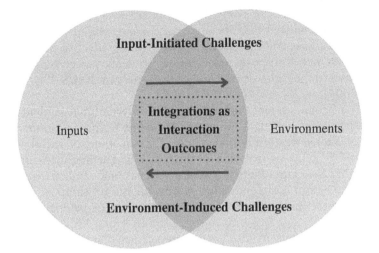

Figure 11.1 Astin's Inputs-Environments-Outputs (IEO) Model (1988, 1993) Revised to Address the Experiences of Asian International Students Studying in Canada

Notes. This revised model shows the interaction between inputs and environments, leading to (1) input-initiated challenges and (2) environment-induced challenges experienced by international students from Asia studying at universities and colleges in Canada. This interaction shapes *integration*, which permeates across the academic, cultural, and social dimensions.

Environment-Induced Challenges

The most pronounced input characteristics for international students from Asia emerge when on campus. For example, international students from Asia become *international* when migrating to a new country. Similarly, most international students from Asia, such as Chinese and Indians, become culturally and racially *minoritized* when relocating to a host country like Canada. Therefore, the new environments international students from Asia occupy construct and socialize the new inputs and associated meanings to them.

Campus environments often facilitate internalizing racial stereotypes and discrimination for international students from Asia. One study interviewed 47 undergraduate and graduate students from China, Japan, and South Korea studying at a large US public university determined that campuses are environments where international students from Eastern Asia encounter and internalize racial stereotypes and hierarchy (Ritter 2013). Similarly, Haider (2018) studied Muslim Pakistani international students who encounter hostile treatment in the US using the concept of double consciousness to show that these students view their religious and national identities not only through their own eyes but also through the newly internalized identity of terrorists and religious others by the host environment. Another study highlighted the effect of duration, revealing that non-European international students perceive discrimination related to their identity the longer they study in the US (Poyrazli and Lopez 2007).

From a broad student engagement lens, international students from Asia experience challenges influenced by White norms on campus. This includes White, Western dominance over Asian students' racial authenticity and feelings of isolation (Ashlee 2019). Furthermore—and like many other race and identity groups—international students from Asia experience monoracism and White-norms on and off campus, which influences where and how they experience a sense of belonging (Ashlee 2019).

Campus environments also perpetuate academic and linguistic norms, challenging and potentially marginalizing international students from Asia. Kuo and Roysircar (2006) discovered that adjusting to new academic and linguistic environments negatively impacts the psychological well-being of many Taiwanese international students when studying in Canada. They also uncovered that perceived prejudice on White dominant campuses exacerbates the adjustment of international students from Asia. Similarly, Louie (2018) reported power asymmetry felt by Chinese international students on a US campus. The findings revealed unequal treatment of Chinese international students receiving very little appreciation for the knowledge they bring and feeling obligated to adjust to the academic and sociocultural norms. Moreover, Eastern Asian international students navigate the Canadian academic environment with different expectations about cultures and norms, facing academic integrity and inclusion issues (Kang 2022). Nonetheless, maintaining close relationships with campus staff and peers is key for international students from Asia when navigating through dilemmas in new environments, as evidenced by two Canadian studies (Popadiuk 2009, 2010).

While the examples above demonstrate the key role of campus environments for constructing new input meanings for international students from Asia, certain campus sectors are more relevant to their inputs—such as cultural newcomers, English language learners, and minority groups—shaping their integration experiences. Kim (2001) criticized Astin's I-E-O model for not distinguishing between the types of environments that students engage in. Specifically, Kim argued that it is the interaction between student inputs and individual-specific environments that exerts the most impact on student outcomes. Therefore, students are most affected by the environments relevant to them, not by the overall campus environment encompassing all students.

Input-Induced Challenges

Distinctive inputs international students from Asia possess risk translating into disadvantages on campuses (Van Horne et al. 2018). An extensive literature review revealed that factors challenging international students the most include navigating immigration status, lacking network connections, and, for many, speaking a foreign language (Zhang and Goodson 2011). However, being an international student from Asia presents additional challenges. Lee et al. (2017) discovered most international students from Asia come from countries socially, culturally, politically, and religiously different from Western civilizations, rendering them a steeper adaptation curve in Western host countries compared to those from Australia, Canada, and the UK (Lee et al. 2017). Studies have reported Asian international students facing issues of discrimination and a sense of othering (Yao 2018), avoidance by domestic students for lacking Western cultural reference points (Peacock and Harrison 2009), and unfamiliarity with the social and academic norms (Sato and Hodge 2009). In Canada, Asian international students experienced similar issues including being excluded and mocked on campus (Houshmand et al. 2014), leading them to form their own sociocultural and academic spheres, marginalized from the campus and host country environments (Scott et al. 2015).

Language is an input of international students from Asia studying in Canada that shapes the availability and hospitality of campus environments. Language proficiency affects integration. English language deficiency is the most reported issue impeding various aspects of campus experiences for international students from Asia (Lin and Day 2014). Commanding a second language in an English-dominant academic environment disadvantages this population, limiting the type and scope of the campuses they can engage in. A case study in Canada discovered that language proficiency means more than a skill to improve for international students from Asia because it is often the source of issue for transition and relationship development on campus (Popadiuk and Marshall 2011). Moreover, the perceived language barrier among international students from Asia often causes them to be reluctant in initiating social interactions and shy away from utilizing resources on campus (Wright and Schartner 2013). This is because some international students from Asia consider English deficiency as an invitation for discrimination (Karuppan and Barari 2010). English fluency has been conceptualized as a "symbolic capital" (Pham and Tran 2015, 291) or power credential (Jon 2012), drawing boundaries between inclusion, exclusion, and discrimination on campus depending on language fluency.

Nationality is another salient input. For example, being a Chinese national invites stereotypes and discrimination from many domestic students

(Yao 2018). First-year Chinese international students in the US perceive racism and othering that undermine their sense of belonging on campus (Yao 2018). Anti-Chinese sentiments in South Korea manifest from verbal aggression and discriminatory behaviors to unfair employment practices (Lee et al. 2017). Likewise, British students avoid connecting with Chinese students who are often perceived as culturally distant, poor English speakers, self-excluding, and lacking cultural reference points (Peacock and Harrison 2009). In summary, many input characteristics translate into disadvantages and challenges on campus for international students from Asia.

Integration as Outcomes

Integration for international students from Asia on a campus has the greatest potential for affecting their possible success on a campus. Academic and social integrations are pressing issues for minority students (Braxton et al. 2004), and they are widely examined as outcomes in the I-E-O model. We borrow the definition of social and academic integration from Tinto (1987) who proposed to assess academic integration based on the feedback students receive from faculty on academic performance and how comfortable students feel about their communication with faculty regarding academic matters. Tinto (1987) also recommended assessing students' social integration by looking at their interaction with peers and their sense of belonging to the student cultures as well as their engagement with various non-academic organizations on campus (Tinto 1987). Additionally, Tierney examines cultural integration using a cultural dichotomy: *cultural suicide* versus *cultural integrity*. While cultural integrity means establishing their own cultural enclave to preserve their culture, cultural suicide means discarding their own culture and fully assimilating into campus culture (Tierney 1999, 82). Below we communicate *academic*, *social*, and *cultural integration* as potential integration challenges for all student populations. However, as we demonstrate below, being Asian and international adds additional layers of challenge from these contexts (Lee and Castiello-Gutiérrez 2019), which we overview.

Academic Integration

International students from Asia experience challenges in academic integration. Although international students are reported as equally, or sometimes even more, engaged in formal academic activities as domestic students (Zhao et al. 2005), international students from Asia are far less likely to seek academic support services on campus (Wright and Schartner 2013). International students from Asia may have these experiences due to a series of factors, from their navigating college academically by themselves include English language barriers, cultural differences, and a lack of understanding of Western classroom norms (Li et al. 2013). For example, their previous understanding about classroom norms deters many international students from Asia from speaking up, engaging in debate, and offering criticism in class, which are interpreted by them as academic struggles (Campbell and Li 2008; Sato and Hodge 2009). Unfortunately, the silence of international students from Asia, largely affected by their previous educational experiences and norms, is often mistaken as disengagement in class (Campbell and Li 2008).

Social Integration

While social integration is a concern for all student populations (Braxton et al. 2004), it is particularly a challenge for international students from Asia. For example, although domestic minority students are often concerned about their social integration on campus, they possess social currency such as linguistic and socio-cultural knowledge that international students from Asia lack. As such, domestic students possess the social networks that international students from Asia do not. For example, Waterman (2012) argued that *home-going behaviors* are crucial to Indigenous students to connect with their families, communities, and spirituality, which helps them persist through college. Similarly, Black students receive motivation and role-model support from services and institutions dedicated to serving them (Palmer et al. 2010). International students from Asia often do not go home frequently due to long distances, for example. Given that international students are often living abroad away from their families and social networks, they are more prone to experiencing loneliness than domestic students, undermining the quality of their studying abroad experience (Sawir et al. 2008). For instance, Tsai et al. (2017) identified that Chinese students reporting a greater level of loneliness also perceive lower self-efficacy. Considering most international students from Asia come from non-English speaking countries, the language barrier exacerbates social isolation in and outside of the classroom (Lee and Castiello-Gutiérrez 2019). Therefore, social integration is a persistent issue for international students from Asia as they consistently report lower levels of social satisfaction and more loneliness than their domestic counterparts (Van Horne et al. 2018; Zhou and Cole 2017).

Cultural Integration

International student populations generally face a dichotomy of cultural integration on campus. To successfully integrate on campus, international students must realign their values and identities to conform to the

dominant culture and norms of Western campuses (Tierney 1999). However, the view of *successful* is biased because it means asking international
students to conform to an institutional environment that does not always
provide what they need, exposing the power inequalities between international students from Asia and domestic students. Because international
students' cultures of origin and previously socialized cultural norms do not
always align with those in the new environments, they end up in the dilemma of either maintaining their "cultural integrity" or committing "cultural suicide" (Tierney 1999, 82). International students from Asia can feel
marginalized on campus into their own cultural enclave, voluntarily and
involuntarily (Peacock and Harrison 2009; Sato and Hodge 2009). Unfortunately, many international students choose to form their own cultural
enclave consisting of those from similar sociocultural roots because they
often do not feel that they are interacting on an equal basis with domestic
students (Schweisfurth and Gu 2009).

Conclusion and Future Directions

This chapter revises Astin's reputable I-E-O model as a way to understand
how the broad population of international students from Asia may experience higher education in Canada. While the model has been applied to international students, in the US context mainly, it rarely considers
international students from Asia in Canada. We highlighted problematic
experiences related to being an international student from Asia, then briefly
explained the original model, our critiques, and the rationales for revision.
We argue that inputs by international students from Asia and the responses
from environments (campus in particular) within the host country are conducive to each other. Specifically, campuses induce and socialize new
meanings for this population based on their input characteristics. Likewise, certain inputs international students from Asia carry initiate various
challenges for integration, mediating the types and extents of the environments available to them. Understanding the intricate interaction between
inputs and environments helps scholars and administrators to deliver more
satisfying support services for this population.

   While we utilize a broad view and definition of international students
from Asia, we acknowledge the diversity among this population and encourage scholars to examine integration challenges associated with their
diverse origins from national and sociocultural to ethnic. Specifically, our
focus on this broader population risks overlooking the diversity such as
the distinction between East and Southeast Asian populations, washing
out the nuances related to those inputs. We also acknowledge variations in
environments, and consider how international students from Asia navigate different environments to derive different integration experiences.

Therefore, we encourage scholars to highlight geographical origin because our revision of the I-E-O model relies on recognizing the diverse input characteristics—the national and cultural landscapes of specific Asian countries—among international students from Asia, which shape how they navigate campus environments and obtain education outcomes.

While international recruitment efforts continue to surge, we encourage campus executives to understand areas that support international populations on campus and their specific needs. Executive leadership can address this by understanding the needs of different student populations by hearing from those who should have this expertise (e.g., international student services leadership, senior student affairs officer). Having these leaders participate in executive decision-making can better inform institutional planning, enrollment, and student-facing areas. Furthermore, assessing how student affairs and international student support services are resourced can determine if these areas have adequate resources to meet diverse student needs. To meet the needs of international students from Asia, we encourage researchers, campus leadership, and practitioners to better address nuances from inputs (e.g., diverse student characteristics from a wide origin background within the broader categorization of international students from Asia) and environments (e.g., physical, political, social, cultural, academic, and demographics) on Canadian campuses.

References

Anderson, Stuart. 2022. "U.S. International Student Enrollment Dropped as Canada's Soared." *Forbes.* https://www.forbes.com/sites/stuartanderson/2022/03/03/us-international-student-enrollment-dropped-as-canadas-soared/?sh=5379111b776e.

Ashlee, Aerial A. 2019. "Engaging Transracial Asian American Adoptee Students." In *Student Engagement in Higher Education: Theoretical Perspectives and Practical Approaches for Diverse Populations*, edited by Stephen John Quaye, Shaun R. Harper, and Sumun L. Pendakur, 14 pages. New York: Routledge.

Astin, Alexander W. 1988. *Achieving Educational Excellence: A Critical Assessment of Priorities and Practices in Higher Education*. San Francisco: Jossey-Bass.

Astin, Alexander W. 1993. *What Matters in College? Four Critical Years Revisited*. San Francisco: Jossey-Bass.

Astin, Alexander, and A. L. Antonio. 2012. *Assessment for Excellence: The Philosophy and Practice of Assessment and Evaluation in Higher Education*. Rowman & Littlefield Publishers.

Bowden, Jana Lay-Hwa, Leonie Tickle, and Kay Naumann. 2021. "The Four Pillars of Tertiary Student Engagement and Success: A Holistic Measurement Approach." *Studies in Higher Education* 46, no. 6: 1207–24. https://doi.org/10.1080/03075079.2019.1672647.

Braxton, John M., Amy S. Hirschy, and Shederick A. McClendon. 2004. "Understanding and Reducing College Student Departure." *ASHE-ERIC Higher Education Report* 30, no. 3. https://eric.ed.gov/?id=ED501184.

Campbell, Jacqui, and Mingsheng Li. 2008. "Asian Students' Voices: An Empirical Study of Asian Students' Learning Experiences at a New Zealand University." *Journal of Studies in International Education* 12, no. 4: 375–96. https://doi.org/10.1177/1028315307299422.

Canadian Bureau of International Education (CBIE). 2022. *International Students in Canada*. https://cbie.ca/infographic/.

Chen, Liang-Hsuan. 2006. "Attracting East Asian Students to Canadian Graduate Schools." *Canadian Journal of Higher Education* 36, no. 2: 77–105.

Fischer, Karin, and Sasha Aslanian. 2021. *Fading Beacon: The U.S. May Never Regain Its Dominance as a Destination for International Students. Here's Why that Matters*. APM Reports. https://www.apmreports.org/episode/2021/08/03/fading-beacon-why-america-is-losing-international-students.

Frenette, Marc, Youjin Choi, and April Doreleyers. 2020. *International Student Enrolment in Postsecondary Education Programs Prior to COVID-19*. Economic Insights, Statistics Canada. Catalogue no. 11-626-X – 2020003 – No. 105, ISSN 1927-503X.

Grayson, J. Paul. 2008. "The Experiences and Outcomes of Domestic and International Students at Four Canadian Universities." *Higher Education Research and Development* 27, no. 3: 215–30. https://doi.org/10.1080/07294360802183788.

Haider, Maheen. 2018. "Double Consciousness: How Pakistani Graduate Students Navigate Their Contested Identities in American Universities." In *Understanding International Students from Asia in American Universities*, edited by Yingyi Ma and Martha Garcia-Murillo, 107–25. Cham: Springer. https://doi.org/10.1007/978-3-319-60394-0_6.

Houshmand, Sarah, Lisa Spanierman, and Romin Tafarodi. 2014. "Excluded and Avoided: Racial Microaggressions Targeting Asian International Students in Canada." *Cultural Diversity and Ethnic Minority Psychology* 20, no. 3: 377–88. https://doi.org/10.1037/a0035404.

Jon, Jae-Eun. 2012. "Power Dynamics with International Students: From the Perspective of Domestic Students in Korean Higher Education." *Higher Education* 64, no. 4: 441–54. https://doi.org/10.1007/s10734-011-9503-2.

Kang, Phoebe Eunkyung. 2022. "Academic Integrity and the Inclusion of East Asian International Students in Canadian Higher Education." In *Handbook of Research on Teaching Strategies for Culturally and Linguistically Diverse International Students*, edited by Clayton Smith and George Zhou, 188–200. Hershey: IGI Global.

Karuppan, Corinne M., and Mahua Barari. 2010. "Perceived Discrimination and International Students' Learning: An Empirical Investigation." *Journal of Higher Education Policy and Management* 33, no. 1: 67–83. https://doi.org/10.1080/1360080X.2011.537013.

Kim, Mikyong Minsun. 2001. "Institutional Effectiveness of Women-only Colleges: Cultivating Students' Desire to Influence Social Conditions." *The Journal of Higher Education* 72, no. 3: 287–321. https://doi.org/10.1080/00221546.2001.11777096.

Kuo, Ben C. H., and Gargi Roysircar. 2006. "An Exploratory Study of Cross-Cultural Adaptation of Adolescent Taiwanese Unaccompanied Sojourners in Canada." *International Journal of Intercultural Relations* 30, no. 2: 159–83.

Lee, Jenny J., and Santiago Castiello-Gutiérrez. 2019. "Engaging International Students." In *Student Engagement in Higher Education*, edited by Stephen John Quaye, Shaun R. Harper, and Sumun L. Pendakur, 107–29. New York: Routledge.

Lee, Jenny, Jae-Eun Jon, and Kiyong Byun. 2017. "Neo-Racism and Neo-Nationalism within East Asia: The Experiences of International Students in South Korea." *Journal of Studies in International Education* 21, no. 2: 136–55. https://doi.org/10.1177/1028315316669903.

Li, Peiwei, Y. Wong Joel, and Toth Paul. 2013. "Asian International Students' Willingness to Seek Counseling: A Mixed-Methods Study." *International Journal for the Advancement of Counselling* 35, no. 1: 1–15. https://doi.org/10.1007/s10447-012-9163-7.

Lin, Shu-Yuan, and Scherz Susan Day. 2014. "Challenges Facing Asian International Graduate Students in the US: Pedagogical Considerations in Higher Education." *Journal of International Students* 4, no. 1: 16–33. https://doi.org/10.32674/jis.v4i1.494.

Louie, Vivian. 2018. "From Elites to Outsiders: How Chinese MBA Students Experience Power Asymmetries in American Universities." In *Understanding International Students from Asia in American Universities*, edited by Yingyi Ma and Martha Garcia-Murillo, 149–71. Cham: Springer. https://doi.org/10.1007/978-3-319-60394-0_8.

National Foundation for American Policy. 2022. *Analysis of U.S. and Canadian International Student Data*. https://nfap.com/wp-content/uploads/2022/03/Analysis-of-International-Student-Data.NFAP-Policy-Brief.March-2022.pdf.

Palmer, Robert T., Ryan J. Davis, and Dina C. Maramba. 2010. "Role of an HBCU in Supporting Academic Success for Underprepared Black Males." *Negro Educational Review* 61, no. 1–4: 85–106. https://eric.ed.gov/?id=EJ908044.

Pang, Guanglong, and Jean Michel Montsion. 2022. "Chinese International Students at Two Canadian Universities: Learning from their Emotional Labor to Re-align Support Services." In *International Student Support and Engagement in Higher Education: Exploring Innovative Practices in Campus, Academic and Professional Support Services*, edited by Janet Boyd and Mutiara Mohamad. New York: Routledge.

Peacock, Nicola, and Neil Harrison. 2009. "'It's So Much Easier to Go with What's Easy' 'Mindfulness' and the Discourse between Home and International Students in the United Kingdom." *Journal of Studies in International Education* 13, no. 4: 487–508. https://doi.org/10.1177/1028315308319508.

Pham, Lien, and Ly Tran. 2015. "Understanding the Symbolic Capital of Intercultural Interactions: A Case Study of International Students in Australia." *International Studies in Sociology of Education* 25, no. 3: 204–24. https://doi.org/10.1080/09620214.2015.1069720.

Pidgeon, Michelle. 2008. "Pushing against the Margins: Indigenous Theorizing of 'Success' and Retention in Higher Education." *Journal of College Student Retention: Research, Theory and Practice* 10, no. 3: 339–60.

Popadiuk, Natalie E. 2009. "Unaccompanied Asian Secondary Students Studying in Canada." *International Journal of Advancement of Counselling* 31, no. 229. https://doi.org/10.1007/s10447-009-9080-6.

Popadiuk, Natalee E. 2010. "Asian International Student Transition to High School in Canada." *Qualitative Report* 15, no. 6: 1523–48.

Popadiuk, Natalee E., and Steve Marshall. 2011. "East Asian International Student Experiences as Learners of English as an Additional Language: Implications for School Counsellors." *Canadian Journal of Counselling and Psychotherapy* 45, no. 3.

Poyrazli, Senel, and Marcos Damian Lopez. 2007. "An Exploratory Study of Perceived Discrimination and Homesickness: A Comparison of International Students and American Students." *The Journal of Psychology* 141, no. 3: 263–80. https://doi.org/10.3200/JRLP.141.3.263-280.

Renn, Kristen A., and Robert D. Reason. 2021. *College Students in the United States: Characteristics, Experiences, and Outcomes*. 2nd edition. Sterling, VA: Stylus.

Renn, Kristen A., and Brandon R. G. Smith. 2022. "Creating and Sustaining Organizational Change to Promote College Student Success in Natural and Open Systems." In *Improving College Student Retention: New Developments in Theory, Research, and Practice*, edited by Robert D. Reason and J. Braxton. Sterling, VA: Stylus.

Ritter, Zachary Stephen. 2013. "Making and Breaking Stereotypes: East Asian International Students' Experiences with Cross-Cultural/Racial Interactions." Dissertation, University of California Press, Los Angeles.

Sato, Takahiro, and Samuel R. Hodge. 2009. Asian International Doctoral Students' Experiences at Two American Universities: Assimilation, Accommodation, and Resistance." *Journal of Diversity in Higher Education* 2, no. 3: 136–48. https://doi.org/10.1037/a0015912.

Sawir, Erlenawati, Simon Marginson, Ana Deumert, Chris Nyland, and Gaby Ramia. 2008. "Loneliness and International Students: An Australian Study." *Journal of Studies in International Education* 12, no. 2: 148–80. https://doi.org/10.1177/1028315307299699.

Schweisfurth, Michele, and Qing Gu. 2009. "Exploring the Experiences of International Students in UK Higher Education: Possibilities and Limits of Interculturality in University Life." *Intercultural Education* 20, no. 5: 463–73. https://doi.org/10.1080/14675980903371332.

Scott, Colin, Saba Safdar, Roopa Desai Trilokekar, and Amira El Masri. 2015. "International Students as 'Ideal Immigrants' in Canada: A Disconnect between Policy Makers Assumptions and the Lived Experiences of International Students." *Comparative and International Education* 43, no. 3. https://doi.org/10.5206/cie-eci.v43i3.9261.

Statistics Canada. 2020. *International Students Accounted for All of the Growth in Postsecondary Enrolments in 2018/2019*. https://www150.statcan.gc.ca/n1/daily-quotidien/201125/dq201125e-eng.htm.

Statistics Canada. 2021. *Enrolments in Canadian Universities and Colleges by Field of Study, 2008/2009 and 2018/2019*. https://www150.statcan.gc.ca/n1/daily-quotidien/201125/t001e-eng.htm.

Tierney, William G. 1999. "Models of Minority College-Going and Retention: Cultural Integrity versus Cultural Suicide." *Journal of Negro Education* 68, no. 1: 80–91. https://doi.org/10.2307/2668211.

Tinto, Vincent. 1987. *Leaving College: Rethinking the Causes and Cures of Student Attrition.* Chicago: University of Chicago Press.

Tsai, William, Kenneth T. Wang, and Meifen Wei. 2017. "Reciprocal Relations between Social Self-Efficacy and Loneliness among Chinese International Students." *Asian American Journal of Psychology* 8, no. 2: 94. https://doi.org/10.1037/aap0000065.

Usher, Alex. 2021. *The State of Postsecondary Education in Canada, 2021.* Toronto: Higher Education Strategy Associates.

Van Horne, Sam, Shuhui Lin, Matthew Anson, and Wayne Jacobson. 2018. "Engagement, Satisfaction, and Belonging of International Undergraduates at US Research Universities." *Journal of International Students* 8, no. 1: 351–74. https://doi.org/10.5281/zenodo.1134313.

Waterman, Stephanie J. 2012. "Home-Going as a Strategy for Success among Haudenosaunee College and University Students." *Journal of Student Affairs Research and Practice* 49, no. 2: 193–209. https://doi.org/10.1515/1949-6605.6378.

Wright, Clare, and Alina Schartner. 2013. " 'I Can't... I Won't?' International Students at the Threshold of Social Interaction." *Journal of Research in International Education* 12, no. 2: 113–28. https://doi.org/10.1177/1475240913491055.

Yao, Christina W. 2018. " 'They Don't Care About You': First-Year Chinese International Students' Experiences with Neo-Racism and Othering on a US Campus." *Journal of the First-Year Experience & Students in Transition* 30, no. 1: 87–101. https://digitalcommons.unl.edu/cehsedadfacpub/84/.

Young, Glenda, David B. Knight, and Denise R. Simmons. 2014. "Co-curricular experiences link to nontechnical skill development for African-American engineers: Communication, teamwork, professionalism, lifelong learning, and reflective behavior skills." In *2014 IEEE Frontiers in Education Conference (FIE) Proceedings*, pp. 1–7. IEEE.

Zhang, Jing, and Patricia Goodson. 2011. "Predictors of International Students' Psychosocial Adjustment to Life in the United States: A Systematic Review." *International Journal of Intercultural Relations* 35, no. 2: 139–62. https://doi.org/10.1016/j.ijintrel.2010.11.011.

Zhao, Chun-Mei, George D. Kuh, and Robert M. Carini. 2005 "A Comparison of International Student and American Student Engagement in Effective Educational Practices." *The Journal of Higher Education* 76, no. 2: 209–31. https://www.jstor.org/stable/3838723.

Zhou, Ji, and Darnell Cole. 2017. "Comparing International and American Students: Involvement in College Life and Overall Satisfaction." *Higher Education* 73: 655–72. https://doi.org/10.1007/s10734-016-9982-2.

Anti-Asian Racism and the Politics of Race

Section III

Anti-Asian Racism and the Politics of Race

12 International Students from Asia at the University of Toronto

How Diversity Discourses Downplay Student Demographics

Elizabeth Buckner, Eun Gi Kim, and Fotini Vlahos

Introduction

Over the past few decades, Canadian universities have significantly increased international student recruitment, with the stated goals of providing students with a more culturally diverse learning environment and supplementing stagnant provincial budgets with international student fees (McCartney 2021; Smith 2016; see also Montsion and Caneo). Today, over half of all international students in Canada come from only two countries: China and India (Buckner et al. 2020), and at the university level, most international students come from China (Leary et al. 2016; Smith 2016).

Both internal and external stakeholders have recognized and criticized a contradiction between the stated goals of internationalization as increasing diversity and the reality of an international student body that is overwhelmingly Chinese (Gertler 2015b; Singh 2017; Stein and de Andreotti 2016; University of Toronto 2008; Wu et al. 2021; see also Das Gupta and Gomez). These concerns place pressure on Canadian universities to appear as diverse as possible, especially when diversity is used as a recruitment tool to attract academically elite international students (Ford and Patterson 2019; Leary et al. 2016; McCartney 2021). Similar concerns exist in American post-secondary institutions. American scholars have coined the term "cosmetic diversity" to describe this phenomenon of exaggerating certain student demographics over others to strategically portray a specific kind of diversity (Ford and Patterson 2019).

When borrowing this idea of cosmetic diversity and applying it to the Canadian higher education context, the specifics of Canadian student demographics must be taken into consideration. Students' ethno-racial backgrounds and international students' presence in Canada differ somewhat from the American context (Buckner et al. 2021). In Canada, the high proportion of Asian students, both domestic and international, has been

DOI: 10.4324/b23160-16

criticized in popular media, often with racist undertones (Guo and Guo 2017; Scott et al. 2015; Wu et al. 2021). To understand how prior work on diversity representations (Ford and Patterson 2019; Miller-Idriss et al. 2019; Omi and Winant 2014) maps to the Canadian context, a closer examination of how Canadian universities portray their Asian international student population to the public is warranted.

In this chapter, we examine the extent to which Canada's largest university – The University of Toronto (UofT) – engages in cosmetic diversity to manage perceptions of its Chinese international students in particular. Specifically, we examine how UofT portrays its international student body in the "most favourable light" (Ford and Patterson 2019, 102) by examining who is highlighted and who is downplayed. We do this through content analysis and close reading of the *UT Magazine*, a magazine published twice annually by the University of Toronto Communications and freely distributed to tens of thousands of alumni.

Diversity Representations as an Institutional Racial Project

To understand how *UT Magazine* discusses international students to its varied internal and external audiences, we draw on prior studies that examine representations of diversity in higher education. Our study begins with the concept of institutional racism, which is distinguished from individual-level attitudes and prejudice. In contrast to individual-level bias, institutional racism occurs when societies and their institutions, policies, and practices systematically privilege individuals from certain races. Scholars explain that to understand how racism works in practice, we must pay attention to "the ways in which both social structures and everyday experiences are racially organized" (Omi and Winant, 2014, 125). In Canadian higher education, universities are predominantly white institutions that operate according to white middle-class norms, yet in recent decades have also sought to portray themselves as highly diverse. In this context, representing diversity constitutes an organizational project for the institution, with universities actively and strategically managing representations of their student bodies (Ford and Patterson 2019; Omi and Winant 2014). We conceptualize this organizational project as a racial project, where the university seeks to reap the benefits associated with being highly diverse without fear of or attention to any consequences. The institutionalization of organizational and racial projects by universities has been corroborated by prior research, which shows that universities engage in strategic representations on their outward-facing documents and websites (Miller-Idriss et al. 2019). Universities seek to highlight the racial, cultural, and religious diversity of their students, often in ways that exaggerate this diversity beyond the demographic reality (Buckner et al. 2021; Ford and Patterson 2019).

In their work, Ford and Patterson (2019) identify three ways that universities employ cosmetic diversity on their public websites. These are omission, aggregation, and addition. For the purposes of this chapter, we will focus on the first two strategies. *Omission* refers specifically to the omission of white students from race data (Ford and Patterson 2019). Omission assumes that the reader understands there is a white presence on campus and therefore, does not need to know or care to know what that presence is, so the institution does not report this prevalence when presenting their student body's racial composition. Omission reinforces the conceptualization of whiteness as an unraced norm to which all non-whites are compared, constituting a racialized "Other." Another institutional strategy for cosmetic diversity is *aggregation*, which occurs when an institution collapses all non-white racial groups into a single "minority" or "ethnic" presence (Ford and Patterson 2019). In doing so, aggregation perpetuates the fallacy of a white/non-white binary defining diversity in ways that do not recognize differences among non-white students. As with omission, aggregation reifies the idea of a white norm and provides little information about the actual prevalence of different races and ethnicities on campus.

This strategic portrayal of diversity on university campuses is concerning for several reasons. Simplistic messages about celebrating diversity may create unrealistic expectations of campus life and may make it more difficult to address experiences of racism (Ahmed 2006). Additionally, cosmetic diversity contributes to perpetuating "diversity mixed messages" (Windscheid et al. 2016, as cited by Ford and Patterson 2019). This is a phenomenon born out of a dissonance between the public image of diversity and the experiences of racialized students, leading to negative outcomes for these students, such as psychological distress and attrition. In the next section, we describe the international student presence at UofT to then be able to connect American literature to the Canadian reality of cosmetic diversity.

International Students at the University of Toronto

In Canada, Ontario hosts the highest number of international students (Leary et al. 2016) and UofT, located in Ontario, is Canada's largest university. This is based on both total student enrollments and international student enrollments across the three campuses: St. George (UTSG); Mississauga (UTM); Scarborough (UTSC), of which UTM and UTSC are predominantly undergraduate institutions. International students at UofT are charged much higher tuition fees than their domestic counterparts, paying anywhere from five to nine times more tuition per annum. This is evidenced by the 2021–2022 fee schedule which shows $6,100 for domestic students versus $58,160 for international students in the Arts and Science programs and $14,180 versus $62,250 in the Applied Science and Engineering programs (University of Toronto 2022).

In addition to choosing UofT as the subject of this chapter for its high international student enrollments, we note that we are based at UofT and as internal stakeholders to the institution's policies, we not only have a personal stake in its policies and practices but are the specific audience targeted by the *UT Magazine*. In part, this research project stems from our own reading of the *UT Magazine* articles that seem increasingly inconsistent with other discussions about international student recruitment within the university.

Not only does UofT house the largest number of international students in Canada, but this percentage has been consistently increasing since 2003 (University of Toronto 2008). In 2017, UofT enrolled international students from 162 countries, and in the 2020–2021 academic year, international students represented 29 percent of undergraduate students and 21 percent of graduate student populations. This increase in international student enrollments largely includes students from India, the United States, South Korea, and, most notably, China (University of Toronto 2022). Chinese international students now comprise roughly 65 percent of UofT undergraduate international students and 43 percent of graduate international student populations (University of Toronto 2021). Having laid out the actual demographics of UofT's international students, we now present our data and analysis of the *UT Magazine* for its strategic use of cosmetic diversity.

Data and Analysis

To understand strategic self-representations, we focus on the *UT Magazine*, a flagship publication issued twice annually by the University of Toronto Communications that targets all UofT alumni, faculty, staff, and students. UofT alumni and alumnae are automatically registered to receive the magazine in print and through email, while other members of the community can easily subscribe to receive a copy. Back issues of *UT Magazine* from 2003 onwards are available online, allowing us to explore a substantial collection of articles that, while written for a more general audience, also articulate what UofT is and how the institution views itself in the world.

For our analysis, we used the keyword "international students," to search UofT archives for all articles addressing international students. This yielded a total of 46 articles from 2003 to 2022. After confirming that each article actually discussed international students, we then coded the full text for key themes, including the reasons for international student recruitment;

awards and scholarships; funding and tuition; supports for international students; global connections; multiculturalism; and the university's reputation. We also coded the countries or nationalities mentioned in the articles and whether the article included visual images. We then synthesized these key themes to identify the overarching messages that *UT Magazine* sends about its international students.

Findings

We found that UofT tells a very particular story about its international students through *UT Magazine*, portraying its recruitment efforts in ways that will garner support from the institution's many stakeholders. This story is that UofT recruiting highly qualified and extremely diverse international students from all over the world and that this improves the academic quality of the university. Below, we deconstruct this overarching message into two main topics: top-tier talent and demographic diversity.

International Students as a Source of Diversity and Top-Tier Talent

UT Magazine telegraphs a story of recruiting highly qualified, top-tier international students from diverse backgrounds. In part, this narrative redirects conversations away from viewing international students as a source of revenue and instead emphasizes how international students contribute to UofT's goal of being a top global university. Since UofT is a provincially supported university, the institution needs to justify to the public its reason for recruiting and enrolling this large proportion of international students. Over the years, the magazine has included many debates over how many international students to recruit towards this goal of high global ranking.

Examining the articles chronologically, we found a shift in the discussion of international student recruitment from a "should we" question in the early 2000s, to a "we should because" stance from 2009 onwards. For example, in a 2007 article titled, "Towards 2030: How will we preserve excellence at the University of Toronto?" then-president David Naylor wrote:

> Our proportion of international students sits at around 10 per cent. Should we recruit more international students to the university? If so, how many students and from where?
>
> (Naylor 2007)

Subsequently, President Naylor began to advocate for more active recruitment of international students by articulating their contribution to globalizing the UofT campus in a 2009 article titled, "Going Global: We must prepare U of T for a borderless world." In this article, President Naylor stated:

> U of T's growing internationalism is a great strength. More than any previous generation, today's students will be global citizens. ... And while U of T is already one of Canada's most diverse universities, we must boost international student recruitment to attract the finest young minds from around the world. ... By increasing the international opportunities available to students and faculty, U of T aims to enhance Canada's capacity to thrive in a world that's more interconnected than ever.
>
> (Naylor 2009)

In this article, President Naylor connects increases in international student recruitment with larger institutional goals through developing international and global perspectives in UofT students and connecting students with each other and with diverse faculty.

Over the years, *UT Magazine* continuously emphasizes the benefits of increased international student recruitment for both current international and domestic students. In an article titled, "Meeting Global Challenges: U of T is teaching future leaders to think creatively across disciplines," published on June 14, 2011, President Naylor added that an increased number of international students and faculty contribute to a "more direct interaction among students and faculty and more informal inter-disciplinary and cross-cultural exchanges" (Naylor 2011). UofT's current Vice-President, International, Joseph Wong, commented in an interview with *UT Magazine* that "Canadian students learn side-by-side with peers who often have direct knowledge of a topic... It's an entirely different learning experience when you can talk to – and learn from – your peers who are from these regions" (Ndikubwayezu et al. 2021). Vice-President Wong emphasized the unique perspectives and experiences that international students bring to globalize the learning of all students in the classroom.

In addition to international students contributing to a global learning environment, many articles in *UT Magazine* discuss international student scholarships and profile recipients. These scholarships include the Jon S. Dellandrea Award for International Students which is awarded to one student annually for exceptional academic achievement and extracurricular leadership (Easton 2006), the Lester B. Pearson scholarships for academic achievements and creativity (Easton 2019; Gertler 2021; Staff 2016; Toller 2017), and the MasterCard Foundation Scholars Program which supports financially disadvantaged students from Africa (Aschaiek 2013). In 2017, the story of a Syrian graduate student who was admitted to UofT on a full scholarship after complications arose with his U.S. visa was also highlighted

(Kaye 2017). These articles mask the previously noted disparity between international and domestic student fees. International students are presented as top-tier talents who receive prestigious scholarships, rather than the reality that most international students still pay full tuition fees, which international students note is their least favorite part of their life at UofT (Chang 2011).

In terms of graduate students, in a 2015 article titled, "A Global Talent Destination: U of T's ability to attract international graduate students is important to our – and Ontario's – long-term success," President Gertler wrote:

> [I]nternational graduate students are making substantial contributions – a fact that deserves greater attention, especially as we celebrate the university's ability to attract top talent and its role in driving the Toronto region's culture of innovation. ... International graduate students – and indeed faculty, staff and students at every level from abroad – enrich and internationalize the university experience for our entire academic community. ... those who return to their countries of origin also make a great impact for the better, while heightening the reputation of U of T – and the Toronto region – as a global talent destination.
>
> (Gertler 2015a)

Recruiting talented international students, therefore, is framed as benefiting not only the immediate university environment and its international reputation but also the region of Toronto more broadly, upon their graduation. In fact, in contrast to the 2007 Naylor article, by 2021, President Gertler celebrated the idea that "at U of T the number of talented international students grew to comprise one-quarter of our student body" (Gertler 2021).

The emphasis on international students as top-tier talent seems to rebut any concerns that international students are recruited primarily for revenue generation (see Beck; Montsion and Caneo). In fact, the idea that international students generate revenue for the university is almost entirely absent, paralleling the omission strategy for cosmetic diversity. Rather than emphasize, or even openly acknowledge, the substantial revenue international students bring to the university, *UT Magazine* instead emphasizes its international students as contributing to its larger academic goals. This strategically pulls the focus to a more palatable area for stakeholders and society at large.

A Diverse International Student Population

In addition to top-tier talent, the *UT Magazine* also sends the message that international students come to UofT from extremely diverse backgrounds.

For example, then Vice-President, International, Ted Sargent, noted in an interview with the Magazine that international students are attracted to UofT as they "want to be part of an institution that values diversity and is interested in creating a global classroom that's inclusive of people from around the world" (Aschaiek 2017). UTSC's Principal Kidd added in a different interview, "No matter who you are, you will see yourself reflected in the student body here. There's a strong sense of, 'we're in this together'" (Webb 2015). Similarly, in a 2017 article titled, "U of T: Still Defying Gravity: President Meric Gertler Looks Ahead to His Second Term," President Gertler writes: "Half of the people in Toronto were born outside of Canada. We can't tell the difference between a domestic student and an international student at U of T – and that's wonderful. It's one of the things that makes our international students feel so welcome here" (Lanthier 2017).

These statements imply that UofT classrooms welcome such global perspectives from international students and that they contribute to increasing the diversity of the UofT campus environment from both domestic and international students. Therefore, a narrative is constructed of a reciprocal and mutually beneficial relationship between international and domestic students who learn together in a global and inclusive campus environment. However, this narrative contradicts decades of scholarship that find international students are often clearly distinguished in classroom environments by their accents, writing norms, or unfamiliarity with domestic curricula (Guo and Guo 2017; Heng 2019; Zhang and Zhou 2010; see also de Oliveira Soares et al., and Luo and Wilkinson). Furthermore, a significant body of research suggests that international students often feel isolated or excluded even on diverse university campuses (Houshmand et al. 2014; Zhou and Zhang 2014).

International student diversity is measured by national origin and the large number of countries represented among the student body is celebrated. For example, articles include statements such as, "Some 137 foreign countries are represented at U of T, with the largest number of students coming from China, the United States and South Korea" (Faught 2003), and "UTSC is more diverse than most Canadian universities. ... 17 percent are international students, with each incoming class representing some 80 countries" (Webb 2015). By emphasizing the total number of nationalities represented on campus as one large group of "diverse countries" *UT Magazine* is engaging in "aggregation," emphasizing the number of countries represented and eliding discussion of their proportional representation.

UT Magazine also engages in omission regarding international students from China. For example, the 2019 article, "The Things They Carried: Students far from home show us the keepsakes that comfort them," profiles students from Zimbabwe, Ukraine, Ecuador, India, Malaysia, and Germany.

While it is unclear how these students were selected to share their stories, it is clear that students from China and South Korea, two of the most prominent sending countries of international students to UofT, were omitted from this article.

Similar to the emphasis on top-tier talent, this skewed representation of the UofT's international student body also appears in *UT Magazine* articles relating to prestigious international student scholarships. In 2006, an international student from Panama was celebrated for receiving the Jon S. Dellandrea Award for International Students, and in 2017 a student from India for the Pearson scholarship. Another article from that same year profiled Pearson scholarship recipients from the United States, Trinidad and Tobago, Armenia, South Korea, and Nigeria (Easton 2006; Gertler 2021; Toller 2017). The complete absence of students from China is striking and constitutes an example of omission, again for Chinese students who constitute more than 60% of all international students at UofT. This practice of omission differs from the kind found by Ford and Patterson (2019), whose use of omission referred to white students in the US. This variance seems to reflect differences in the national context and our particular focus on international students.

Celebrating Diversity, Downplaying Demographics

In this study, we deconstructed how UofT portrays its international students to its diverse internal and external stakeholders through a close reading of its flagship publication, *UT Magazine*. We argued that *UT Magazine* is a tool through which UofT engages in a racial institutional project of cosmetic diversity, specifically through the use of aggregation and omission in its portrayals of its international student body. By shifting the narrative from international students as financial resources to international students as a highly diverse source of top-tier talent, UofT aims to make its increased recruitment of international students more palatable to internal and external stakeholders. In a similar vein, through aggregation and omission, UofT aims to assuage stakeholder concerns that Canadian universities are "too Asian" (Wu et al. 2021). Despite the reality of UofT's international student body being two-thirds Chinese, *UT Magazine* consistently downplays the presence of its Chinese international students. This is done either by aggregating all international students into one "diversity" category or by omitting Chinese students entirely from articles that specifically highlight the diversity of the university's international students.

Our primary concern with the current practice of celebrating diversity but downplaying actual demographics is that, in doing so, UofT is sidestepping many important conversations about its international students and their experiences on campus. Ahmed (2006) explains that when an institution celebrates its image as a highly diverse and inclusive space, it can actually make it more difficult for internal stakeholders, including students, staff, and faculty, to acknowledge racism and to have their lived experiences of racism and micro-aggressions acknowledged by the institution (Guo and Guo 2017; Heng 2019; Zhang and Zhou 2010; Zhou and Zhang 2014). Given the prevalence of anti-Asian discrimination in Canada, cosmetic diversity is perpetuating a serious issue by simultaneously minimizing the most prominent international student demographic and maximizing false expectations about campus diversity. Research should continue to hold institutions accountable for the use and presentation of demographic information so that the consequences for international students are considered and addressed, therefore minimizing the impact of racial projects.

References

Ahmed, Sara. (2006). Doing Diversity Work in Higher Education in Australia. *Educational Philosophy and Theory* 38, no. 6: 745–768.

Aschaiek, Sharon. (2013). Supporting African Scholars: A $22.5-Million Donation from MasterCard Foundation Will Bring Bright Young Students to U of T. *University of Toronto Magazine*, June 19. https://magazine.utoronto.ca/people/students/supporting-african-scholars-mastercard-foundation/.

Aschaiek, Sharon. (2017). U of T Gains Global Edge: Applications from Several Countries Soar as International Students Rethink Where to Attend University. *University of Toronto Magazine*, April 20. https://magazine.utoronto.ca/campus/u-of-t-gains-global-edge-international-students-ted-sargent-sharon-aschaiek/.

Buckner, Elizabeth, Scott Clerk, Adriana Marroquin, and You Zhang. (2020). Strategic Benefits, Symbolic Commitments: How Canadian Colleges and Universities Frame Internationalization. *Canadian Journal of Higher Education/Revue canadienne d'enseignement supérieur* 50, no. 4: 20–36.

Buckner, Elizabeth, Punita Lumb, Zahra Jafarova, Phoebe Kang, Adriana Marroquin, and You Zhang. (2021). Diversity without Race: How University Internationalization Strategies Discuss International Students. *Journal of International Students* 11, no. S1: 32–49. https://doi.org/10.32674/jis.v11iS1.3842.

Chang, Suzanna. (2011, June 2). Faces of '14 after First Year: What Six First-Year Students Have to Say about Their Experiences at U of T So Far. *University of Toronto Magazine*. https://magazine.utoronto.ca/people/students/reflections-on-freshman-year-first-year-at-university-of-toronto/.

Easton, Megan. (2006, June 10). Awards of Excellence: U of T Alumni Association (UTAA) Awards of Excellence Ceremony. *University of Toronto Magazine*. https://magazine.utoronto.ca/people/alumni-donors/u-of-t-alumni-awards-of-excellence-2006/.

Easton, Megan. (2019, April 23). Her Extraordinary Journey: Judith Schurek Fled the Hungarian Revolution and Studied at U of T. Now, She Supports Scholarships for International Students. *University of Toronto Magazine*. https://magazine.utoronto.ca/people/alumni-donors/her-extraordinary-journey/.

Faught, Brad. (2003, June 13). Global Village: Once a Private Residence, Cumberland House Is Now a Thriving Social Centre for Almost 4,000 International Students. *University of Toronto Magazine*. https://magazine.utoronto.ca/campus/places/cumberland-house-international-student-centre-u-of-t/.

Ford, Karly Sarita, and Ashley N. Patterson. (2019). "Cosmetic Diversity": University Websites and the Transformation of Race Categories. *Journal of Diversity in Higher Education* 12, no. 2: 99–114. https://doi.org/10.1037/dhe0000092.

Gertler, Meric S. (2015a, April 1). A Global Talent Destination: U of T's Ability to Attract International Graduate Students Is Important to Our – and Ontario's – Long-Term Success. *University of Toronto Magazine*. https://magazine.utoronto.ca/campus/a-global-talent-destination-international-graduate-students-meric-gertler/.

Gertler, Meric S. (2015b, October). *Three Priorities: A Discussion Paper*. University of Toronto. https://threepriorities.utoronto.ca/wp-content/uploads/2015/10/Three-Priorities-Discussion-Paper.pdf.

Gertler, Meric S. (2021, April 22). Attracting Top Talent to Canada: Canada Could Invest in a "Moonshot" to Recruit the World's Outstanding Scientists Engineers, Artists and Scholars. *University of Toronto Magazine*. https://magazine.utoronto.ca/research-ideas/culture-society/attracting-top-talent-to-canada-meric-gertler/.

Guo, Yan, and Shibao Guo. (2017). Internationalization of Canadian Higher Education: Discrepancies between Policies and International Student Experiences. *Studies in Higher Education* 42, no. 5: 851–868. http://doi.org/10.1080/030750 79.2017.1293874.

Heng, Tang T. (2019). Understanding the Heterogeneity of International Students' Experiences: A Case Study of Chinese International Students in U.S. Universities. *Journal of Studies in International Education* 23, no. 5: 607–623. https://doi.org/10.1177/1028315319829880.

Houshmand, Sara, Lisa B. Spanierman, and Romin W. Tafarodi. (2014). Excluded and Avoided: Racial Microaggressions Targeting Asian International Students in Canada. *Cultural Diversity and Ethnic Minority Psychology* 20, no. 3: 377–388. https://doi.org/10.1037/a0035404.

Kaye, Marcia. (2017, September 13). For This Syrian Grad Student, a Fresh Start: Denied Re-Entry into the U.S. to Complete His Studies in Public Health, Khaled Almilaji Finds a Warm Welcome at U of T. *University of Toronto Magazine*. https://magazine.utoronto.ca/people/students/for-this-syrian-grad-student-a-fresh-start-khaled-almilaji-marcia-kaye/.

Lanthier, Jennifer. (2017, September 17). U of T: Still Defying Gravity: President Meric Gertler Looks Ahead to His Second Term. *University of Toronto Magazine*. https://magazine.utoronto.ca/campus/u-of-t-still-defying-gravity-meric-gertler-jennifer-lanthier/.

Leary, Tamara, Keith Hotchkiss, and Alana Robb. (2016). "International Students." In Cox, D. G. H. and Strange, C. C. (Eds), *Serving Diverse Students in Canadian Higher Education*. (pp. 100–127). Montreal & Kingston: McGill-Queen's University Press.

McCartney, Dale M. (2021). A Brief History of 50 Years of International Student Policy in Canada. *Canadian Journal of Higher Education* 51, no. 3: 33–50.

Miller-Idriss, Cynthia, Jonathan Z. Friedman, and Jennifer Auerbach. (2019). Jumping, Horizon Gazing, and Arms Wide: Marketing Imagery and the Meaning of Study Abroad in the USA. *Higher Education* 78, no. 6: 1091–1107.

Naylor, David. (2007, September 21). Towards 2030: How Will We Preserve Excellence at the University of Toronto? *University of Toronto Magazine.* https://magazine.utoronto.ca/campus/towards-2030-david-naylor-u-of-t-plan-for-future/.

Naylor, David. (2009, March 16). Going Global: We Must Prepare U of T for a Borderless World. *University of Toronto Magazine.* https://magazine.utoronto.ca/campus/going-global-2/.

Naylor, David. (2011, June 14). Meeting Global Challenges: U of T Is Teaching Future Leaders to Think Creatively across Disciplines. *University of Toronto Magazine.* https://magazine.utoronto.ca/campus/university-of-toronto-as-a-global-institution/.

Ndikubwayezu, Gilber, Scott Anderson, Megan Easton, Rebecca Gao, Matthew DiMera, and Cynthia Macdonald. (2021, September 23). Come from Away: These Seven International Students and Alumni Are among the Thousands Who Contribute to Scholarly and Cultural Life at U of T. *University of Toronto Magazine.* https://magazine.utoronto.ca/people/students/come-from-away-international-students/.

Omi, Michael, and Howard Winant. (2014). *Racial Formation in the United States.* New York: Routledge/Taylor and Francis Group.

Scott, Colin, Saba Safdar, Roopa Desai Trilokekar, and Amira El Masri. (2015). International Students as "Ideal Immigrants" in Canada: A Disconnect between Policy Makers' Assumptions and the Lived Experiences of International Students. *Comparative and International Education* 43, no. 3. https://doi.org/10.5206/cie-eci.v43i3.9261.

Singh, Simran. (2017). "UBC International Students 'Displace' Domestic Students in Some Academic Programs: REPORT." *The Daily Hive* (May 17, 2017). https://dailyhive.com/vancouver/ubc-foreign-domestic-students.

Smith, Clayton. (2016). International Student Success. *Strategic Enrollment Management Quarterly* 4, no. 2: 61–73.

Staff. (2016, December 19). Pearson Scholarships Aim to Attract World's Brightest Students: Program Named for Lester B. Pearson Would Offer 37 International Students Full Tuition for Four Years. *University of Toronto Magazine.* https://magazine.utoronto.ca/campus/pearson-scholarships-aim-to-attract-worlds-brightest-students-to-u-of-t/.

Stein, Sharon, and Vanessa Oliveira de Andreotti. (2016). Cash, Competition, or Charity: International Students and the Global Imaginary. *Higher Education* 72, no. 2: 225–239. https://doi.org/10.1007/s10734-015-9949-8.

Toller, Carol. (2017, September 13). On a Mission of Compassion: The Recipient of a Lester B. Pearson International Scholarship, Deborah Emilia Solomon Wants to Devote Her Engineering Career "to the Service of Others". *University of Toronto Magazine.* https://magazine.utoronto.ca/people/students/on-a-mission-of-compassion-deborah-emilia-solomon-lester-b-pearson-international-scholarship-carol-toller/.

University of Toronto. (2008). *Towards 2030: A Third Century of Excellence at the University of Toronto, A Synthesis Report.* http://www.towards2030.utoronto.ca/files/2030_REDUXv7.pdf.

University of Toronto. (2021, February 8). *Enrolment Report 2020-21.* https://planningandbudget.utoronto.ca/wp-content/uploads/2021/06/Enrolment-Report-2020-21-FINAL.pdf.
University of Toronto. (2022, March 1). *Tuition Fee Schedules for Publicly-Funded Programs 2022-23.* https://planningandbudget.utoronto.ca/wp-content/uploads/2022/04/2022-23-Tuition-Fee-Report_FINAL-Mar-31-2022.pdf.
Webb, Margaret. (2015, December 10). A Life in Blue and White: From Champion Student Athlete to UTSC's Principal Bruce Kidd Ushers in a New Era at the University's Eastern Campus. *University of Toronto Magazine.* https://magazine.utoronto.ca/people/faculty-staff/bruce-kidd-a-life-in-blue-and-white-new-era-at-utsc-margaret-webb/.
Windscheid, Leon, Lynn Bowes-Sperry, Deborah L. Kidder, Ho Kwan Cheung, Michèle Morner, and Filip Lievens. (2016). Actions Speak Louder Than Words: Outsiders' Perceptions of Diversity Mixed Messages. *Journal of Applied Psychology* 101, no. 9: 1329–1341. https://doi.org/10.1037/apl0000107.
Wu, Cary, Abidin Kusno, Ann H. Kim, Carol Liao, Dennis Kao, Guida Man, Hae Yeon Choo, Jing Zhao, Min Zhou, and Muyang Li. (2021). "As Asian Canadian Scholars, We Must #StopAsianHate by Fighting All Forms of Racism." *The Conversation, Canada* (April 15). https://theconversation.com/as-asian-canadian-scholars-we-must-stopasianhate-by-fighting-all-forms-of-racism-157743.
Zhang, Zuochen, and George Zhou. (2010). Understanding Chinese International Students at a Canadian University: Perspectives, Expectations, and Experiences. *Comparative and International Education* 39, no. 3. https://doi.org/10.5206/cie-eci.v39i3.9162.
Zhou, George, and Zuochen Zhang. (2014). A Study of the First Year International Students at a Canadian University: Challenges and Experiences with Social Integration. *Comparative and International Education* 43, no. 2. https://doi.org/10.5206/cie-eci.v43i2.9253.

13 An East Coast Racial Reckoning

International Students and the Politics of Race at Dalhousie University

Ajay Parasram, Madison Gateman, and Amaan Kazmi

Introduction: Canada's Ocean Playground?

A hundred years ago, the Bluenose Schooner was launched in Nova Scotia. Today its image adorns provincial license plates with the slogan, "Canada's Ocean Playground." Global perceptions of Canada, in general, and the east coast city of Halifax, in particular, tend to emphasize rugged coasts, thick wool toques, and foot stomping sea shanties paired with the welcoming roar of "sociables" as pub dwellers down their India Pale Ales and iconic rum and cokes. This social experience awaits any tourist "on the Halifax pier," but once the season is over, it is the international students clustered around, what Kwak et al. in this volume describe as, the "intellectual periphery" of Halifax's five universities that mainly comprise the "come from aways". As winter descends, students begin to see that beneath the shanties, rum, and "India" pale ales lurks uncomfortable imperial nostalgia that works to undermine public engagement with the legacies of race inherited through a web of empire that constitutes Halifax.

Established in 1818, Dalhousie University has been present for most of the settler-colonial period. Now in its third century, the university is taking steps to try to reconcile its role in supporting the enslavement of Africans and the theft and genocide of Mi'kmaw land and people. At the same time, building the complement of international students is a priority for Dalhousie, and while there is no ostensible connection between the two, diversification and decolonization are related tasks in the Canadian academe. In this chapter, we focus on Dalhousie's third-century efforts to "internationalize" as a core part of the university's strategic priorities with close attention to the last decade. We situate the institutional plan amidst the evolving politics of race in Halifax. In section one, we discuss efforts to expand the university's ability to attract and retain international students. In section two, we describe the politics of race in Halifax to better understand the campus as an embedded part of the city. In section three, we discuss some of our findings based on interviews with Chinese and Indian international

DOI: 10.4324/b23160-17

students to privilege the voice and experiences of those "come from aways" studying in Halifax. We conclude with some early observations about how student experiences speak to some measured success but also a need for greater institutional calibration of services with respect to the rapidly changing urban environment.

International Students by the Numbers

In 2013, international students comprised 14.5% of the student population at Dalhousie. This increased to 18.6% in 2016 and 21% in 2019 (*International Opportunities With Countries Of Focus* 2018 and *Dalhousie University's International Strategy* 2017, 8). According to the latest 2021–2026 Strategic Plan, international enrolment at Dalhousie has grown by more than 300% over the last decade, with students coming to Dalhousie from more than 120 countries (*Canada's International Education Strategy (2019–2024)* 2020).

The majority of international students come from China and India. For example, in September 2019, of the 1531 new international students enrolled at Dalhousie, 518 were from China and 310 were from India (*Dalhousie University's International Strategy* 2017). Notably, this dominance of Indian and Chinese international students reflects larger Canada-wide enrollment trends. When examining recent data released by Immigration, Refugees, and Citizenship Canada (IRCC), 621,565 study visas for international students were issued in 2021. Of this 621,565 total students, Indian students accounted for 217,410 of the study visas issued, with Chinese students at 105,265 (*ICEF* 2022). This is over half of all the study visas issued for international students from two source countries alone.

Finally, of the 4,200 international students that came to Dalhousie in 2019, 70% came to study as undergraduate students and 30% came for graduate studies (*International Opportunities With Countries Of Focus* 2018). The majority of international students are coming to Dalhousie to join the Faculties of Science, Management, Engineering, and Computer Science, although as discussed below, Dalhousie's strategic planners have repeatedly emphasized the need to diversify the source countries and programs that international students are enrolling in (*Internationalization and global engagement at Dalhousie* 2020, 11).

Budget and International Student Tuition Fees

In 2008, 54% of Dalhousie's revenue came from predominantly government sources, with only 34% coming from tuition and fees. In the most recent 2022 budget, 44.3 percent of Dalhousie's day-to-day operating funds are set to come from the provincial government, with 45.7 percent coming from tuition fees (Balser and Nason 2019). Nova Scotia committed to increasing its financial contribution to Dalhousie's (and other institutions') operational budget annually by 1% between 2019 – 2024 in exchange for an agreement to cap annual tuition increases at 3% per year for Nova Scotian students. This agreement does not apply to international students, however, and while the increase in public investment is welcome, it needs to be understood in the context of a 10% decrease in public funding relative to other funding over the last decade (Laroche 2019). International undergraduate students beginning studies in September 2021 were required to pay an additional $8,430 per term, on top of their regular tuition fees (which range from $5,393-$12,955 per term). For Masters students (non-thesis based), this fee was $16,860 per year on top of their regular tuition fees (which vary from $8,300-$28,000 for full-time studies) (*International and Exchange students – International tuition fees* 2022). As of Sept. 2019, doctoral students are no longer charged differential fees, so they pay what domestic students do, making the financial situation of international students quite varied by level of study.

Since at least 2013, but likely for much longer, these differential fees for international students have been controversial in the Dalhousie community. In the December 2013 *100 Days of Listening Report* (2013), the committee noted that "the differential fee for international graduate students is compromising Dalhousie's competitiveness in attracting top graduate students, posing a hardship for students and for researchers". The *Report* noted that the university "has had to rely to a great extent on increasing enrolment to balance the budget as a result of declining government support and constrained tuition increases" (*100 days of Listening final report – Dalhousie University* 2013, 126). Dalhousie has used this same justification for a decade – that the tuition fees of international students are required to be so high to offload the cost of running the university and government cuts.

This controversy became more public in 2019 when Dalhousie's Budget Advisory Committee (BAC) recommended dramatic increases in international tuition fees. These increases included an additional $1,473 per year over four years for international students in undergraduate and non-thesis master's programs. For 2019–2020, this amounted to an average increase of 8.1% (Balser and Nason 2019). In response to this increase, Dalhousie International Students' Association (DISA) hosted a rally in April 2019 outside the university's Halifax campus and delivered a petition calling for an end to the high tuition fees paid by international students. This petition was signed by more than 1,000 students (Gillis 2019). In response to this outcry, the BAC argued that tuition fees were "the only avenue available to the university to increase revenue and ensure our programs, our people, and our supports and services can receive sustainable funding" (Balser and Nason 2019). The BAC continues that although international students add greatly to the diversity and richness of the campus, they put a larger strain on university support and teaching systems than domestic students do.

"Internationalization" at Dalhousie

This dramatic expansion of Dalhousie's international student population over the past decade, and the tuition revenue that comes with it, is not accidental. In fact, it represents a well-documented and concerted effort on the part of Dalhousie's decision-makers to attract and retain more international students in recent years. As Beck notes in this volume, internationalization is an "ideological frame" in Canadian universities, and we can see this develop institutionally in strategic plans published over the last decade.

In his first 100 working days in office, former Dalhousie President Richard Florizone undertook a structured program of meetings, consultations, and data gathering with stakeholders and the general public to determine the strategic direction of the university. Overall, thousands of people connected with Florizone in more than 40 large group consultations, 500 smaller meetings, and over 700 online submissions. The *100 Days of Listening Report* from December 2013 was the final report from these consultations, and it serves as a helpful first source to better understand subsequent strategic planning since 2013 (McNutt 2014).

International students featured heavily in the *Report*, particularly the issue of retention between first and second year, where Dalhousie was about 7% below comparator universities. According to the *Report*, "this is a major indicator from students that the university needs to provide more support for international students to assist their transition to Halifax and Canada and to support their academic success while at Dalhousie" (*100 days of Listening final report – Dalhousie University* 2013, 62–68). Moreover, the report noted that success in the future relies on helping "students integrate into the Dalhousie community well and achieve academic success" (*100 days of Listening final report – Dalhousie University* 2013, 53). The *Report* noted that in the next 3–5 years, Dalhousie Student Services plans to focus on student academic success supports, particularly strengthening and integrating career counselling and planning with advising and access services for all students, and "paying particular attention to improving academic supports to improve successful persistence of international students" (*100 days of Listening final report – Dalhousie University* 2013, 66). No recent data has been released by Dalhousie related to how successful these efforts at improving retention have been, however, in its most recent strategy (published April 2021 and discussed below), Dalhousie continues to emphasize the need to "strengthen and maximize retention" (*Exceptional student experience* 2022).

The *100 Days of Listening Report* also referenced Dalhousie's broader international strategy, which was first approved by the Dalhousie Board of Governors on December 19, 2013, and later revised and re-published in April 2017. Dalhousie's International Strategy (2017–2020) is titled "From A National University to An International University: Building on International Opportunities That Inspire" (*Dalhousie University's International Strategy* 2017). Dalhousie has yet to publish an updated version of its international strategy.

In brief, Dalhousie's international strategy from 2013 until now has focused on international recruitment, international mobility, internationalization of academic programs, support to and retention of international students, international research and development and the engagement of international alumni. The primary focus of this chapter is on international student support and retention, although international recruitment (primarily the recruitment of students from Asia) and the internationalization of academic programs (the introduction of global perspectives in programs and the development of intercultural competence) are also relevant.

In terms of institutional student supports, Dalhousie recognizes that "much needs to be done beyond language training, for example, to support international students so they can succeed in academic, social, cultural and economic contexts" (*Dalhousie University's International Strategy* 2017, 10–11). Existing supports for international students are spread across several units as well as within the individual Faculties. For example, the Writing Centre, College of Continuing Education, and Advising and Accommodation Services all support international students in different ways at Dalhousie, particularly through language and academic supports. This matches similar strategies as other Canadian institutions, although it does not go as far as some in terms of orienting students to the settler-colonial context and urban environment beyond the university (see Luo and Wilkinson; Oliveira Soares et. al.). In addition, the Dalhousie International Centre in Halifax, Nova Scotia, exists to "support international students throughout their time at Dalhousie University" and to offer "services and programs designed to ease their transition to life in Canada and at Dal, to help our students succeed academically, and prepare for graduation and beyond" (*About the International Centre* 2022). Finally, on-campus student-run organizations such as the Dalhousie International Students' Association, the Dalhousie Student Union, the Dalhousie Black, Indigenous, and People of Colour Caucus (BIPOCUS), Department-specific groups (such as the Computer Science Society, Engineering Societies,

Management Society, etc.) and Geographical/Religious/Cultural groups (such as the Dalhousie Chinese Society, Indian Subcontinental Students Association) offer additional, peer-based supports to students. International students have also told us that much of the networking – both social and academic – takes place on social media platforms, so international students are self-organizing to support themselves, especially in the context of the COVID-19 pandemic.

In addition to the *100 Days Report* and the *International Strategy*, there have been two strategic directions since 2013. The first was approved by the Dalhousie Board of Governors on 24 June 2014 and was based in part on the findings published in the *100 Days Report*. What came forth was *Inspiration and Impact: Dalhousie Strategic Direction 2014–2018*. Annual progress reports from the strategic plan reveal a heavy focus on international student retention, and to a lesser extent, student supports. Much of what was captured in this first Strategic Direction was captured in the six key areas of the international strategy.

Additionally, of note in this strategic plan was the identification of inclusion and diversity as one of the university's critical priorities under Charter 5.2. In early January 2015, President Richard Florizone accelerated and intensified the work under Charter 5.2. This included input from faculty, staff, and students from diverse communities across the university, and the outcome of this work was the publication of the "Belong: Supporting an Inclusive and Diverse University" report in March 2015. The report asked: "What would Dalhousie look like if all of us felt we truly belonged?" According to the report:

> Our meetings confirmed pervasive, and often extreme, experiences of isolation and marginality. Many students, faculty, and staff reported profound levels of disrespect... The challenges of exclusion due to hierarchies and bureaucracy are too often compounded by systemic misogyny, sexism, racism, ethnocentrism, heterosexism, colonialism, socioeconomic disadvantage, ableism, ageism, sexualized violence, harassment, and discrimination. In many cases, exclusion and marginalization are unintentional – a matter of unquestioned assumptions, lack of knowledge, or inadequate skill. While that may make it a challenge to recognize the barriers to inclusion, the effects of exclusion are profound, even when not intentional.
>
> (6–7)

From here, the approach taken by the Report was one that focused "not only on the institutional mechanisms required to support an inclusive and diverse university, but also on the ways in which each of us must take responsibility for supporting inclusion and diversity" (Belong 2015: 7).

194   *Ajay Parasram et al.*

The committee called for everyone – from members of the senior administration to members of student social clubs – to build an understanding of how we (intentionally and unintentionally) include and exclude members of our community; to take steps to bridge and respect differences; and to hold ourselves accountable for change. A new Vice-Provost position was established in 2019 and named for Equity and Inclusion, and new institutional measures across the university have been underway since. Much of the emphasis and purpose of these initiatives were domestic in nature, specifically in terms of developing better ways of serving the Indigenous and African Nova Scotian students who have been historically harmed and underserved by the university over its history. As Das Gupta and Gomez in this volume argue, however, using international students as a marker of equity, diversity, and inclusion (EDI) is rife with problems as their integration into the university comes on fundamentally inequitable terms due to the enormous differences in tuition.

Finally, in April 2021, Dalhousie's Board of Governors approved Dalhousie's 2021–2026 Strategic Plan, titled "Our Third Century Promise", or "Si'st Kasqimtlnaqnipunqekl Teli L'wi'tmasimk" in Mi'kmaw. This recent strategic direction echoes many of the same themes as the previous strategic plan: delivering "excellent student support programs and services that increase student retention by reflecting evolving student needs and identities", and "expanded recruitment, retention, and academic success of international students" (*Exceptional student experience* 2022). Moreover, the most recent strategic plan emphasizes the work of Dalhousie's Diversity and Inclusiveness Strategy and prioritizes "actions that reflect Dalhousie's commitment to an anti-racist culture" (*Inclusive excellence* 2022). Dalhousie is currently planning for the implementation of these goals, which when published will offer further insight into how Dalhousie plans to increase retention, offer international students additional support, and commit to an "anti-racist culture" in practice.

Racial Politics in Halifax

The politics of race in Halifax has a long and evolving history, though anti-Black and anti-Indigenous racism, have shaped its long-term dynamics. The destruction of Africville, a historic and independent community of people of African ancestry in the 1960s, overlapped with the rise of the civil rights movement in Nova Scotia and the Black radical tradition embodied by community leaders like siblings Burnley Allen "Rocky" Jones and Lynn Jones. Collaboration between the African Nova Scotian community and Mi'kmaw community has led to important programs like the Indigenous Blacks and Mi'kmaq Initiative housed in the Dalhousie Law School, and the Transition Year Program housed in the College of Continuing Education.

Although there have been important institutional wins over the last several decades, this is more testimony to the organizational and political acumen of community leaders that have worked to carve out this institutional space and protect it over decades. Racial politics in Halifax has been historically hostile to confronting structural white supremacy within institutions and the city, even when very modest attempts were made by people like Mi'kmaw historian Dan Paul to consider name changes and statue removals of colonial officials like Edward Cornwallis who is responsible for scalping proclamations paying different levels of reward for the scalps of Mi'kmaq men, women, and children (Paul 2006). Despite being a hub of imperial trade relations connecting the Caribbean, Africa, Britain, and Canada, white Nova Scotians have been both fragile and hostile in confronting any contemporary implications of these historical imbrications (Parasram 2019).

In the last decade, key flashpoints in the politics of race include the increased presence and visibility of international students and new immigrants, many of whom are non-white. Movements against settler-colonial "development" projects that do not respect treaty obligations with Mi'kmaq people in their design and scope like the failed Alton Gas project have been lightning rod issues, simultaneously drawing ire from some settlers and inspiring solidarity building across racial lines as well (Pictou 2021). Recently the question of sovereignty with respect to Mi'kmaq fisheries came to a boil, with white settler fishers violently attacking Mi'kmaq fishing boats and lobster storage facilities, all with little intervention from provincial and federal governments and police forces (Parasram, forthcoming 2023). The movement for Black Lives, with leaders such as the poet and professor El Jones, has been leading public discussion about the need to defund the police and refund society, considering extreme racial discrimination in policing that continues to this day (Ajadi, et al. 2022). Since 2015 Nova Scotians have been coming to terms with the findings of the Truth and Reconciliation Commission report, which has put a spotlight on what Indigenous survivors have always known: Canadian institutions ostensibly built to "educate" were instead genocidal regimes designed to either assimilate or destroy Indigenous people and culture.

The surface-level representation of Halifax as a fun and friendly party town speaks to what scholars have described in other geographical contexts as one of "ignorance, ambivalence, and acknowledgement" as well as "settler-insecurity" (Reid-Hresko and Warren 2022; Midzain-Gobin 2021). Into this slow cooker of racial politics, international students have been arriving in increasingly larger numbers and increasingly from places that were also connected to the web of the British Empire, most notably India and China. This broad society-level context does not tell the full story of racial politics, as there are many everyday expressions of racial tension in the city stemming from microaggressions to violent attacks against people of color and Indigenous people.

Student Experiences

We conducted semi-structured interviews with 10 international students at Dalhousie who come from China (2) and India (8). Of the 10, two identify as female and eight identify as male. One identifies as bisexual, and the rest are heterosexual. Nine come from middle-class backgrounds in their respective countries, while one is working class. All students come from STEM disciplines. One student was based at Dalhousie's Agricultural campus in the nearby town of Truro, and thus is not living in the Halifax area. The observations of our interviewees speak to the human experience of race and racialization amidst the university's developing internationalization strategies. Importantly, while most students were well informed about the many avenues Dalhousie offers to support students, aside from a few positive experiences with the writing center and International Student Centre, most students noted they would be more inclined to turn to their families back home and immediate friend circle for help long before consulting the university.

Interestingly, most students said they have not experienced any significant racism, though during the interview, they would often go on to outline everyday examples of racism. These everyday examples include instances in public spaces, such as the grocery store, where people might imply that they do not belong due to linguistic or cultural difference from the white majority population. Most students say they did not experience racism in the classroom and on campus, though during the interviews they noted challenging power dynamics in navigating relationships with professors and other students. The more overt racism they experienced came in public places off campus, including transportation, hospitals, and places of work. One student explained that he experienced a great deal of micromanagement and aggression from a white supervisor at the grocery store that he worked at, ultimately leading him to resign and instead work at a small grocery store catering to Asian clientele and managed by a person from their hometown. When asked what made the new job comfortable, he recounted that his boss trusted him to get his work done as he saw fit, that it was understood that he could study while working and communicate with family and friends back home so long as customers were always given priority.

All students agree that the Canada that they had imagined was different from the Canada they experienced, though not in uniform ways. For example, some students were surprised to find how poorly organized public transportation was in the cities of Halifax and Truro, while others experienced moving through the city with relative ease. This is partially due to the urban geography of the city itself, with students living near campus more likely to have positive experiences with transit. In one instance, "Davendra" described the overt racism he and another international student experienced in a taxi, where the driver told him, "Canadians do not want international students, they only want their money."

Finding housing was difficult for many. One student, "Rajesh," living off-campus, told us that he had to stay for two months in an Airbnb because of a shortage in housing. Moreover, he also felt that Canadian students were being favored over international students for placement in residences, all while international students face extra hurdles to find employment. Rajesh made offers on 20 apartments before finally finding one, suggesting that it is not only housing supply but also the preference of landlords for "Canadians" that plays a role in the housing instability faced by international students. Rajesh's experience of Dalhousie's apathetic attitude towards its international students reminded one author (Amaan) of his first few days of coming to terms with invisibility in Kjipuktuk. International students had been advised to arrive a few days before Canadian students for "international orientation" and, even though they had bought meal plans, no provision was made for their meals during those days.

Another student, "Lin," who was able to find housing noted that she lived with six other people and had to schedule times to access common facilities, especially due to the COVID-19 pandemic. Interestingly, this student's perception of Canada was radically different from all others interviewed in part because rather than spending most of her time with other international students or domestic Canadian students, she ended up developing friendships with Indigenous students. Lin learned about Mi'kmaw culture early on, as she attended the annual Mawio'mi early in her studies at Dalhousie. A Mawio'mi in Mi'kmaw culture refers to a gathering of spiritual and cultural significance. Indigenous students at Dalhousie started the tradition of hosting a Mawio'mi for the first time in 2010, and it has been an annual event ever since, aside for during the early stages of the COVID-19 pandemic when gatherings were not permitted (Benwah 2005; Reeder 2018). After attending the Mawio'mi, Lin visited the Indigenous Students' Centre and took an interest in the Mi'kmaw language. As a Mandarin speaker, she understands and values specificity in language and found similarities between Mandarin and Mi'kmaw without needing to sieve either through English or French. Lin reported feeling much more welcome and accepted when at the Indigenous Student Centre as compared with the International Centre and on campus more generally.

Aside from Lin's experience, most international students we spoke with found that the culture on campus was not very diverse, but in fact very siloed and cliquey. As Rajesh described it to us, "[I]t's so silent here," compared with "back home." As he explains, "[M]ost of the talk is transactional … people don't have time here for anything besides their work." The experience of eating in the dining hall was described as one in which you stuck to people from your country of origin. Moreover, despite efforts to develop friendships with Canadian students, most international students found it much easier to develop relationships with other international students. For example one Chinese student, "Jing," told us, she experienced her first Indian meal after being invited to the home of a classmate from India: "It was a new experience for me because she [the Indian friend] used [her] hands to take the food … she gave me a spoon and it was the first time I ate Indian food, it is really, really good [and] nice." It was clear that for most students, they equated "Canadian" with "white" although noted that the "Canadian" students regardless of their racial background tended to stay away from international students for one reason or another.

The students noted that the COVID-19 pandemic introduced specific kinds of challenges due to online learning. Students were split on their views about online, hybrid, and in-person teaching, though most admitted that there was less isolation when the option for in-person learning returned. They relied mostly on social media forums to get information from within their national diaspora groups, and most suggested that interacting with the formal university spaces set up for them like the International Centre or Writing Centre was not very practically useful. One student, Akash, was very enthusiastic about these spaces, however. For many students, Dalhousie was not the number one choice of institution, but the open racism in the United States since 2016 was an important part of many students' decision to come to Canada. While many students expressed a desire to stay in Canada, most indicated they would seek their next degree or strive to make a permanent home outside of Nova Scotia.

Conclusions

While the institutional efforts aimed at internationalization and, to a lesser extent, decolonization, have played an important role in the growth of international students at Dalhousie, the degree to which students are well prepared to navigate life in a settler-colonial city that is struggling to come to terms with its colonial past and present is suspect. International students were largely unaware of Canada's ongoing colonial project until arriving in Canada and interacting with Indigenous students, as Lin explained to us and as Luo and Wilkinson explain in this volume. Retention and student satisfaction with life in Halifax and nearby areas remains an important challenge linking the politics of race more generally to the ideological frame of internationalization at the university (see Beck) With respect to existing services and spaces serving international students at Dalhousie, there appears to be some important work needed to calibrate these services in a way that is more linked to the urban politics (i.e., housing, race, integration opportunities) to ensure that core material concerns such as safe and sustainable housing on the one hand, and interpersonal concerns such as bridging cultural divides between multicultural domestic students and international students can be fostered. To be clear, these kinds of relationships are developing on their own, especially within student-led spaces such as the Mawio'io, intramural sports, or peer-driven social media, but to some extent the existing institutional spaces do not appear to be the go-to hubs for information, help, and opportunities. it is not the case that these relationships are not being formed. By contrasting the institutional developments of the last decades with the lived experiences of international students from India and China, it is clear that the presence of some institutional support at the university is not adequately calibrated to helping students navigate the racial politics of the city of Halifax. The struggles to include domestic students in international social networks were noted by many, and students speculated that the economic pressures faced by both domestic and international students tended to keep everyone too busy to meaningfully get to know one another. It is clear that institutional measures cannot be treated separately from the broader political and economic milieu the university is based in. While international students from Asia rarely reported instances of racism on campus and did not often use university services, some degree of preparation for the racial politics of Halifax would surely help them navigate the city.

References

"100 Days of Listening Final Report – Dalhousie University." 2013. *Issuu*. December 23. https://issuu.com/dalhousieuniversity/docs/100days-report-01-full-dec23/25.

"About the International Centre." 2022. Dalhousie University International Centre. Accessed June 30. https://www.dal.ca/campus_life/international-centre/contact-us/about-us.html.

Ajadi, Tari, Critchley, Harry, Jones, El, and Rodgers, Julia. 2022. "Defunding The Police: Defining The Way Forward for HRM." January 22. https://www.halifax.ca/sites/default/files/documents/city-hall/boards-committees-commissions/220117bopc1021.pdf.

Balser, Teri, and Ian Nason. 2019. "Responding to Your Feedback: International Fees and Supports at Dalhousie." *Dalhousie News*. April 5. https://www.dal.ca/news/2019/04/05/responding-to-your-feedback--international-fees-and-supports-at-.html.

Beagan, Brenda, et al. 2015. "Belong: Supporting an Inclusive and Diverse University." Report and Recommendations of the Committee for Dalhousie's Strategic Initiative on Diversity and Inclusiveness (Charter 5.2). March 5. https://cdn.dal.

ca/content/dam/dalhousie/pdf/sites/biosignal-lab/dalhousie_belong_report. PDF.
lt_f05db60d1e03d8cb96ce3e1597faecdc.res/dalhousie_belong_report.PDF
Benwah, Jasen Sylvester. 2005. *LNU'K – Mi'kmaq History and People: The Pow Wow or Mawio'mi*. July 25. https://www.benoitfirstnation.ca/mikmaw_article31_powwow.html.
Canada, Global Affairs. 2020. "Canada's International Education Strategy (2019-2024)." *GAC*. October 19. https://www.international.gc.ca/education/strategy-2019-2024-strategie.aspx?lang=eng+https%3A%2F%2Fcdn.dal.ca%2Fcontent%2Fdam%2Fdalhousie%2Fpdf%2Fabout%2FStrategic-Planning%2FDalhousie-University-Strategic-Plan-2021-2026.pdf.
"Dalhousie University's International Strategy (Plan 2017-2020)." 2017. https://cdn.dal.ca/content/dam/dalhousie/pdf/dept/international-relations/DALHOUSIE%20INTERNATIONAL%20STRATEGY%202017-2020-June-2018.pdf.
"Exceptional Student Experience." 2022. *Dalhousie University Strategic Plan (2021-26)*. Accessed June 30. https://www.dal.ca/about-dal/leadership-and-vision/strategic-plan/our-shared-plan/exceptional-student-experience.html.
Gillis, Wyatt. 2019. "Halifax Students Demand End to High Tuition Fees for International Students." *Thestar.com*. April 9. https://www.thestar.com/halifax/2019/04/09/halifax-students-demand-end-to-high-tuition-fees-for-international-students.html.
"Inclusive Excellence." 2022. *Dalhousie University Strategic Plan (2021-26)*. Accessed June 30. https://www.dal.ca/about-dal/leadership-and-vision/strategic-plan/our-shared-plan/inclusive-excellence.html.
"International and Exchange Students – International Tuition Fees." 2022. *Dalhousie University – Money Matters*. Accessed June 30. https://www.dal.ca/admissions/money_matters/tuition_payments/Tuition_Fees/International_Students.html.
"International Opportunities with Countries of Focus." 2018. Dalhousie University. https://cdn.dal.ca/content/dam/dalhousie/pdf/dept/international-relations/International%20Opportunties%20-%20Faculty%20Consultations%202018.pdf.
"International Student Numbers in Canada Rebounded Close to Pre-Pandemic Levels in 2021." 2022. *ICEF Monitor – Market Intelligence for International Student Recruitment*. April 21. https://monitor.icef.com/2022/03/international-student-numbers-in-canada-rebounded-close-to-pre-pandemic-levels-in-2021/.
"Internationalization and Global Engagement at Dalhousie." 2020. April 16. https://cdn.dal.ca/content/dam/dalhousie/pdf/about/Strategic-Planning/Internationalization-and-Global-Engagement.pdf.
Laroche, Jean. 2019. "Province Increases Funding to Universities by 1% per Year | CBC News." *CBC News*. CBC/Radio Canada. September 13. https://www.cbc.ca/news/canada/nova-scotia/province-increases-funding-to-universities-by-1-per-year-1.5282477.
McNutt, Ryan. 2014. "200 Pages of Reading for 100 Days of Listening." *Dalhousie News*. January 16. https://www.dal.ca/news/2014/01/23/200-pages-of-reading-for-100-days-of-listening.html.
Midzain-Gobin, Liam. 2021. "Comfort and Insecurity in the Reproduction of Settler Coloniality." *Critical Studies on Security* 9, no. 3: 212–25. doi:10.1080/21624887.2021.1936834.

Parasram, Ajay. 2019. "Pathological White Fragility and the Canadian Nation." *Studies in Political Economy* 100, no. 2: 194–207. doi:10.1080/07078552.2019. 1646457.

Parasram, Ajay. 2023 (forthcoming). "Pluriversal Sovereignty and the State of IR" *Review of International Studies.*

Paul, Daniel N. 2006. *We Were Not the Savages, First Nations History: The Collision between European and Native… American Civilizations.* Halifax: Fernwood Publishing.

Pictou, Sherry. 2021. "Welastoqiyik and Mi'kmaq Grandmothers – Land/Water Defenders Sharing and Learning Circle: Generating Knowledge for Action." https://www.kairoscanada.org/wp-content/uploads/2021/09/Grandmothers_ Land_Defense_Report_Pictou_2021.pdf.

Reeder, Matt. 2018. "Dal's 9th-Annual Mawio'mi a Chance for Celebration and Reflection." *Dalhousie News.* October 5. https://www.dal.ca/news/2018/10/05/ dal-s-9th-annual-mawio-mi-a-chance-for-celebration-and-reflectio.html.

Reid-Hresko, John, and Jeff R. Warren. 2022. "'A Lot of What We Ride Is Their Land': White Settler Canadian Understandings of Mountain Biking, Indigeneity, and Recreational Colonialism." *Sociology of Sport Journal* 39, no. 1: 108–17. doi:10.1123/ssj.2020-0161.

"Third Century Promise: Dalhousie's 2021-26 Strategic Plan." 2022. *Dalhousie University Strategic Plan (2021–26).* Accessed June 30. https://www.dal.ca/ about-dal/leadership-and-vision/strategic-plan.html.

14 International Students from Asia in a Mid-sized Canadian University

A University of Manitoba Case Study

Yazhi Luo and Lori Wilkinson

Introduction

Although it is not wrong to regard universities as the place for communicating information, ideas, and ideologies, it is unrealistic and naïve to assume that post-secondary institutions are welcoming to all. International research has demonstrated the marginalization experienced by racial minorities and international students (Dovchin 2020). Students from racialized backgrounds report having experienced racism of various kinds and on various levels from being verbally abused to being physically attacked and being side-lined for programs and services to being differentiated by rules and regulations (Brown and Jones 2011). International students are confronted by obstacles ranging from language and cultural differences and pedagogical disparities to a lack of social and financial support for adaptation, but the sufficiency of institutional policies is seldom critically considered as a reason for these challenges (Lee 2015; also see Pang and Smith and de Oliveira Soares et al.). The lack of appropriate international student services and complex federal regulations, coupled with racism and marginalization, increases the burden for international students to navigate their way through their university career.

In order to understand the context of international student integration at the University of Manitoba, we need to understand the history of the land which our institution sits. In this chapter, we describe the traditional land context and discuss various initiatives that are meant to educate the campus community about Indigenous peoples. We then examine the strategies and facilities for equity, diversity, and inclusion at the University of Manitoba and consider how they influence Indigenous and international student experiences in this community. We end the chapter by discussing racism on campus and how the University has responded. Using this context, we can better understand the experiences of international students from Asia on the University of Manitoba campus.

DOI: 10.4324/b23160-18

We Live and Use Traditional Lands

As the University of Manitoba and the City of Winnipeg are situated on Treaty 1 territory, understanding the history and the guardianship of our land has an important influence on our understanding of the experiences of international students on campus. While land acknowledgements have been used by universities and other legal entities in Canada for over a decade, as they have become more commonplace, their influence on our way of thinking has started to wane, and certainly, these treaty acknowledgements have done nothing to reduce the inequality that Indigenous peoples face in 21st-century Canada (Hergesheimer 2016). The University of Manitoba has instituted a land acknowledgement for several years and the institution is now actively striving to develop policy and programming, along with changes to the institutional structure, to better recognize the very important contributions that Indigenous peoples have made to the university, city, province, and country.

The University of Manitoba, established in 1877, is the first university in Western Canada and is located in Winnipeg, the capital city of Manitoba. It is located on the original lands of Anishinaabe, Cree, Oji-Cree, Dakota, and Dene Peoples, and is located on the homeland of the Métis Nation. Drinking water is sourced from Shoal Lake 40 First Nation, an Ojibwa community straddling the provincial borders of Manitoba and Ontario. Shoal Lake has provided clean drinking water, without charge, to the City of Winnipeg since the construction of an aqueduct was completed in 1919 (City of Winnipeg 2022; Shoal Lake First Nation 2019). The aqueduct was built over a traditional burial ground, and the original village was forcibly resettled to make way for the construction, leaving the First Nation virtually isolated for over 100 years until the construction of the "Freedom Road" was completed in 2019 and provided a four-season road to connect the community (Indigenous Services Canada 2019). Despite living on the shores of a body of safe and drinkable water, Shoal Lake band members had to rely on water imported from Kenora to have safe drinking water due to a boil water advisory that lasted 24 years (City of Winnipeg 2022) until the construction of a new water treatment plant was completed in September 2021.

Having some knowledge of territorial acknowledgement allows a discussion of the University of Manitoba in relation to international students and their experiences on campus. In 2021, 2,614 students self-declared an Indigenous status, including First Nations, Métis, Inuit or other heritage (Office of Institutional Analysis 2021b), which makes up 8.4% of the student body, making the University of Manitoba one of the universities with the largest enrolment of Indigenous students in Canada. Among self-declared students, 56% identify as Métis, 41% as First Nations, and 1% as

Inuit (Office of Institutional Analysis 2021b). Students who self-identify with an Indigenous heritage make up 8.9% of undergraduate and 6.1% of graduate students at the University. Enrolment among Indigenous students is slowly growing, increasing from 8.3% of students in 2020 to 8.4% in 2021 (Office of Institutional Analysis 2021c). Sadly, however, Indigenous students remain well under-represented in terms of their actual proportion of the population. The 2021 Census shows that Indigenous people make up 18% of Manitoba's total population and Winnipeg is the census metropolitan area with the largest Indigenous population in Canada with 12.45% of its population having an Indigenous ancestry (Statistics Canada, 2022).

International Students at the University of Manitoba

Currently, the University is home to 31,037 undergraduate and graduate students, with international students representing 115 countries and making up 20.5% of undergraduate students, 35.6% of graduate students, and 22.1% of the overall student population (Office of Institutional Analysis 2021d). Compared to 2020, international student enrolment increased by 7% in 2021, making this the fastest growing segment of the student population. The newest report for the citizenship of students in November 2020 showed that the majority of international students (86.5%) come from Asia (59.5%) and Africa (27%), with China, Nigeria, and India being the top three countries of origin (Office of Institutional Analysis 2021a).

Table 14.1 shows that in 2021, the top five academic programs attracted 87.9% of international undergraduate student enrolment, a slight increase from 2019. The Faculty of Arts and Faculty of Science remain consistent as the top two most popular programs of enrolment for international students. "University 1" is a unique program at the University of Manitoba meant to introduce "undecided" first-year students to different faculties, programs, and majors during their first year without having to "commit"

Table 14.1 Programs with the highest proportions of international *undergraduate* students, University of Manitoba, 2019–2021

Undergraduate Faculty/Program	2021 (%)	2020 (%)	2019 (%)
Science	35.7	34.8	33.0
Arts	27.2	25.0	24.2
University 1	10.8	12.7	14.1
Asper School of Business	8.0	9.1	9.6
Price Faculty of Engineering	6.2	5.7	5.6

Source: Office of Institutional Analysis (2019, 2020, 2021e).

Table 14.2 Programs with the highest proportion of international *graduate* students, University of Manitoba, 2019–2021

Graduate Faculty/Program	2021 (%)	2020 (%)	2019 (%)
Price Faculty of Engineering	19.9	23.3	23.2
Science	16.5	16.2	16.6
Asper School of Business	10.1	8.3	9.5
Max Rady College of Medicine	9.2	9.1	8.2
Arts	9.0	9.8	9.4

Source: Office of Institutional Analysis (2019, 2020, 2021e)

to a faculty. At the start of the COVID-19 pandemic in 2020, more students joined University 1 for their first year in university, while enrolment for science, arts, and engineering decreased. This is a change to recent trends. The proportion of international students entering arts and science programs has been consistently increasing, whereas fewer freshmen are choosing to enrol in University 1, a trend also seen among domestic students.

Table 14.2 shows the international student distribution across the top five graduate programs of admission. In 2021, these five programs enrolled 64.6% of all international graduate students, compared to 66.7% in 2020 and 66.9% in 2019. Like most universities, the largest number of international graduate students choose to study science-related programs. Comparing 2019 to 2021, the enrolment percentages for these five programs remain fairly stable, with little fluctuation in the distribution of international students.

Table 14.3 shows that students from Asia are the largest number of students, making up 13% of the total student body. The largest number come from China (1,135) followed by India (1,104). Another 716 are from Bangladesh. The next largest group, however, is much smaller, numbering 336 students from Vietnam. Other notable countries include Pakistan (201) and Sri Lanka (121).

This table, however, gives an incomplete impression of the ethnic and cultural identities of the University of Manitoba. Other than age and gender, no other demographic characteristics are collected and published by the University and the results of the survey are inconclusive given the extremely low response rate from students, faculty, and staff. A newly created Equity Diversity and Inclusion (EDI) Committee, established in 2019, commissioned a survey in the Fall of 2020, and its first recommendation involved the significant absence of visible and invisible minorities (their language) among campus faculty, staff, and administration (President's Taskforce 2020). Although the University is hiring more Indigenous

Table 14.3 International Students by Country of Origin (Asia only), University of Manitoba, 2021[1]

Country or Region	Full-Time	Part-Time	Total
Bangladesh	664	52	716
China	991	144	1,135
Hong Kong	78	7	85
India	1,054	50	1,104
Indonesia	37	3	40
Japan	19	1	20
Kazakhstan	21	3	24
Korea, South	99	14	113
Kyrgyzstan	6	0	6
Malaysia	40	3	43
Mongolia	3	0	3
Myanmar	5	1	6
Nepal	17	0	17
Pakistan	186	15	201
Philippines	16	1	17
Singapore	4	0	4
Sri Lanka	119	2	121
Taiwan	17	4	21
Thailand	4	0	4
Vietnam	310	26	336
Other Asian Countries or Regions[2]	4	1	5
Total Asian International Students	3,694	327	4,021
Other International Students	2,478	289	2,767
Total International Students	6,172	616	6,788
Total Canadian Students	19,707	4,462	24,169

Source: Office of Institutional Analysis University of Manitoba (2021a).

Notes:
[1] Includes graduate and undergraduate students, Joint Master's students from both the University of Manitoba and the University of Winnipeg, and Distance Education students. Also includes all Post-Graduate Medical Education (PGME) students; therefore, the total may vary from other reports. Excludes B.Sc. (Dentistry) and B.Sc. (Medicine) students. Names of countries may have changed since data were collected.
[2] Includes countries with fewer than three students.

peoples and racialized faculty and staff, many are hired and subsequently leave the institution, usually due to better working conditions and pay. The committee also observed that the service commitments for Indigenous peoples and racialized faculty and staff were significantly larger than expected for white faculty and staff members. For racialized students in particular, the lack of staff and faculty in positions of authority or in teaching positions has meant very little space for interaction and learning from non-white faculty members.

Another interesting finding of the EDI Taskforce (2020: 49) was that a small proportion of staff and faculty wished that all University community members "assimilate to the language and culture of Manitoba in order to remain a part of the university community and even wanted to see an 'English only' rule instituted on campus". The recommendations outlined in this report also indicate a major shortfall in academic and writing supports for English as an additional language for international students. They also note the lack of assistance in completing visa and permanent resident forms and that the University is well behind in providing this type of service compared with other institutions.

Services for International Students

The University of Manitoba has a variety of services to assist international students in their transition to life and studies in Canada. When international students first arrive on campus, the International Centre hosts orientation sessions specifically designed for them to navigate life at the university and in Canada. These orientations include information on course selection and registration, academic integrity, living on campus, sexual violence awareness, financial preparedness and so on. Later on, they provide immigration services including legal advice on transitioning from a study visa to permanent residency. Orientation sessions also provide an environment for new international students to connect with one another and to meet Canadian students.

In terms of academic services, the University of Manitoba has several programs dedicated to international students, the most popular being the international student advisors. They can aid with personal or academic matters, as well as provide information regarding student visas and immigration processes. Other academic services include the Academic Learning Centre and the English Language Centre, but other than the "Homestay" program provided by the English Language Centre – which offers an opportunity for international students to live with a local Canadian family and to explore and experience local activities and Canadian culture – they do not cater to international students specifically. This has caused problems, particularly when language difficulties create issues with academic integrity.

In terms of financial support, international students are eligible for some scholarships and bursaries, but the selection is limited (see Das Gupta and Gomez). Overall, international students are not eligible for most of the scholarships and bursaries that are offered to Canadian students since the conditions under which scholarships and bursaries are awarded often specify that only permanent residents and Canadian citizens are eligible. There are two notable exceptions. Upon entry to the University of Manitoba, both undergraduate and graduate international students are eligible for entrance scholarships and subsequent scholarships after completing certain requirements. International graduate students are eligible for the University of Manitoba Graduate Fellowship. The University of Manitoba Bursary is also available for international student applications, and many departments within the university have internal awards for students based on academic merit. Other than these subsidies, many other scholarships have citizenship restrictions which prevent international students from applying.

The university also has an emergency loan program that provides short-term assistance to students who are experiencing unexpected financial difficulties, and international students are eligible to apply for this type of assistance. We do not have information on the number of international students who rely on the emergency loan program. During the COVID-19 pandemic when the University and other places of businesses were closed for long periods of time, the COVID-19 emergency loans program was available to international students who were hit extraordinarily hard given that a primary source of income for them, off- and on-campus work, had closed. They were, however, ineligible for the Canada Emergency Student Benefit (CESB) which was offered to Canadian citizens and permanent residents who were enrolled in post-secondary institutions in 2020 (Canada Revenue Agency 2022). Given that many international students depend upon the income they receive from working part-time jobs, the exclusion from this benefit had a significant influence on their ability to remain in Canada and many returned home as a result. At the time of writing, it is unknown how many students were forced to abandon their studies in Canada due to financial hardship during the COVID-19 pandemic.

Other than services provided by the University, international students have created their own organizations on campus as ways to provide help and connection. The University of Manitoba International Student Organization, founded on March 30, 2018, was created by a group of international students who wanted to use their experiences to help other international students integrate into the University and Winnipeg community. Some of their goals include promoting activism to strengthen and help members of the international community, promoting diversity and awareness of diversity, responding to the needs of international students to ensure their wellbeing, and working closely with the International Centre to help international students to the best of their abilities. International students from different countries have also organized their own associations.

Indigenous Students and International Students: Connecting

In the summer of 2015, the National Centre for Truth and Reconciliation (NCTR) opened its doors at the University of Manitoba (NCTR 2015).

Its purpose is to provide a safe and accessible archive of the statements and evidence gathered during the Truth and Reconciliation Commission of Canada which released its report in 1995 and to share the stories of the residential school survivors. Many international students have never heard about the atrocities committed against Indigenous peoples until they have arrived in Canada (see Parasram et al.). One of the observations made by a co-author of this chapter is that although students who have experienced the secondary education in system seem to know a bit about residential schools, overall, both Canadian-born and international students are still largely unexposed to this violent history. Locating the NCTR at the University of Manitoba provides all our students with important opportunities to learn and study from our past. This is one small but necessary step in addressing racism that is institutionally and systemically embedded within our practices.

What other efforts have been made by the University to introduce international students to the culture and history of Indigenous peoples in Manitoba? During International Orientation week, one session on Indigenous history and reconciliation is offered. Over a one-hour block, students are presented with a brief history of Indigenous peoples. It is not known how many students take advantage of this learning opportunity. Having this course made available throughout the year might encourage more international students to learn about our Indigenous peoples.

The University has also instituted a new graduation requirement for students in most faculties. Starting in Fall 2021, all new students are required to pass a three-credit hour course in Indigenous studies (University of Manitoba News 2021). In addition to providing a much-needed educational resource for all students, the intention of the policy is also to address the National Truth and Reconciliation's Call to Action #57 (NTRC 2022). The classes are offered in several departments and faculties.

Migizii Agamik, also known as Bald Eagle Lodge, is the home of the Indigenous Students' Centre. The University's official website describes it as a "home away from home" for Indigenous students (University of Manitoba 2022). Designed by Prairie architects, Migizii Agamik emphasizes the traditional teachings of Indigenous peoples, and is home to the Indigenous Student Centre, the University of Manitoba Indigenous Students' Association, the Office of Indigenous Engagement, and Access and Aboriginal Focus Programs. It houses a Circle Room that is a sacred, collaborative space for ceremonies, meetings, classes, and other traditions.

Given that the University of Manitoba is home to more than 2,600 Indigenous students, Migizii Agamik plays an important role in helping educate all students about Indigenous peoples and their history. As part of their team, Migizii Agamik has an Indigenous recruitment team to help Indigenous peoples become students and succeed in their degrees, and the Indigenous Student Centre is focused on welcoming and supporting Indigenous students, providing academic and social guidance, advocating for Indigenous needs, and creating a safe space for the community. The Indigenous Student Centre also offers students opportunity to learn about First Nations, Inuit and Métis culture by providing cultural support programs such as the annual Traditional Graduation PowWow and the Full Moon Ceremonies.

There are few opportunities for Indigenous students to meet and get to know international students in a formalized, university-sanctioned manner (see Parasram et al.). Because international student services and Indigenous student services are housed in different institutional departments, there is little interaction between the two. While students can and do intermingle and meet one another outside of university-sanctioned events, the administration does very little to provide opportunities for the two units to work together and bring their students together. This is a fundamental flaw in the institutional structure of the university and this separated structure also affects international students.

Racism on Campus

The University is not immune to racism within its community at all levels – from student to staff to faculty to administration (see Pang and Smith; Das Gupta and Gomez). The President's Taskforce on EDI (2020) provides evidence and individual reports regarding racism and colonialism on campus. In addition to overt acts of racism (examples discussed below), the committee observed that the experience of racism is particularly pronounced for first year international students (President's Taskforce 2020). One student commented that "white supremacy and lowkey racism is still very much a part of my every day experience" on campus. Racialized students and faculty also have been "carded" by Campus Security. Carding is the act of being asked for identification to prove that an individual rightly belongs on campus. Incidents of carding have occurred during "normal aspects of campus life or work like going to the office, using a photocopier, or looking for your keys to open an office door" (President's Taskforce 2020: 46; see also Das Gupta and Gomez).

In Fall 2018, the campus community awoke to find posters stating "It's OK to be white" plastered on campus (Markusa 2018). The slogan "it's ok to be white" is a common "dog whistle" used by white supremacist and alt-right groups to troll anti-racist institutions and the media. Disguised as an innocuous message, the statement is used by modern racial supremacist groups as a way of asserting their authority. The posters have appeared at other Canadian and American universities, including the University of Regina and the University of Waterloo (Markusa 2018). It is the place where these posters were located on campus that reinforces their racist intent. At the University of Manitoba, the posters appeared outside the Department of Native Studies, Migizii Agamik and the Gender Studies Program. The placement of these posters in these locations specifically undermines the supposedly innocuous nature of the message "it's okay to be white". It is a subtle message to these departments and institutions that their presence is not welcome. For many international students, this message underscores the unwelcome reception that many of them experience when they come to Canada.

These posters are just one of thousands of racist acts that happen every day. Some are reported to authorities, but most are not. Outside the Universities, police reported a 37% increase in hate crimes reported in 2021, the highest number since reporting began in 2009 (Moreau 2022). For hate crimes directed towards East and Southeast Asians, the number of crimes reported to police increased 301% in a single year. Crimes against Indigenous peoples increased by 152% and crimes against Black Canadians increased by 92% (Moreau 2022). While speculation is that the increase in police reported hate crime is correlated with the pandemic and its related social restrictions, evidence suggests that racially motivated hate crime has been on the rise for over a decade and that there are other institutional and systemic causes of racism that also influence the higher reporting rates we see off-and on-campus. At this time the University of Manitoba does not collect or report incidents of racism on campus.

University Response to Racism

Like other post-secondary institutions in Canada, racism rears its ugly head at the University of Manitoba. And, like other institutions, it was incredibly slow to fully undertake anything more than just lip service to addressing the fundamental issues that sustain racism on our campus. The lack of sufficient financial support for international students, the lack of international- and Indigenous-student-oriented services, and the tendency of regarding international enrolment as fulfilment of the EDI agenda speak volume to the slow response the institution has made towards discrimination and racism (see Das Gupta and Gomez). There have, however, been some positive initiatives.

In September 2020, the Rady Faculty of Health Sciences passed the *Disruption of all forms of Racism Policy* (UM Today 2020), partly in response

212 Yazhi Luo and Lori Wilkinson

to the findings of the President's Taskforce (2020). It was the first institutional anti-racism policy passed by a post-secondary institution in Canada (Wilson 2022). In this report, racialized and Indigenous students reported that racism was a particular problem in the Rady Health Faculty. This is not surprising, given that Winnipeg has a history of ignoring the health needs of its Indigenous peoples. For example, in 2008, Brian Sinclair died after spending 34 hours waiting for care in the Emergency Room at the Health Sciences Centre. He was suffering from a treatable urinary tract infection (CBC 2013). Staff believed he was intoxicated and ignored him. In 2017, the Brian Sinclair Working Group produced a report and recommendations regarding the treatment of Indigenous peoples in Manitoba Health Care settings.

The introduction of the *Disruption of Racism Policy* on the Rady campus has spurred other initiatives to combat racism on campus. In March 2022, the University introduced the anti-racism taskforce to work on identifying, addressing, and eliminating all forms of racism on campus. As part of this initiative, two new executive positions were announced—the Executive Lead for Equity, Diversity, and Inclusion and a new Vice President for Indigenous Affairs.

Students have also led the charge against racism. The University of Manitoba Bisons joined other post-secondary institutions in the province to create a video and statement against racism that is featured prominently on the University's website (Wesmen Athletics, Bison Sports, Bobcats Sports 2020). Researchers in the Faculty of Kinesiology and Recreation Studies, along with the Faculty of Arts and Immigration Partnerships of Winnipeg, are partnering to provide research and programming to prevent racism in sport. Their campaign, "Sport is not an equal playing field" (Anti-Racism in Sport 2022) includes a report, events, templates for sporting bodies, and training to assist players, parents, coaches, officials, and board members to identify, address, and prevent racism from within and outside the sporting ranks.

Conclusion

It is clear from this discussion that racism is alive and well at the University of Manitoba, as it is at other Canadian institutions. The University has responded in several ways to identify and address racism. Although they have made some progress in addressing the problem, there is clearly a long way to go.

Regarding the experiences of Asian students specifically, this chapter reveals that in addition to addressing racism, this group of students has experienced inequality in terms of access to services and bursaries scholarships.

Its own internal reporting (President's Task Force 2020) indicates that international students, especially those having English as an additional language, require additional writing and academic supports which are currently not available or under-resourced. Additional investment into this infrastructure would greatly improve the outcomes for these students. What is markedly absent from the public documents and discussion is the unequal access to bursaries and scholarships for international students. A majority of international students are ineligible for these awards simply because the donors have required that recipients be Canadian citizens or permanent residents. This practice continues today with new scholarships and bursaries excluding international students for no apparent rationale. We suggest that the University decline such donations and educate would-be donors about the cultural and international diversity of the student body. It would be beneficial if the Tri-Council (the main funding body for academics in Canada) also followed suit as these awards are prestigious and unfairly disadvantage otherwise qualified international students. Given that international students pay tuition that is twice or three times what Canadian citizens pay and that 73% of international students remain in Canada upon graduation (Crossman et al. 2022), the inequity in services and access to scholarships and bursaries needs to be addressed in order to smoothen the transition from international student to Canadian citizen.

Universities also need to do more to educate international students about Indigenous peoples and their histories. Without this knowledge, society is doomed to maintain the status quo in terms of the maltreatment of our Indigenous brothers and sisters. Universities can do more than just offer required courses in Indigenous studies. They can strive to provide events and spaces that bring international and Indigenous students together so that they may learn from one another and make genuine connections and friendships. As participants in the National Truth and Reconciliation report, the University of Manitoba in particular should lead the way in making these opportunities available to all students.

References

Anti-Racism in Sport. 2022. Sport Is Not an Equal Playing Field. Authors: Sarah Teetzel, Leisha Straichan, Craig Brown and Lori Wilkinson. Winnipeg: Immigration Partnership Winnipeg. Accessed online at https://antiracisminsport.ca/.

Brian Sinclair Working Group. 2017. Out of Sight: A Summary of the Events Leading Up to Brian Sinclair's Death and the Inquest That Examined It and the Interim Recommendations of the Brian Sinclair Working Group. Winnipeg. Accessed online at https://libguides.lib.umanitoba.ca/ld.php?content_id=33973085.

Brown, Lorraine, and Ian Jones. 2011. "Encounters with Racism and the International Student Experience." *Studies in Higher Education* 38, no. 7: 1004–1019.

Canada Revenue Agency. 2022. Canada Emergency Student Benefit-Eligibility Criteria. Ottawa: CRA. Accessed online https://www.canada.ca/en/revenue-agency/services/benefits/emergency-student-benefit/cesb-who-apply.html.

CBC. 2013. "Brian Sinclair Ignored by Winnipeg ER: Report." CBC News online. September 5. Accessed online at https://www.cbc.ca/news/canada/manitoba/brian-sinclair-ignored-by-winnipeg-er-report-1.1385107.

City of Winnipeg. 2022. Shoal Lake and Winnipeg's Drinking Water. March 2022. Winnipeg: Department of Water and Waste. Accessed online at https://winnipeg.ca/waterandwaste/water/shoallake.stm.

Crossman, Eden, Youjin Choi, Yuqian Lu, and Feng Hou. 2022. International Students as a Source of Labour Supply: Summary of Recent Trends. Ottawa: Statistics Canada. Accessed online at https://www150.statcan.gc.ca/n1/pub/36-28-0001/2022003/article/00001-eng.htm.

Dovchin, Sender. 2020. "The Psychological Damages of Linguistic Racism and International Students in Australia." *International Journal of Bilingual Education and Bilingualism* 23, no. 7: 804–818.

Hergesheimer, Joshua. 2016. "Unceded Territory: Meaningfully Acknowledging the Coast Salish Peoples." *Megaphone*. March 18. Accessed online at https://www.megaphonemagazine.com/unceded_territory.

Indigenous Services Canada. 2019. Shoal Lake 40 Welcomes the Opening of Freedom Road. Ottawa: Indigenous Services Canada. Accessed online at https://www.sac-isc.gc.ca/eng/1567348217295/1567348299590?wbdisable=true.

Lee, Jenny J. 2015. "International Student Experiences of Neo-Racism and Discrimination." *International Higher Education* 44: 3–5.

Markusa, Marcy. 2018. "Q and A: Lori Wilkinson Explains Why 'It's OK to Be White' Posters Are Not OK." CBC News online. November 9. Accessed online at https://www.cbc.ca/news/canada/manitoba/lori-wilkinson-racism-university-manitoba-1.4897478.

Moreau, Greg. 2022. Police Reported Crime Statistics in Canada. Catalog 85-002-X. Ottawa: Statistics Canada. Accessed online at https://www150.statcan.gc.ca/n1/pub/85-002-x/2022001/article/00013-eng.htm.

National Centre Truth and Reconciliation Commission. 2015. Message from the Executive Director. Winnipeg: National Centre for Truth and Reconciliation, University of Manitoba. Accessed online at https://nctr.ca/about/who-we-are/message-from-the-director/.

National Centre Truth and Reconciliation Commission. 2022. TRC Website. Winnipeg: University of Manitoba. Accessed online at https://nctr.ca/about/history-of-the-trc/trc-website/.

Office of Institutional Analysis. 2019. International Undergraduate and Graduate Students by Faculty/College/School, Fall Term 2019 as of November 1. Winnipeg: University of Manitoba. Accessed online at https://umanitoba.ca/institutional-analysis/sites/institutional-analysis/files/2021-08/International_Students_Faculty_College_School_Fall_2019.pdf.

Office of Institutional Analysis. 2020. International Undergraduate and Graduate Students by Faculty/College/School, Fall Term 2020 as of November 1. Winnipeg: University of Manitoba. Accessed online at https://umanitoba.ca/institutional-analysis/

sites/institutional-analysis/files/2021-08/International_Students_Faculty_College_
School_Fall_2020.pdf.
Office of Institutional Analysis. 2021a. Students by Citizenship-University of Man-
itoba Fall Term 2021 as of November 1. Winnipeg: University of Manitoba.
Accessed online at https://umanitoba.ca/institutional-analysis/sites/institutional-
analysis/files/2022-07/Students_by_Citizenship_F21.pdf.
Office of Institutional Analysis. 2021b. A Profile of Canadian Indigenous Students,
Fall Term, 2021. Winnipeg: University of Manitoba. Accessed online at https://
umanitoba.ca/institutional-analysis/sites/institutional-analysis/files/2022-01/
indigenous_profile_21.pdf.
Office of Institutional Analysis. 2021c. Canadian Indigenous Students by Faculty/
College/School Compared to the Overall Student Population, Fall 2021. Winnipeg:
University of Manitoba. Accessed online at https://umanitoba.ca/institutional-
analysis/sites/institutional-analysis/files/2022-01/canadian_indigenous_students_
faculty_college_school_overall_population_21.pdf.
Office of Institutional Analysis. 2021d. University of Manitoba Fall Term Enrolment (as at November 1) Summary Report, November 9, 2022. Winnipeg: University of Manitoba. Accessed online at https://umanitoba.ca/institutional-analysis/
sites/institutional-analysis/files/2022-11/summary_report_F22.pdf.
Office of Institutional Analysis. 2021e. International Undergraduate and Graduate
Students by Faculty/College/School, Fall Term 2021 as of November 1. Winnipeg:
University of Manitoba. Accessed online at https://umanitoba.ca/institutional-
analysis/sites/institutional-analysis/files/2022-02/international_students_faculty_
college_school_fall_2021.pdf.
President's Taskforce on Equity Diversity and Inclusion. 2020. *President's Task
Force on Equity Diversity and Inclusion Final Report.* Winnipeg: University of
Manitoba. Accessed online at https://umanitoba.ca/sites/default/files/2021-06/
presidents_task_force_on_edi_final_report.pdf.
Shoal Lake #40 First Nation. 2019. Water-Protecting and Preserving and Supplying
Winnipeg's Water. Shoal Lake, ON: Shoal Lake First Nation. Accessed online at
https://www.sl40.ca/water.htm.
Statistics Canada. 2022. "Indigenous Identity by Registered Indian or Treaty Sta-
tus, Canada." Retrieved in May 8 2023 at https://www150.statcan.gc.ca/t1/tbl1/
en/tv.action?pid=9810026501&pickMembers%5B0%5D=1.110&pickMembers
%5B1%5D=2.1&pickMembers%5B2%5D=3.1&pickMembers%5B3
%5D=4.1.
UM Today. 2019. "Presidents Message on Confronting Anti-Indigenous Racism
Collectively." UM Today. February 7. Accessed online at https://news.umanitoba.
ca/presidents-message-on-confronting-anti-indigenous-racism-collectively/.
UM Today. 2020. "Disruption of All Forms of Racism Policy Approved." UM
Today. September 1. Accessed online at https://news.umanitoba.ca/disruption-
of-all-forms-of-racism-policy-approved/.
University of Manitoba. 2022. Indigenous Connect. Winnipeg: University of Manitoba.
Accessed online at https://umanitoba.ca/admin/indigenous_connect/5558.html.
University of Manitoba News. 2021. "Faculty of Arts Introduces Indigenous
Content Requirement." UM Today-News. January 11. Accessed online at https://

news.umanitoba.ca/disruption-of-all-forms-of-racism-policy-approved/https://
news.umanitoba.ca/faculty-of-arts-introduces-indigenous-content-requirement/.
Wesmen Athletics, Bison Sports, Bobcats Sports. 2020. "Wesman, Bisons, Bobcats
Athletes Unite against Racism." YouTube. Accessed online at https://www.
youtube.com/watch?v=RCMYRhya4kU.
Wilson, Jonathan. 2022. "Walking the Talk." UM Today. March 3. Accessed online at https://news.umanitoba.ca/walking-the-talk/.

15 Neo-racism, Neo-nationalism, and the Recruitment of Chinese International Students to Canada in the Era of the Pandemic

You Zhang, Shangcao Yuan, and Phoebe Kang

Introduction

Anti-Asian racism has been exacerbated since the COVID-19 pandemic, affecting the Asian community, particularly Asians of Chinese descent in Canada (Guo and Guo 2021). Against this background, media coverage in China on anti-Asian racism in top English-speaking destination countries has ramped up (Romann 2021), which potentially heightens Chinese students' awareness of anti-Asian racism in major international student destination countries, such as Canada. Oliveira Soares et al. in this volume note that racism is one of the principal challenges Chinese international students face in Canada. This is echoed by research that highlights the experience of exclusion that Chinese international students experience (see Tavares). Moreover, the rising anti-Asian sentiments in major Western countries are also influenced by the growing tensions between China and the US, which also affected China's relations with Canada. Against this background, emerging research focuses on the racism faced by Chinese international students currently in destination countries (Chen 2021 and Zhanga, Bowb, and Bowc 2020). Moreover, there have been concerns on whether the rising tensions in international relations and racism would deter Chinese international students (Allen and Ye 2021), yet little empirical research has been conducted to understand how exacerbated anti-Asian racism and increasing awareness partly facilitated by increased media coverage affect the perceptions of potential international students in China and their study abroad considerations.

Chinese international students have been consistently one of the largest groups of international students in Canada (Canadian Bureau of International Education 2022). According to the sample from the survey by the Canadian Bureau of International Education (CBIE), Chinese international students consist of around 25% of the total international students

DOI: 10.4324/b23160-19

in Canada (see Kim, Abdulkarim, and Payne). Moreover, Canada has been competing intensely with other destination countries such as the US, the UK, and Australia for Chinese international students. Therefore, it is important to investigate how potential Chinese international students are affected by increasing reports of unfriendly treatments in Canada. Through a survey and semi-structured interviews of Chinese university students, this study aims at understanding how potential international students in China, the top exporting country for international students, perceive anti-Asian racism in Canada, one of the top international student destination countries, and whether and how anti-Asian racism affects their study abroad plans.

Our findings suggest that students are increasingly aware of anti-Asian racism in Canada and are bothered by the occurrence of the incidents. In addition, students report much more negative impression of Canada. Moreover, students report that anti-Asian racism is among the factors that students consider but does not serve as the determinant of students' choice. Yet students' concern of anti-Asian racism is closely linked with safety, meaning that students tend to think that anti-Asian racism may threaten their safety. Moreover, Chinese students tend to think that the anti-Asian racism experienced by Chinese international students is related to their country of origin, namely China, which has been experiencing worsening relations with Western countries such as the US and Canada recently. Based on our findings, we argue that the rising occurrence of neo-racism towards Asians, particularly Chinese students, coupled with neo-nationalism, might eventually affect the recruitment of Chinese international students, which remains one of the largest groups of international students in Canada. This study has implications for other major destinations countries.

Conceptual Framework

We employ the notions of 'neo-racism' and 'neo-nationalism' as our conceptual framework for this study. Neo-racism refers to a "new racism" based on negative perceptions about an individual's culture of origin, in addition to their race (Lee, Jon, and Byun 2017, 141). This discrimination is based on cultural order and stereotypes in that people from certain cultures are discriminated against because they are from countries that are perceived as inferior to Western countries. In essence, "good" or "better" cultures become the basis of discrimination and racism (see Tavares). In this study, neo-racism might be manifest as certain stereotypes are associated with Chinese international students, such as working in high-tech industry and thus taking jobs from local people or performing well in science. We apply this concept in this study to see if future Chinese international students' understanding of anti-Asian racism corresponds with the notion of neo-racism, or discrimination based on the cultural stereotypes associated with national identity, how cultural stereotypes are manifested in the context of the pandemic, and how students' study abroad plans to Canada are affected.

We also draw on "neo-nationalism". As Lee, Jon, and Byun (2017) note, with the influence of increased internationalization, "national identity is being reproduced and reconceptualized as a form of global competition" (142). This global competition relates to global hierarchies in economic and political power. The new version of nationalism encompasses a sense of national distinctiveness and power. Societal boundaries are reinforced by negative attitudes against those who are perceived to be lower in power or those who are rivalries in the global hierarchy (Lee, Jon, and Byun 2017). The COVID-19 pandemic has heightened the drastic changes in geo-political tensions and impacted on intrastate and interstate shifts. Canada's foreign policy aligning with the US government's position against China created political tensions between Canada and China. This is partly manifested in the incidents of Meng Wanzhou and "two Michaels".[1] As such, we draw neo-nationalism to understand how potential Chinese international students perceive the exacerbated anti-Asian racism in Canada in the context of the pandemic and rising political tensions.

Overall, since there is rising violence against the Asian population and this has been portrayed in the media, we hypothesize that prospective Chinese students might link the violence with the neo-racism and neo-nationalism associated with their Chinese identity, which might affect their sense of safety if they study in Canada.

Literature Review

Canada continues to attract international students and remain as one of the top study abroad destinations. Prior to the COVID-19 pandemic, according to the Statistics Canada (2020), international students accounted for all the growth in post-secondary enrolments in Canada during the 2018/2019 academic year. In 2022, Immigration, Refugees and Citizenship Canada (IRCC) reported that Canada saw nearly 450,000 new study permits take effect last year, the figure broke the highest number set in 2019. However, discrimination against international students is prevalent across major Western countries, including Canada (Guo and Guo 2021 and Stein and de Andreotti 2016).

In Canada, racism and discrimination are concealed by a multicultural harmony on the surface, but racism is deeply rooted in Canadian history (Cui 2019). Racism and discrimination are inhibiting factors affecting international student experiences in Canadian universities (see Luo and Wilkinson; Kim et al.). According to Smith (2016), international students, faculty and service providers all identified racism and discrimination as emerging concerns. His study reviews anecdotal reports on the observations of discrimination in class or incidents of racism and discrimination around the university campus. Moreover, Lee and Rice (2007) found that while racism and discrimination are not significant issues for international students from Europe, it is a concern for most international students, or international students as a whole. A study conducted in South Korea by Jon (2012) found that English proficiency has strong implications for potential power differentials and discrimination between international students and domestic students. In Canada, this native speakerism perpetuates the marginalization of international students whose first language is not English (see Tavares) or French in Francophone universities in Canada (see Olivera Soares et al.). Furthermore, a university's emphasis on the international students having to "adapt" or "adjust" is a deficit perspective, and may effectively involve placing all the responsibility for change on international students, and none on the university (see Montsion and Caneo).

Existing literature emphasizes the need for raised awareness of potential discrimination by the university community and the institution. Lee and Rice (2007) suggest that institutions become more aware that discrimination based on nation of origin exists in many forms. There seems to be no shortage of literature on international student experiences; however, there is a lack of research on how prospective international students perceive racism and whether and how it affects their study abroad decisions. This study is particularly important in a time of rising political tensions between China and major Western countries.

Methods and Data

We use the mixed method approach, combining a survey and follow-up interviews to understand how anti-Asian racism affects potential Chinese international students' study abroad plans. The combination of surveys and interviews allows us to gain a comprehensive understanding of the topic. First, the survey with potential Chinese international students gives us a broad picture of the extent to which students are aware of anti-Asian racism and the extent of its impact on students' impression of major destination countries, including Canada. The survey was designed to understand students' current plans regarding studying abroad, the destination of choice, important factors that motivate them to study abroad, and questions related to their awareness of anti-Asian racism. We used the convenient sampling method to administer the online survey to Chinese students currently in China and studying overseas through our personal connections. Convenient sampling is not the optimal method as it does not ensure sampling representativeness. This is the limitation of the study. However, we received a significant number of completed surveys (N=173) from Chinese students in 58 universities, including 33 Chinese universities and 25 universities in the US, UK, Canada, Japan, Singapore, France, and Australia.

Among the 173 students, 130 or 75% of them are currently in China and 43 or 25% of them are currently studying abroad. In addition, among the 130 students, 42 or 32% of them are planning to study abroad in the near future. It is important to note that this percentage is higher than China's outbound mobility rate, which stood at 2.26% (UNESCO Institute for Statistics 2019). This means that this survey is over-represented by students who intend to study abroad. However, this also enables us to reach our target population of students planning to study abroad, which will illuminate the purpose of the study on how anti-Asian racism affects students' study abroad plans. We used descriptive analysis of the survey data to understand students' awareness of anti-Asian racism and the impression of Canada in the context of being aware of anti-Asian racism.

While the survey gives a general understanding of the extent to which Chinese students are aware of anti-Asian racism and its potential impact on students' impressions of Canada, it does not provide insights on how Chinese students understand anti-Asian racism and how anti-Asian racism affects their study abroad plans. This is important as most Chinese students may not have extensive lived experience in Western countries; it is not clear how they understand anti-Asian racism while being far from where it happens. Moreover, the survey also does not shed light on whether and how anti-Asian racism affects students' study abroad decisions. Do students choose not to study abroad solely because of the rampant anti-Asian racist incidents? How does anti-Asian racism affect students' plans, in consideration of many other factors such as reputation and travel restrictions posed by the COVID-19 pandemic? As such, we conducted semi-structured follow-up interviews with ten Chinese students who have or had plans to study abroad for degree programs to understand their perspective of anti-Asian racism and how it affects their study abroad plans.

The interviews were conducted online and recorded with participants' consent. The recordings were transcribed and uploaded to Nvivo for coding. We used the emergent coding method (Charmaz 2006) to identify patterns and themes with particular attention to factors that students consider regarding their destination choice, students' understanding of anti-Asian racism, and how anti-Asian racism affects students' study abroad plans.

Survey Findings

In the survey, we asked students the extent of their awareness of anti-Asian racism in major English-speaking destination countries, which country has received the most media coverage of anti-Asian racism incidents, how students feel about the occurrence of anti-Asian racism, and how the occurrence of anti-Asian racism affects their impression of major destination countries.

In terms of students' preferred destination countries to study abroad, our survey suggests that Chinese students prefer to study in English-speaking countries or neighboring countries/regions. As Table 15.1 suggests, the US, the UK, and Hong Kong[2] are the top three destination countries/regions. Other popular destinations are Canada, Europe, Australia, which are major Western countries or regions that receive international students. In addition, Chinese students also reported being interested in neighboring countries such as Japan, Singapore, and South Korea. These countries all have significant ties with China and are geographically close. Particularly, Singapore is an English-speaking neighboring country, which particularly attracts Chinese students.

In terms of students' awareness of anti-Asian racism, we find that among the 173 students, 92% of the students (N=159) reported that they are aware of anti-Asian racism in the US, compared to 72% about Australia,

Table 15.1 Top destinations for study abroad

Countries	Percent (%)	Number
United States	27.92	55
United Kingdom	24.87	49
China (Hong Kong)	12.69	25
Canada	11.68	23
Europe	6.09	12
Australia	6.09	12
Japan	5.08	10
Singapore	4.06	8
South Korea	1.52	3
Total	100.00	197*

Note
* This is a multiple-choice question. Students are asked to choose three preferred destinations, therefore the total number (N = 199) surpasses the total number of students who completed the survey (N = 173).

Table 15.2 Number and percentage of Chinese students aware of anti-Asian racism

Country	Awareness of Anti-Asian Racism	Total	Percent (%)
Australia	124	173	72
Canada	96	173	55
USA	159	173	92
UK	103	173	60

60% about the UK, and 55% about Canada (see Table 15.2). Although awareness of Canada's anti-Asian racism is the lowest, with 55% of the students being aware, it still surpasses half of the respondents. Among the 96 students that reported having awareness of anti-Asian racism in Canada, 74% of them are university students in China. Namely, they are not living abroad and are unlikely to gain this knowledge from personal experience but from the media, friends or family living overseas, or personal experience if they had lived in Canada before.

In addition, most students reported being emotionally affected by these anti-Asian racism incidents. For example, a total of 118 students (or around 68% of the students) reported being slightly bothered (around 34%) or very bothered (around 35%) by anti-Asian racism in Canada, compared to around 22% of the students who reported that they were not affected, or around 3% reported that they think the incidents may be overstated. Among these students, around 79% of them are living in China, suggesting that the occurrence of anti-Asian incidents emotionally affects students even when they are not currently in Canada or the country where the anti-Asian incidents occurred.

In addition to the awareness and emotional impact of anti-Asian racism, we are also interested in the extent to which a country's image will be affected by the occurrence of anti-Asian racism in this country. A country's image is important, particularly for potential international students, as many of the students' decision to study abroad is also affected by how well-received the country is among students (Ghazarian 2016). According to the survey, not surprisingly, 68 students reported that Canada's image is slightly more negative and 51 students reported that Canada's image is much more negative. In other words, 119 students or around 69% of the students reported a negative impression of Canada caused by anti-Asian racism incidents.

In summary, the survey findings suggest that Chinese students' preferred destinations for study abroad have not gone through significant changes. They still prefer Western countries, particularly English-speaking countries. However, there are strong regional contenders for Chinese international students such as Singapore, Hong Kong, Japan, and South Korea. In terms of Canada, it is still the fourth popular destination country, although still lagging behind the US, the UK, and Hong Kong. Moreover, over half of the respondents are aware of anti-Asian racism incidents in Canada and 69% of the students reported a negative impression of Canada due to anti-Asian racism incidents. This suggests that Canada is not necessarily in an optimistic position in attracting international students, since it is still less popular compared to the US and the UK and it faces regional competitors such as Hong Kong and Singapore. Particularly, regional competitors may be in a favorable position during COVID-19 since students may prefer destinations that are close to their homes.

Interview Findings

The survey provided us a general understanding of Chinese students' awareness of anti-Asian racism and its impacts on students' emotions and their impression of Canada as a destination country. Based on this general understanding, in the interviews, we further asked the potential international students in China how they understand anti-Asian racism, including the causes for anti-Asian racism, what they mainly consider in choosing destination countries, and how anti-Asian racism has affected their study abroad plans.

Chinese students spell out four reasons why Chinese international students face racism in Western countries. First, the students believed that Chinese people historically immigrated "illegally" to Western countries such as Canada and the US and did low-status labor work. Second, students believe that there has been a prevalent perception in Western countries that the COVID-19 disease originated from China and Chinese people, including Chinese international students, have brought the virus to other countries. This perception fueled racist incidents against Chinese people. Students believe that these two reasons are in effect about Western countries' negative impressions on China based on their stereotypes of Chinese people and can be considered as causes of racism. Thirdly, students believe that the rise of China in the global economy may have threatened the Western world's traditional superior status in the world. As one participant mentioned, "China has become stronger, probably they (Western countries) think that (Chinese people) will take their jobs and may even pose threats to their development, and they want to stop countries like China from growing, I think." Fourthly, on the contrary, some participants attributed Chinese international students' encounter with racism and/or discrimination to the current economic gaps between China and developed Western countries. One participant said "Such discrimination against Japanese students is relatively less, right? I think the fundamental reason is the overall national strength, e.g., international influence of the country. We (China) have a much smaller average GDP than Western countries". Chinese students believe that Chinese international students are discriminated against because China's economic rise may harm the interests of Western countries and China's current average GDP still positions China inferiorly in the global hierarchy.

Regarding Canada as a potential destination country, our findings suggest that Canada was a less popular choice for studying abroad compared with other English-speaking countries such as the US and UK. This was even more obvious when Canada is considered to have the same disadvantages with other English-speaking countries. For example, one student reported that since the long distance from China was a negative factor for both the US and Canada, he would rather choose the US than Canada. The perceived lower academic prestige of Canadian universities was referred to as the most important reason. In effect, many interviewees lacked a basic understanding of Canadian higher education landscapes. One participant reported that "in my impression, the academic research of scholars in Canada is not as strong, of course, this might be because I don't know Canada very much, therefore, when I consider choosing academic advisors, I first think about scholars in the UK and the US". In addition, the deteriorating international relations between China and Canada in the past few years has also been a concern for those potential international students in China. The Meng Wanzhou incident (CBC News 2021) was referred to as one reason for not considering Canada as a good study abroad choice.

Finally, although the COVID-19 pandemic has heightened the awareness of potential international students in China about the rising anti-Asian racism in Western countries, including Canada, anti-Asian racism was not a deciding factor for them when they selected the destination country. They considered more about academic quality and reputation, safety, and distance. They believed that racism is a widespread issue existing not just in Western countries but also in Asian countries, including China. Moreover, they believed that anti-Asian racism or even racism in general has been a long-standing issue in Western countries and would not be resolved within a short time. Thus, they, to some extent, accepted anti-Asian racism as an existing reality in Western countries. That said, those students did perceive anti-Asian racism as an influencing factor as they associated anti-Asian racism with personal safety. As explicitly pointed by one participant, "I think (my parents') concern about anti-Asian racism is in effect the concern about my personal safety". Once they felt immediate threat to their safety, anti-Asian racism could significantly influence their selection of the destination country. When they learned or even felt that incidents associated with anti-Asian racism happened much in a country or city, they chose to avoid such countries and cities while selecting their study abroad destinations.

Moreover, to stay safe, many students reported that they would prefer to stay within their own ethnic or cultural communities despite their desire to communicate with local students and experience local cultures.

Discussion and Conclusion

This study intends to understand the impact of anti-Asian racism on international student mobility in Canada. Particularly, it is interested in how future Chinese international students, one of the largest groups of international students, understand anti-Asian racism in Western countries, and whether anti-Asian racism affects their study abroad plans, and if so, how.

We found that the participating students' understanding of why Chinese students are targeted for racism and discriminated against, especially during the COVID-19 pandemic aligned with the intertwined notions of neo-racism and neo-nationalism. This finding is corroborated by other chapters in this volume (see Kim et al. and Tavares). Both neo-racism and neo-nationalism emphasize one's country of origin or national identity as an important cause for encountering discrimination. All the reasons participants identified were related to Chinese students' national identity. For example, Chinese students believed that Chinese people are targeted due to long-standing cultural stereotypes about the inferiority of Chinese people. The cultural stereotypes of Chinese people are reinforced by the pandemic, which is thought to originate in China and spread to the world. In addition, participants spoke about both China's rise and challenge to Western countries and the economic gap between China and the Western countries. These two seemingly contradictory reasons point to the sense of neo-nationalism, which essentially derives from intense economic and political competition in the global economy. This suggests that neo-nationalism plays a role in Chinese students' perception of destination countries, anti-Asian racism, and their study abroad considerations. Moreover, our research participants associated the violent incidences, stemming from neo-racism and neo-nationalism, with their own sense of safety, worrying that their lives might be endangered in Canada.

As such, our findings point to the potential adverse effects of anti-Asian racism on international student recruitment in Canada, despite the seemingly bright picture of the rising number of international students in Canada. Compared to other Anglophone destination countries, Canada has some advantages in attracting international students such as its safety and friendly immigration policy (Zhang, O'Shea, and Mou 2021). However, our findings suggest that even though they are still in China, most Chinese students reported that they are aware of anti-Asian racism in Canada and are emotionally bothered by the occurrence of these incidents. They also reported a negative impression of Canada because of anti-Asian racist incidents.

This finding suggests that future Chinese international students, with the help of social media and the Internet, have the capacity to do research on the social environments of destinations countries, and potentially make decisions based on their research. Moreover, their social network plays a role in their awareness. Students are likely to have knowledge of anti-Asian racism from their family members, friends and even acquaintances, whose accounts may emotionally affect them. In a nutshell, students' awareness of anti-Asian racism in Canada serves as a negative factor in bringing down Canada's reputation as a friendly destination country for international students.

In addition, we find that students' sense of safety is closely linked to anti-Asian racism. We argue that the occurrence of anti-Asian racism and its relations with students' sense of safety jeopardizes Canada's advantage as a safe country in attracting international students. Moreover, students' changing perception of Canada as a safe country may affect their perceptions of Canadian higher education institutions, where they study and interact with the local communities. As such, we argue that it is imperative for Canadian institutions to ensure international students that their safety and combating anti-Asian racism are priorities for institutions. In addition, these efforts should not stay on the surface but should be reflected in tangible initiatives. For example, we recommend institutions ensure that offices for international students provide necessary platforms for international students to express their concerns, take steps to prevent anti-Asian racism on and even beyond campus, and have feasible plans to protect students when racist incidents happen. Moreover, international students are not included in Canadian universities' equity, diversity and inclusion (EDI) efforts (Tamtik and Guenter 2019). Yet, our research shows that racism affects Chinese international students. Therefore, it is important for Canadian universities to effectively incorporate international students into their EDI efforts.

Our findings also raise concerns about internationalization at home. As students are concerned about their safety and well-being given rising anti-Asian racism, some students indicated that they would prefer to stay in their familiar social and cultural groups even if they study abroad. On the one hand, this may not be beneficial for international students' own experience as part of their educational experience should include interacting with students from other racial and cultural backgrounds. On the other hand, international students staying among their own group will not benefit domestic students, who can benefit from learning with and socializing with international students.

Our study only focuses on potential Chinese international students. Future research could extend the inquiry towards other Asian international students, such as in South Korea, Japan and Southeast Asian countries, to understand if their perception of anti-Asian racism is different from Chinese international students. Moreover, future research could focus on institutional initiatives in the intersection of anti-Asian racism and international student experience, to understand whether these initiatives are present and how they support building a friendly environment. Future research could also include examining the impact of neo-racism on the Chinese international students' experience in their destination country in the era of reinforced nationalism during and post COVID-19 pandemic.

Notes

1 Meng Wanzhou, the chief financial officer of Huawei Technologies, was accused of committing fraud to circumvent US sanctions against Iran. Canadian police arrested Meng at the behest of a US extradition request on December 1 of 2018. On Dec. 10, 2018, former Canadian diplomat Michael Kovrig and entrepreneur Michael Spavor, known as the "two Michaels" were detained on espionage charges in China, nine days after Meng was arrested in Canada.
2 Although Hong Kong is a special administrative region of People's Republic of China, in this study, we focused on prospective international students from mainland China. First, Hong Kong's social, economic, political, and cultural environment including its education system is visibly different than that of mainland China, and thus we suppose that Hong Kong students' perceptions and study abroad considerations might differ from students from mainland China. In addition, for students from mainland China, Hong Kong has been considered as a popular study "abroad" destination aside from Western countries such as the US, UK, and Canada due to its internationalized educational system.

References

Allen, Ryan, and Ying Ye. 2021. "Why Deteriorating Relations, Xenophobia, and Safety Concerns Will Deter Chinese International Student Mobility to the United States." *Journal of International Students* 11, no. 2: i–vii.
Canadian Bureau of International Education. 2022. "Where Do Inbound Students Come From?" 2022. https://cbie.ca/infographic/.
CBC News. 2021. "The Meng Wanzhou Huawei Saga: A Timeline." September 24, 2021. https://www.cbc.ca/news/meng-wanzhou-huawei-kovrig-spavor-1.6188472.
Charmaz, Kathy. 2006. *Constructing Grounded Theory: A Practical Guide through Qualitative Analysis*. London, Thousand Oaks, New Delhi: Sage.
Chen, Chen. 2021. *Navigating Racial Discrimination as Transnational Actors: Racial Experiences of Asian International Students in the US under the Covid-19 Pandemic*. Albany: State University of New York.
Cui, Dan. 2019. "Model Minority Stereotype and Racialized Habitus: Chinese Canadian Youth Struggling with Racial Discrimination at School." *Journal of Childhood Studies* 44: 70–84.

Ghazarian, Peter G. 2016. "Country Image and the Study Abroad Destination Choice of Students from Mainland China." *Journal of International Students* 6 (3): 700–11.

Guo, Shibao, and Yan Guo. 2021. "Combating Anti-Asian Racism and Xenophobia in Canada: Toward Pandemic Anti-Racism Education in Post-COVID-19." *Beijing International Review of Education* 3 (2): 187–211.

Jon, Jae-Eun. 2012. "Power Dynamics with International Students: From the Perspective of Domestic Students in Korean Higher Education." *Higher Education* 64 (4): 441–54.

Lee, Jenny J., and Charles Rice. 2007. "Welcome to America? International Student Perceptions of Discrimination." *Higher Education* 53 (3): 381–409.

Lee, Jenny, Jae-Eun Jon, and Kiyong Byun. 2017. "Neo-Racism and Neo-Nationalism within East Asia: The Experiences of International Students in South Korea." *Journal of Studies in International Education* 21 (2): 136–55. https://doi.org/10.1177/1028315316669903.

Romann, Alfred. 2021. "Anti-Asian Racism in Canada's West Rising." *China Daily*, May 8, 2021. https://global.chinadaily.com.cn/a/202105/08/WS6095cb0fa31024ad0babc969.html.

Smith, Clayton. 2016. "International Student Success." *Strategic Enrollment Management Quarterly* 4 (2): 61–73.

Statistics Canada. 2020. "Financial Information of Universities for the 2018/2019 School Year and Projected Impact of COVID–19 for 2020/2021." October 8, 2020. https://www150.statcan.gc.ca/n1/daily-quotidien/201008/dq201008b-eng.htm.

Stein, Sharon, and Vanessa Oliveira de Andreotti. 2016. "Cash, Competition, or Charity: International Students and the Global Imaginary." *Higher Education* 72 (2): 225–39. https://doi.org/10.1007/s10734-015-9949-8.

Tamtik, Merli, and Melissa Guenter. 2019. "Policy Analysis of Equity, Diversity and Inclusion Strategies in Canadian Universities – How Far Have We Come?" *Canadian Journal of Higher Education/Revue Canadienne d'enseignement Supérieur* 49 (3): 41–56.

UNESCO Institute for Statistics. 2019. "Outbound Mobility Ratio by Host Region." 2019. http://data.uis.unesco.org/.

Zhang, You, Michael O'Shea, and Leping Mou. 2021. "International Students' Motivations and Decisions to Do a PhD in Canada: Proposing a Three-Layer Push-Pull Framework." *Canadian Journal of Higher Education/Revue Canadienne d'enseignement Supérieur* 51 (2): 61–73.

Zhanga, Bin, Curtis O. Bowb, and Jennifer M. Bowc. 2020. "The Intersection of Racism and Xenophobia on the Rise Amid COVID-19 Pandemic: A Qualitative Study Investigating Experiences of Asian Chinese International Students in America." *Revista Argentina de Clínica Psicológica* 29 (5): 1145–56.

16 The Racial Experiences of International Students from Korea During the Pandemic

Ann H. Kim, Angie Y. Chung, Mihyon Jeon, Thomas R. Klassen, Min-Jung Kwak, Hyunjung Shin, and Patricia Trudel

Introduction

The SARS-CoV-2/COVID-19 pandemic spurred a historic rise in blatant anti-Asian violence and aggressions rooted in a dominant ideology of whiteness. The dismantling of White privilege is all the more critical in light of persistent anti-Black and anti-Indigenous racism. Recent media exposure and coverage as well as the stories shared here demonstrate that international postsecondary students are not sheltered from abuse and violence; perpetrators do not distinguish the immigration status of victims. However, the students' position as temporary residents and their status within universities may highlight some important differences in how they perceive and deal with racialized encounters. In this chapter, we focus on international students from South Korea, who may not have had significant racial experiences prior to their studies abroad, to provide an important perspective for understanding the meaning and impact of racialized encounters. We examine their descriptions of anti-Asian incidents and interactions during the pandemic using data from focus groups in four cities: Toronto, Saskatoon, Halifax, and Albany. In our analysis of international students' stories, we draw comparisons across sites and we consider the implications of anti-Asian racism for postsecondary institutions.

Anti-Asian Racism

This chapter combines Asian Critical Race Theory, or AsianCrit (Iftikar and Museus 2018; Yoo, Gabriel, and Okazaki 2022), and Bowser's theory of racism (2017) that elaborates on three components of enduring racism: cultural, institutional, and individual to understand the ways in which the interplay of the perpetual foreigner stereotype (Tuan 1999) is explicit in the rise of anti-Asian racism during the COVID-19 pandemic (Li and Nicholson 2020). Asian Critical Race Theory "is a conceptual lens for understanding the unique ways in which race and racism shape the lives

DOI: 10.4324/b23160-20

and identities of Asian Americans in society" (Yoo et al. 2022, 565). It expands on Critical Race Theory in education by focusing on Asian history, context, and diversity, and how structural, institutional, and cultural anti-Asian racism supports White supremacy (Yoo et al. 2022).

The historical insertion of diverse Asian groups in an enduring matrix of Black–White racism solidifies White supremacy and Black inferiority. This cultural and ideological matrix informs institutional racism which produces and maintains a racial hierarchy and therefore justifies racial beliefs and actions at the individual level (Bowser 2017, 582). The series of laws against Asian people, rooted in an ideology of the Yellow Peril, such as banning most immigration from Asia to Canada and the US until the mid-1900s and the denial of voting rights, as well as the riots and murders during and since that period, exemplifies the historical implication of cultural attitudes in institutional and individual racism.

The enduring narratives of the Yellow Peril (e.g., Asian people, culture, and objects are diseased and to be feared), the alien, and the meek have homogenized all who appear to be "from China" as a target for discrimination and scapegoating during the current pandemic (Li and Nicholson 2020). The current racial climate vis-à-vis Asians in North America, and the precarious and temporary status of international students, make Asian international students increasingly vulnerable to racial microaggression, institutional racism, and racial violence. Studies show that the psychological well-being, feelings of isolation/loneliness, and safety of international students from Asia are impacted by racial and ethnic stereotypes, gender, acculturative stress, as well as racial microaggressions and discrimination (Green and Kim 2005; Houshmand, Spanierman, and Tafarodi 2014; Lee, Koeske, and Sales 2004; Liu, Wong, and Tsai 2016; Park 2020).

For international students, racialized experiences are inextricably linked to colonialism, whiteness, and English language proficiency (see Parasram et al.; Park 2020; Yeo, Mendenhall, Harwood, and Huntt 2019). The act of going to Canada, the US, or another Western country to study and acquire English linguistic and cultural capital is itself reflective of the desirability to acculturate and connect with White and Western people. Once there, Korean and Asian international students further internalize existing race relations and often directly experience social isolation and marginalization (Park 2020). More specifically, forms of microaggression included social exclusion and avoidance, linguicism (ridiculing accents), and rendering invisible among others (Houshmand et al. 2014). Dealing with gender and racial stereotypes was also a common experience among students (Green and Kim 2005; Houshmand et al. 2014).

In an interesting study that explored racism against Asian students, Yeo et al. (2019) surveyed Asian domestic students who were mistaken for international students and, like Houshmand et al. (2014), found similar experiences of xenophobia and microaggressions related to race, nationality, accents, and language proficiency. These shared experiences among international students and non-international students illustrate the deep entrenchment of the perpetual foreigner stereotype. In other words, Asian students' experiences are tied to ideologies of being non-White, non-English speaking, and migrant.

The COVID-19 pandemic has underscored this reality and the endurance of anti-Asian racism. A recent survey of US students showed higher perceived discrimination compared to students who were surveyed prior to the pandemic (Haft and Zhou 2021). Another study suggests that anti-Asian racism may be more widespread than realized (Hahm et al. 2021). Finally, recent media articles about the virus and anti-Asian racism revealed the indestructibility of the Yellow Peril and forever foreigner stereotypes (Yang, Nhan, and Tung 2021). While exposing the structural, cultural, and individual basis of anti-Asian racism, these studies also show that racial discrimination and aggression in its many forms lead to loneliness and decreased life satisfaction (Liu et al. 2016) as well as acculturative stress and psychological distress (Lee et al. 2004; Yang et al. 2021).

In the current North American context, where race and racism are widely discussed themes, the perspectives of international students from Asia become increasingly vital, as they "often have different ways of understanding the concepts of race, ethnicity and identity, and how these concepts apply to them" (Lee 2017). The application of an AsianCrit lens becomes an important tool to understand the intersection of the perpetual foreigner and model minority stereotypes in the racialized experiences of international students from Asia before and during the pandemic.

Methods and sample

This chapter highlights the experiences of seven international students, four in Canada and three in the US, who participated in virtual semi-structured focus group discussions in January and February of 2021, about a year after the start of the COVID-19 pandemic. These seven participants are part of a larger study of 28 subjects across eight focus groups; two groups in each of the four sites: Albany in the US, and Halifax, Saskatoon, and Toronto in Canada. Most of the participants – who were undergraduate students or recently graduated – were not on student visas but we focus this chapter on the seven international students from Korea to illustrate the intersection of nationality, race, English language ability, and gender.

All of the international students in the sample participated in the first-generation focus group in each site although three of those groups (Halifax, Saskatoon, Toronto) included domestic students as well. Segmented by generational status due to the potentially different ways in which they experienced and understood racial incidents, the first-generation focus groups were composed of participants who arrived at the age of 13 years or older. The second focus group comprised current and recently graduated university students who were either born in Canada or the US or arrived under the age of 13 years. Given the mix of participant backgrounds in terms of their length of stay in Canada or the US, participants were encouraged to speak in the language with which they felt most comfortable (i.e., English or Korean). All transcripts were translated fully into English.

Respondents' length of time living in Canada or the US ranged from as little as five months to approximately nine years. We provide a brief profile of each of the international students with a pseudonym:

(1) Kibeom is a 23-year-old male undergraduate student living in a dormitory in Albany.
(2) Chanjong is a 26-year-old male undergraduate student living in Albany.
(3) Jaeyeon is a 22-year-old female recent graduate living in Albany with friends.
(4) Chulwoo is a 21-year-old male undergraduate student living in a dormitory in Halifax.
(5) Hyejin is a 19-year-old female undergraduate student living in a homestay in Halifax.
(6) Sukyung is a 24-year-old female undergraduate student residing in Saskatoon.
(7) Yeonseo is a 23-year-old female undergraduate student living in London (Canada) and participated in the Toronto group.

Shared experiences and context-dependent descriptions

A small number of participants experienced direct and explicit anti-Asian violence and discrimination during the first year of the pandemic (January 2020 to January 2021), although most students acknowledged that they experienced racism prior to the pandemic and shared at least one account. The absence of an increase can be attributed to previous experiences during the initial years of study in Canada and the US, prior to the pandemic. The majority of the Korean international students reported that they moved from smaller-sized cities or rural towns of initial settlement to bigger cities where their universities are located.

An international student in Saskatoon echoed that "racism gets worse in smaller cities" (Sukyung, Saskatoon) and she wondered if it is due to "the lack of opportunities to be exposed to diversity." While she was studying in a high school located in a small city in Manitoba, someone threw a rock at her and broke her phone, and at another time, garbage was thrown at her while she was eating lunch in the school cafeteria. She noticed these incidents happened when she was with other Asian students, which to her meant they were clearly targeted racist acts. Jaeyeon, an international student in Albany, also shared her experience of overt racialization on a local bus:

> And on the bus, some high school students sprayed these sprays that smell like fart and pointed at me and my roommates, yelling that we did it, saying "That Chinese" or "Those Chinese people" did it. Eventually, the bus driver said that until they are quiet, the bus is not moving and other people on the bus along with the driver made them stop but even that was a little ... it felt as though they wanted to screw us over by spraying their spray and blaming it on us. And honestly, these are small incidents and if these are the only incidents in 7 years, that's a pretty small number ... so I don't particularly live with some discontent, but sometimes I realize that I am a [minority] in this country.
>
> (Jaeyeon, Albany)

Students in the US and Canada commented that racism was more overt and severe in rural towns/smaller cities with fewer Koreans as these places are also less diverse generally than more populous cities.

Participants also recollected more subtle and covert forms of racialization while living and studying in Canada and the US. In these cases, many were confused and wondered whether these incidents could be considered racial discrimination. Sue et al. (2007) describe racial microaggressions as verbal/nonverbal and intentional/unintentional acts which can take place in the form of environmental slights, insults, jokes, and snubs. Usually, these derogatory and hostile communications leave targeted persons feeling isolated and puzzled as they were victimized solely based on their membership with racial minority groups. Sue et al. (2007) categorized racial microaggressions into four different forms: microassaults, microinsults, microinvalidation, and environmental microaggressions. Environmental microaggressions occur at the institutional level where in which a certain group of students is recruited and admitted via institution-specific policies and programs. Microassaults are the most explicit form of microaggressions in which individuals intentionally express and act out based on biased viewpoints. Another experience of racialization shared by Jaeyeon in Albany exemplifies a typical form of microassault acted out by a TA (Teaching Assistant):

> There is this one TA who is notorious as a racist. One time, we did a presentation, and all four group members were People of Colour -- it

was me, one Pakistani member, another Black student, and I don't remember the [identity of the] last member... but the TA asked us more questions and began fighting with one of our team members during the presentation. But the TA is well known as someone that you shouldn't get caught with in the program.

(Jaeyeon, Albany)

Microinsults are often expressed as positive statements and compliments while hiding insensitivity, slights, and rudeness towards the target group with bias. The real issue with microinsults is that people express or act out this form of racialization without consciousness or guilt. The targeted individuals often try to dismiss such incidents as daily happenings even if they are clearly feeling uncomfortable. For example, Sukyung, in Saskatoon, stated, "[A]fter I arrived in Saskatoon, I tried a few part-time jobs at first, and during then, there were a lot of people greeting me with "Ni-hao or putting their hands together and bowing their heads. Like that. But there was so much of that, and I think it's not something that I can label as racial discrimination. That was more of a daily occurrence." Furthermore, the racial microinvalidations even nullify the psychological feelings and beliefs of those racial minority persons who faced exclusion and mistreatment. Chanjong, an international student in Albany, shared his experience of assisting his friend at a local coffee shop.

My friend was ordering coffee there [at a local coffee shop] and although she had clearly ordered a Caramel Macchiato, they kept giving her an Americano. And so, my friend tried telling them that she had clearly ordered a Caramel Macchiato and that this was the wrong order, politely, and even so, they responded to her as if saying, "You just take whatever we give you and go." So, I went to talk to them, and my English isn't great but I did stay here for a little longer so I can speak a little more comfortably. When I talked to them, they said that they were sorry and that it was because they couldn't understand what she was saying.

(Chanjong, Albany)

Due to experiences like these, which were common, participants may not have noticed any major shift or increase since the start of the pandemic. Moreover, at the time of the interview, three of the four international students in Canada, and one of the three students in the US, were moving back and forth from Korea due to the pandemic and subsequent transition to the virtual delivery of university classes. As a result, they did not have "many experiences on campus" during the pandemic (Chulwoo, Halifax). One of these three students stayed in Canada for about a year since the pandemic started before returning to Korea, but she said she "stayed at home" most of the time during this period. The other student moved to another city due to the temporary closure of campus.

Yet, several international students explicitly described racial incidents and interactions during the pandemic and their impact on them. For students in both Canada and the US, most of these racialized encounters occurred in public spaces. For example, one respondent (Hyejin, Halifax), who, like Sukyung from Saskatoon, also experienced "really bad" racism during her high school years in a rural town in Eastern Canada prior to the pandemic, felt "as though racism started all over again" during the pandemic. She heard, "Hey Corona," and, "There's Corona," on the street, and felt "as though a wall has appeared." Another respondent, Yeonseo, from Toronto, commented that she "felt scared and felt a sense of risk" when going outside alone due to media reports on attacks on Asians, even though she "didn't actually experience any discrimination." This respondent stated her sense of "difference between me and White people" expanded further during the pandemic.

As for international students in the US, two students reported incidents of racism in public spaces (a bus stop and a mall). One respondent was waiting for a bus when a group of youths looked at her and remarked about catching the virus from the crosswalk button (Jaeyeon, Albany). A male respondent also felt victimized when a group of youth at a mall pointed at him and made it clear they were keeping their distance (Chanjong, Albany). These public acts of exclusion and aggression were similar among respondents in Canada and the US. The main difference in their description of racial incidents and interactions during the pandemic was the US students' naming of Black youth as the perpetrators of the racism against them (both examples in the US involved Black youth). It is important to highlight that, at no point during the discussion, did we ask about the perpetrator's race so it is notable when respondents offered this information. There were no additional comments about race related to those incidents. The respondents in Canada did not identify the race of their aggressors.

Claire J. Kim (2020), in a conversation about a forthcoming book, *Asian Americans in an Anti-Black World*, points out that Asian people have historically understood their racial position in relation to White people. While this is important, she argues that it omits a critical part of the structure that constructs Blackness as undesirable. We know perpetrators of hate tend to be White (Wong 2021), but we assume, with globalized processes of colonialism and the hegemony of White supremacist ideology, perpetrators come from all backgrounds. There are at least two ways to explain why international students in the US identified the race of perpetrators in contrast to their counterparts in Canada. First, there are systemic and individual differences between the two countries. It may be the case that there is heightened race awareness in the US relative to Canada, particularly where there are entrenched assumptions of the proclivities of crime attributed to certain racial groups as well as the violent history of Black–Korean race relations. Specifically, might there be less race-based stratified thinking and a greater awareness of race-bias and self-reflection among the students in Canada due to a more tolerant and accepting society? Or related to this is that self-selection may be operating, where students with more progressive values are attracted to Canada versus the US. As Michael Adams (2022), from the polling firm Environics Institute, observes through recent polls, the US is more diverged than Canada on how they value diversity.

A second, and perhaps a more plausible, explanation is that perpetrators in Canada were White but students did not feel the need to identify their race because whiteness carries an invisible and universal quality. In other words, participants subconsciously or consciously assumed we would know they meant White perpetrators, hence they did not name them, which, in effect, renders White perpetrators as unknown, invisible, unlabelled, and free from shame and condemnation. While none of the Korean international students who experienced hate encounters in Canada identified their perpetrator's race, one participant above felt an increasing distance with White people after hearing and reading about anti-Asian violence in the media. This speaks volumes about the impact on race dynamics even where a person indirectly suffers from acts of hate.

It is clear that international students' experiences of racism and racialization were similar across Canada and the US during the pandemic. Many racial encounters occurred in public spaces, with comments and behaviors that illustrate the enduring trope of fear and disease. We also found the racial context within places matters as students recalled incidents in different ways, shaped by race relations, race ideology, and race discourse.

The place of institutions

In terms of students' sense of belonging, none of the three US students reported that they feel a sense of belonging to the US, similar to international students in Canada. Many students, however, commented that they felt more comfortable on campus than off campus: "I do have some sense of belonging to my school but because the US is such a big country, I don't yet have a sense of belonging to the country itself" (Kibeom, Albany). This respondent also remarked how he feels like a foreigner off campus and worries that he will face another hate incident.

International student participants were mixed in their views regarding the level of responsibility of universities in dealing with racial microaggressions. The prior experience of participants seems to greatly influence their perceptions about the role universities can play. For example, Jaeyeon in Albany, who had a hard time entering the US during the pandemic, found no help from her university and stated, "...in a circumstance like that, if the schools can simply declare that these people are our students and they must enter, I think even that would be good." She felt the university should take stronger measures to "protect their students" and to provide international students with supportive resources such as places (e.g., an international student office) or people (e.g., international student officers). She believed an international student officer would work better than anti-racism education as she was uncertain that education about racial discrimination would work, since it was doubtful people would listen. This was echoed by other students, both international and domestic.

In general, however, international students were more likely than domestic students to feel there is little the university does or can do. For example, Sukyung in Saskatoon did not see anything for universities to do given her overall positive experiences on campus. Yeonseo in Toronto perceived that universities cannot provide much help to change attitudes and behaviors more broadly. She continued, "Universities are also large organization[s] and even if lots of people attend university, there are bound to be people who are isolated, so I don't think universities can be of big help."

In contrast, domestic students were more likely to call for regulations and protections within universities such as penalties for offensive remarks or acts against Asian American students and they tended to be in the US. One male participant, a domestic student in Albany, argued for governmental policies to protect Koreans or other Asians so that they can receive "proper protection." A female domestic student, also in Albany, felt the need to hire more minority faculty members.

In summary, international students from Korea felt universities were places of safety given the hostile environment off-campus during the pandemic. Yet, several felt they had a role to play that had less to do with public education and more to do with direct support services to international students.

Discussion

The status of international students is a key feature of the experience of racism among Korean postsecondary students in Canada and the United States. It is a legal status that many Korean domestic students once held and, as such, it seems somewhat arbitrary to demarcate students by legal status to understand racialization. However, when asked about their identity, some focus group participants made clear that the acquisition of permanent residency/citizenship status influenced their sense of belonging.

One of the female domestic students, in Toronto, who arrived as an international student explained:

When I first arrived, because I came on a student visa, in terms of my sense of belonging, I identified myself as fully Korean. I thought of myself as a Korean foreign student who just came here to learn English. Since this was my self-identity, when I met White people or people of diverse races, it felt new and I felt a sense of distance because of the differences in ethnic cultures. Then, I really enjoyed living in Canada and began feeling that I want to live here. So, my family and I applied for permanent residency and obtained it, and I started to feel as though my identity is shifting from being Korean to Canadian.

Considering the ways in which international students dealt with experiences of racialization, the lack of language proficiency is not the single most important factor that prevents them from reacting more assertively to discrimination (see de Oliveira Soares et al.). It is also linked to acquiring a sense of belonging to the host society and recognizing themselves to be full members of the community with associated rights. As noted earlier in this chapter, immigration status does not provide shelter or immunity from experiencing direct and explicit anti-Asian violence or more subtle and covert forms of racial discrimination.

Universities in Canada and the United States, along with national and subnational governments, actively recruit international students, including those from East Asia. Prior to the start of the pandemic in 2019, more than 6.1 million postsecondary students around the world crossed a border to study, more than twice the number just a dozen years earlier (OECD 2021, 215) and Asian students accounted for more than half of all international students. The United States, Canada, Australia, and the United Kingdom are the top destinations for international students, in part due to the desirability of studying in English. In addition to offering instruction in English, an important attraction for potential students and their parents is the perceived openness and liberalism of the societies (Klassen and Menges 2020). Surveys of international students in Canada find that one of the major reasons for choosing to study in the country is that it "offers a society that (generally) is tolerant and not discriminatory" (CBIE 2021).

Thus, the institutions that directly benefit and interact with international students bear a responsibility to them and to foster an open and accepting institution and society (see Das Gupta and Gomez). However, the findings from the focus group discussions illustrate that international students have borne a particular burden during the pandemic – a burden tied to legal status and language ability that intersects with race. While our findings do not allow us to determine whether the extent of anti-Asian or anti-Korean discrimination increased during the pandemic, it is clear that international students from Korea in Canada and the US have been the targets of direct and explicit anti-Asian violence and more covert forms of racial discrimination. And although students in the focus groups wished that their institutions would take a larger role in combating racism, most felt resigned that this would not occur.

The experiences shared in this chapter demonstrate the ongoing racialization of Asian people as tied to migration histories, language and accent discrimination, and location, consistent with the AsianCrit perspective that argues for understanding anti-Asian racism as unique to history and context. While incidents occurred among individuals, typically off-campus, and were similar across the two countries, we discern the cultural and institutional underpinnings in taunts of difference and disease in line with Bowser (2017). Culturally, students themselves pointed to changes in moving from smaller (perceived to be more homogenous) to larger, and arguably more diverse, cities, where they felt to be less of a target. Institutionally, by neglect; universities were not seen as helpful to students or equipped to promote equity awareness and education and thus, social change. Moreover, the ways in which participants described perpetrators appear to reflect race-biased ideology as White perpetrators seemed to remain unnamed, unlabeled, and evade reproach. These results demonstrate the need for the active engagement of universities in anti-racism work more generally, and in offering support to international students for experiences that occur both on- and off-campus.

Acknowledgments

This work was supported by the Core University Program for Korean Studies through the Ministry of Education of the Republic of Korea and the Korean Studies Promotion Service of the Academy of Korean Studies (AKS-2018-OLU-2250001).

References

Adams, Michael. 2022. "We're Witnessing the Continuing Cultural Divergence of Canada and the United States." *The Globe and Mail*, January 2, 2022. https://www.theglobeandmail.com/opinion/article-were-witnessing-the-continuing-cultural-divergence-of-canada-and-the/.

Bowser, Benjamin P. 2017. "Racism: Origin and Theory." *Journal of Black Studies* 48, no. 6: 572–590.

CBIE. 2021. "International Student Survey." Canadian Bureau for International Education. Accessed August 2, 2022. https://cbie.ca/survey.

Green, Denise O. N., and Eunyoung Kim. 2005. "Experiences of Korean Female Doctoral Students in Academe: Raising Voice against Gender and Racial Stereotypes." *Journal of College Student Development* 46: 487–500. Project MUSE.

Haft, Stephanie L., and Qing Zhou. 2021. "An Outbreak of Xenophobia: Perceived Discrimination and Anxiety in Chinese American College Students before and during the COVID-19 Pandemic." *International Journal of Psychology* 56, no. 4: 522–531. https://doi.org/10.1002/ijop.12740.

Hahm, Hyeouk Chris, Casey D. Xavier Hall, Kana T. Garcia, Anna Cavallino, Yoonsook Ha, Yvette C. Cozier, and Cindy Liu. 2021. "Experiences of COVID-19-Related Anti-Asian Discrimination and Affective Reactions in a Multiple Race Sample of U.S. Young Adults." *BMC Public Health* 21: 1563. https://doi.org/10.1186/s12889-021-11559-1.

Houshmand, Sara, Lisa B. Spanierman, and Romin W. Tafarodi. 2014. "Excluded and Avoided: Racial Microaggressions Targeting Asian International Students in Canada." *Cultural Diversity & Ethnic Minority Psychology* 20, no. 3: 377–388. http://doi:10.1037/a0035404.

Iftikar, Jon S., and Samuel D. Museus. 2018. "On the Utility of Asian Critical (AsianCrit) Theory in the Field of Education." *International Journal of Qualitative Studies in Education* 31, no. 10: 935–949.

Kim, Claire J. 2020. "A Conversation with Professor Claire Jean Kim on Her Upcoming Book: *Asian Americans in an Anti-Black World.*" Korean Office for Research and Education (KORE) Event, York University, Toronto, November 12, 2020. https://kore.info.yorku.ca/event/asian-americans-in-an-anti-black-world.

Klassen, Thomas R., and Christine Menges. 2020. *The Essential Guide to Studying Abroad: From Success in the Classroom to a Fulfilling Career.* Abington, Oxon: Routledge.

Lee, Sherrie. 2017. "Exploring the Social and Academic Experiences of International Students in Higher Education Institutions." *Journal of International Students* 7, no. 1: 160. Gale Academic OneFile. Accessed August 3, 2022. https://link.gale.com/apps/doc/A478824544/AONE?u=yorku_main&sid=bookmark-AONE&xid=224d5b97.

Lee, Jee-Sook, Gary F. Koeske, and Esther Sales. 2004. "Social Support Buffering of Acculturative Stress: A Study of Mental Health Symptoms among Korean International Students." *International Journal of Intercultural Relations* 28, no. 5: 399–414. https://doi.org/10.1016/j.ijintrel.2004.08.005.

Li, Yao, and Harvey L. Nicholson Jr. 2020. "When 'Model Minorities' Become 'Yellow Peril' – Othering and the Racialization of Asian Americans in the COVID-19 Pandemic." *Sociology Compass* 15: 1–13. https://doi.org/10.1111/soc4.12849.

Liu, Tao, Joel Y. Wong, and Pei-Chun Tsai. 2016. "Conditional Mediation Models of Intersecting Identities among Female Asian International Students." *The Counseling Psychologist* 44: 411–441. https://doi.org/10.1177/0011000016637200.

OECD. 2021. "Education at a Glance." Organisation for Economic Co-operation and Development. Accessed August 2, 2022. https://www.oecd.org/education/education-at-a-glance.

Park, Sung-Chun. 2020. *Korean International Students and the Making of Racialized Transnational Elites.* Lanham, MD: Lexington Books.

Sue, Derald Wing, Christina M. Capodilupo, Gina C. Torino, Jennifer M. Bucceri, Aisha M. B. Holder, Kevin L. Nadal, and Marta Esquilin. 2007. "Racial Microaggressions in Everyday Life: Implications for Clinical practice." *American Psychologist* 62, no. 4: 271–286. https://doi.org/10.1037/0003-066X.62.4.271.

Tuan, Mia. 1999. *Forever Foreigners or Honorary Whites?: The Asian Ethnic Experience.* New Brunswick: Rutgers University Press.

Wong, Janelle. 2021. "Beyond the Headlines: Review of National Anti-Asian Hate Incident Reporting/Data Collection Published over 2019-2021." Unpublished Report, June 7. Last accessed May 31, 2022. https://docs.google.com/document/d/19llMUCDHX-hLKru-cnDCq0BirlpNgF07W3f-q0J0ko4/edit.

Yang, Joyce P., Emily R. Nhan, and Elizabeth L. Tung. 2021. "COVID-19 Anti-Asian Racism and Race-Based Stress: A Phenomenological Qualitative Media Analysis." *American Psychological Association Psychological Trauma: Theory, Research, Practice, and Policy.* https://doi.org/10.1037/tra0001131.

Yeo, Hyejin Tina, Ruby Mendenhall, Stacy Anne Harwood, and Margaret Browne Huntt. 2019. "Asian International Student and Asian American Student: Mistaken Identity and Racial Microaggressions." *Journal of international students* 9, no. 1: 39–65. https://www.ojed.org/index.php/jis/article/view/278.

Yoo, Hyung Chol, Abigail K. Gabriel, and Sumie Okazaki. 2022. "Advancing Research within Asian American Psychology Using Asian Critical Race Theory and an Asian Americanist Perspective." *Journal of Humanistic Psychology* 62, no.4:563–590.https://journals.sagepub.com/doi/10.1177/00221678211062721.

Conclusion

Building on Success from the Bottom-up? Institutional Challenges, Racialized Experiences, and Opportunities for Further Research

Jean Michel Montsion, Ann H. Kim, and Elizabeth Buckner

Introduction

The Government of Canada's 2019–2024 *Building on Success: International Education Strategy* was led by three federal departments: International Trade Diversification; Employment, Workforce Development and Labour; and Immigration, Refugees and Citizenship. The Minister of International Trade Diversification frames this strategy and its benefits as follows:

> International education is an essential pillar of Canada's long-term competitiveness. Canadians who study abroad gain exposure to new cultures and ideas, stimulating innovation and developing important cross-cultural competencies. Students from abroad who study in Canada bring the same benefits to our shores. If they choose to immigrate to Canada, they contribute to Canada's economic success. Those who choose to return to their countries become life-long ambassadors for Canada and for Canadian values.
>
> (Government of Canada 2019, i)

In this view, international students, no matter their nationality or background, can contribute economically to Canada, either indirectly or directly. In line with this rationale, the Minister of Employment, Workforce Development and Labour specifies how "skills training [i.e., adaptability, problem-solving, resilience and intercultural competencies] will strengthen Canada's workforce and create the conditions to compete successfully in global markets" (Government of Canada 2019, ii). And as a matter of student migration, the Minister of Immigration, Refugees and Citizenship adds that this "strategy builds on the attributes that have made Canada a destination of choice for international students"

DOI: 10.4324/b23160-21

(Government of Canada 2019, iii). Put together, this framing of Canada's second international education strategy clearly articulates the federal government's interest in recruiting international students – or what we refer to as the federalization of education migration. At the same time, it shows significant silences in how such an experience is understood, with concrete ramifications on how official support is designed and delivered (Tamtik, Trilokekar and Jones 2020).

Of note, this federal strategy combines a focus on Canadian students studying abroad and on international students to Canada. In both cases, intercultural exposure and global competencies are presented in ways that center Canadian students and how Canada can, through exposing them to outside contexts, benefit from other ideas, cultures, and peoples. Such a perspective reifies a conservative norm and a false interpretation of who Canadian students are and what Canadian society is, even if, in practice, it has been shaped by successive waves of immigration, notably from Asia, since the 1970s (Wong and Guo 2015). In this view, the nationality and cultural background of international students are filtered through an economic and extractive mindset, reducing cultures and intercultural experiences to skills and competencies that will benefit.

Canadian students, companies, and the society at large. And yet, these intercultural advantages do not appear to be supported by the data (see Kim, Abdulkarim, and Payne). Although helpful to give some visibility to international students in national conversations about international education, such an emphasis denaturalizes how cultural contact and change occur and limits how the contributions of international students are perceived, especially during their studies (Belkhodja 2013; Kymlicka 2014). This can be explained by a focus away from what international students can bring on their own terms and closer to how they will fit in and benefit mainstream Canadian society.

One key absence in the framing of this strategy and in its objectives is the recognition of some of the key challenges experienced by international students in Canada. Implying that cross-cultural learning and inter-cultural encounters are simple, linear, and smooth processes, this revised federal strategy does not put front and center the several obstacles to academic success international students face, notably off-campus realities. Whether it is finding adequate and affordable housing, coping with an increasing cost of living, or experiencing everyday racism, the challenges that face international students to Canadian universities are plenty, and acknowledging them explicitly by federal departments and agencies can provide an honest look into this reality, while rendering possible public discussions on improving such living conditions (Scott et al. 2015). One of the key issues here for a federal approach to international education is the necessity of not representing Canada as a monolith. With a message that all of Canada will benefit from recruiting and retaining international students, how these benefits are lived differently across the country, where and for whom tensions and problems arise, and how to address these inequities are all important aspects to investigate further. By not centering postsecondary education institutions and their primary role in supporting student integration, *Building on Success* disregards the importance of the myriad struggles students face and the institutional challenges Canadian universities confront in supporting them.

In this concluding chapter, we reflect on how a national conversation about international education cannot be a top-down process and indicators of success must account for institutional and student experiences. Despite significant similarities across Canada and the structuring effect of national policies, notably in immigration, a conversation starting from the plural and diverse experiences of international students from Asia in Canadian universities will lead to a more realistic, albeit more complex, state of affairs on current institutional challenges. While understanding the prime structuring role of Canada's diverse local and provincial contexts is key to foreground institutional improvements, Canadian universities must also be seen as microcosms of larger Canadian trends and social realities, hence making their adaptions to increasing numbers of international students from Asia not only a concern of the postsecondary education sector, but of all tiers of governments and of Canadian society as a whole. Building on these realizations, we can shed new light on some of the most immediate institutional challenges to Canadian universities in better supporting and including international students from Asia. While none of these are easy tasks, thinking through how to bridge internationalization and related strategic priorities, like anti-racism and strengths-oriented support services, may lead to new, more inclusive ways. In this view, a future research agenda will necessarily focus on how to understand the different local student experiences across Canada, most notably amid a turn to virtual learning as experienced during the COVID-19 pandemic, to bridge more systematically academic studies of migration, racialization, and educational journeys and to situate such institutional challenges and student experiences within a study of the political economy of international education in Canada.

Local Contexts and the National Experience

The structuring role of local and provincial policies and frameworks in shaping the experiences of international students from Asia is key in a critical study of the institutional challenges faced by Canadian universities. As local actors, these institutions are necessarily integrated into particular historical configurations and public discussions on how to address issues emerging from increased local diversity (Narh and Buzzelli 2022). Questions of inclusion and exclusion, notably stemming from racialization processes and equity concerns, are lived and deployed differently across Canada, hence making Canadian university sites where these local formations are experienced. Whereas some of the chapters in the first section of the collection demonstrate that there are national pressures and similar concerns for universities across Canada, when it comes to internationalization, equity and anti-racism, transfer credits, as well as research partnerships, such pressures and concerns are lived differently, based on a distinct, local texturing (see Buckner, Knight-Grofe and Eden; Chan and Matsushita; Montsion and Caneo). As Kwak, Lo, Pang and Wang show, locations in Canada will not only provide distinct experiences based on their integration of global knowledge networks but they will also attract different profiles of international students from Asia. Whether it is related to academic and societal transitions to life in Canada or questions of navigating local ethnic politics, the structuring impact of local contexts is found in daily life encounters as well as in media coverage and university communication campaigns. As chapters in the final section exemplify, the social realities of international students from Asia intersect and are incorporated into local configurations of power in unique ways across Canada, highlighting for instance how their integration cannot be isolated from questions of equity for Indigenous students in Winnipeg (see Luo and Wilkinson), of the politics of race as evolving locally in Halifax (see Parasram, Gateman and Kazmi), and of the politics of language as experienced in Montréal (see De Oliveira Soares, Magnan, Liu and Melo Araneda). While having some resonance across Canada, such local assemblages of power relations provide a basis on which differential experiences can be understood, along with the ways in which the institutional challenges of Canadian universities are framed.

However, such a realization does not mean that the experiences of international students from Asia in specific locales, and in particular institutions, cannot be understood as part of broader trends and social realities of Canadian society. Rather than being conceived of as bubbles within and separate from society, or as "ivory towers," postsecondary education institutions can be framed as mirrors or microcosms of Canadian society. Societal questions related to immigration and settlement and key challenges such as housing, cost of life, and employment, echo in the experiences of international students from Asia in Canadian universities, along with their encounters with racism, linguistic differences, and instances of exclusion and marginalization (see Yu; Pang and Smith; Tavares). Similarly, Canada's historical configuration in terms of structures of oppression (i.e., sexism, racism, neo-racism, classism, homophobia, and ableism) is shaping student experiences and perceptions in distinct manners, often reflective of the ways in which such structures are integrated to the local context they inhabit (see Kim, Abdulkarim and Payne; Zhang, Yuan and Kang). For example, anti-Asian racism lived on campuses cannot be assessed separately from the rise of anti-Asian racist incidents since the beginning of the COVID-19 pandemic, building notably on mainstream racist and xenophobic reactions to the number of students of Asian descent in universities (Guo and Guo 2021). It is no surprise that, as in Canadian society, in general, international students from Asia face such challenging experiences by relying on particular social networks, including some that are culturally and linguistically more familiar. Often misunderstood, participation in such support networks has been sometimes opposed to the integration strategies of Canadian universities for such students (Montsion 2018). Such reactions to the ways in which international students from Asia self-organize reflect a broader societal critique towards the ways in which migrants to Canada have self-isolated from Canadian mainstream society, which echoes xenophobic tropes often found in public debates throughout Canadian history and society.

Challenges and Opportunities for Universities

One key goal of many contributors in this collection is to document, examine, and assess how the increasing focus on internationalization in Canadian universities since the late 1990s has unfolded and impacted other dimensions of these institutions and of Canadian academic life (see Beck; Das Gupta and Gomez; Buckner, Knight-Grofe and Eden; Buckner, Kim and Vlahos; Luo and Wilkinson). Many factors have been presented with respect to the context in which internationalization strategies were structured, including the financial constraints imposed by provincial governments and the need for Canadian postsecondary institutions to integrate the global knowledge economy and to compete globally for students (De Wit 2011; Jones 2004). A significant impact of internationalization as a strategy has been the concrete consequences on the everyday life of these institutions, notably as incoming international students and research partnerships have accumulated. Whereas, during the same period of time, Canadian universities have made progress in addressing questions of equity, diversity, and inclusion (EDI), anti-racism, and decolonization, it is of note that several potential connections that could be made with internationalization have yet to be established, from integrating the perspectives of international students from Asia into these discussions to creating opportunities and spaces that are designed to be more inclusive and welcoming for them. With increasingly internationalized student bodies, clear connections to equity and anti-racist requests to universities can be found, like developing less-Eurocentric curricula (see Yu). The challenge and related opportunity for postsecondary education institutions is to bridge key priorities of their internationalization strategies to other strategic goals, as such connections would improve the integration of international students from Asia, notably as it relates to EDI, anti-racism, and decolonization.

Bridging internationalization to other branches of the university might also influence how the integration and support of international students is conceived, away from a deficit-focused mindset. Deficit-thinking has been the historical norm in Canadian universities and continues to underpin many institutions' approach to student support services. It starts with identifying the areas in which students lack abilities in order to achieve institutional standards. Support services are then designed from the standpoint of the obstacles specific groups face in succeeding academically. In this view, students are seen as having shortcomings that targeted services will be able to address, if said students put the work into improving themselves (Shields et al. 2005). No matter the intent behind this approach, it raises many concerns. It reifies an abstract and unspoken norm of the "mainstream student," that is a White, middle-class, Canadian, full-time student, who is also young, able-bodied, and non-accented in the institution's language of instruction. Implicitly, it views any deviation from the norm as an obstacle that may affect the students' likelihood of success. More importantly, such a mindset restricts the ways in which students can contribute to their institutions. For instance, the several dominant languages spoken by students, international or domestic, are often conceived as an obstacle to mastering English or French, the main languages of instruction in Canadian universities. However, most of these institutions have yet to adopt a plurilingual approach to language training like it exists in Europe (Council of Europe 2001). Within such a framework, students are not conceived of as lacking abilities in English or French. Their linguistic backgrounds are rather mobilized and incorporated to language acquisition services, utilizing plurilingualism to integrate rather than isolate students (Pennycook 2010). The challenge and opportunity of Canadian universities, as presented in some of the chapters in this collection, is therefore to rethink support services beyond deficit-thinking (see Montsion and Caneo; De Oliveira Soares, Magnan, Liu, and Melo Araneda). Whereas redesigned services might involve many similar activities, the ways in which they are conceived and presented could de-emphasize instilling dominant Eurocentric norms, to understand students' wide-ranging knowledges, diverse worldviews, life experiences, and multi-national communities and support networks as critical factors in their success.

Absent in many of these institutional discussions about international students, as highlighted directly and indirectly in many of the chapters, is how the status of international student makes students vulnerable to various forms of discrimination and further marginalization (see Kim, Abdulkarim and Payne; Yu; Tavares; Kim, Chung, Jeon, Klassen, Kwak, Shin and Trudel). When focusing on the intersectionalities of the racial, gender, and class experiences, among others, in understanding student experiences (Belle 2020), the status of a visitor on Canadian ground is often forgotten as a key category of analysis. Concretely, Canadian institutions have regulations that restrict international students from accessing opportunities offered to all other students (see Luo and Wilkinson). Along with the high (and unregulated) tuition fees international students pay to study in Canada, their lack of citizenship or permanent residency status is an added, but often unacknowledged, structure of oppression. In light of the Combahee River Collective and legacy in examining and understanding social inequalities (Hill Collins 2000; Smith 1978), we consider international student status as an interlocking oppression, along with sexism, racism, classism, homophobia, and ableism, in shaping the experiences of international students from Asia. Highlighting the inner workings of interlocking oppressions helps connect how systems of oppression, globally defined, are experienced in daily life, including the status of international student which emerges from the xenophobic tenets of nation-state citizenship regimes and results in a clear demarcation between who can or cannot apply for specific scholarships or work opportunities, regardless of the academic merit of the candidate (Hulko 2009). A study of interlocking oppressions brings visibility to social markers that are commonly conceived of as unproblematic and only additive to other conditions, whereas the status of international student is a lived category and social marker that does not simply add to one's experience but rather shapes how they are integrated in society as a whole (Belle 2020).

Future Research Agenda

Some avenues for future research in support of improving the experiences of international students from Asia in universities across Canada have been identified throughout this collection. Given the transformative impact of the COVID-19 pandemic on the daily operations of the postsecondary education sector, the increasing presence and use of virtual learning has and will necessarily impact these experiences. E-learning has been on the rise over the last 20 years, but its connection to the internationalization strategies of universities, even before the pandemic, could be studied more explicitly. While the COVID-19 pandemic has led to an increasing number of anti-Asian racist incidents in the country, the ways in which e-learning intersects with and is shaped by varying local contexts across Canada requires further examination (Guo and Guo 2021). Requiring international students to adjust to virtual classes, academic, and social events has led these institutions to develop complex solutions to reconciling in-person and virtual activities and reconfiguring the university experience. The pandemic forced connections between online pedagogical practices, public health restrictions, and the living, working, and studying conditions of international students, well beyond the walls of the university. It exacerbated iniquities for international students to Canada, including some that have even experienced their studies from their home country while paying exorbitant tuition, and others have faced particular difficulties while in Canada, notably being excluded from many federal relief programs (Firang and Mensah 2022). More scholarship is needed to document and assess such iniquities, by combining studies of virtual learning to internationalization, of virtual learning to student migrations, and the structuring aspects of local and provincial contexts on student experiences.

Similarly, the complex and plural combinations by which migration and racialization intersect with the educational journeys of international students from Asia can be examined more systematically. International students are often depicted as an exception to immigration discussions due to their purposeful and temporary status, even if they are solely dependent on immigration policies and guidelines. Similarly, their economic contribution is often portrayed as conditional to finding employment after graduation, even if they contribute and work during their studies. Their experiences of racialization and racism are often diluted as either part of broader racial configurations or conflated with the experiences of Canadian citizens and permanent residents. While the field of international student migration to Canada is growing, such studies either follow a specific group of students with the same nationality or cultural background or provide national overviews of all students, with no real incorporation of such background in the analysis (Narh and Buzzelli 2022; Sondhi 2017; Walton-Roberts 2015). More studies are needed to bridge the gap between country-specific and national overview analyses, focusing specifically on how the social processes at play (i.e., migration, racialization, and education) intersect, interlock, and support each other. Aside from studies documenting the challenges, obstacles, and iniquities lived by students (Belkhodja 2013; Firang and Mensah 2022; Scott et al. 2015), a better grasp of how the combination of social processes further marginalize international students from Asia, and overlook their presence, contribution, and lived experiences, would allow us to address directly the ways in which changes and improvements can be made.

Coming back to the current phase of the federalization of education migration, it seems appropriate, as a final point, to suggest a more systematic examination of the political economy of international education. Student experiences and institutional challenges can be better understood by contextualizing their importance and role within the sector of international education, including what they mean for several stakeholders involved and how they relate to new directions of universities in designing their next internationalization strategies (Tamtik, Trilokekar and Jones 2020). As with adult education in universities more broadly, in Canada and abroad (Sumner 2008; Torres and Schugurensky 2002; Woolley 2018), research on international students can highlight the connections between the state (including all levels of government), the private sector, universities, and other institutionalized groups benefiting from the mobility of international students coming to Canada, as well as individuals, such as students themselves, their friends, networks, and communities, in shaping the ecosystem by which the business of international education thrives. It would also provide some system-wide explanations for the treatment of international students, some of the discriminatory regulations they encounter, and some of the reasons why changes to improve their experiences, including through the migration process, are difficult to implement. More importantly, understanding the contours of a political economy of international education will lead to a better understanding of how the realities of international students from Asia mesh with local social realities, societal perceptions of this student group, and everyday interactions. As *Building Success* is reductively geared towards how this country benefits from the business of international education, the narrative and indicators of success must be pluralized to include improved living conditions, institutional treatment, and overall integration of students in Canadian universities and into Canadian society.

References

Belkhodja, Chedly. 2013. *Improving the Assessment of International Students' Contribution to Canadian Society*. Knowledge Synthesis. Pathways to Prosperity Canada (last accessed August 21, 2022). http://quebec.p2pcanada.ca/wp-content/blogs.dir/1/files/2014/02/International-Students-Contribution-to-Canadian-Society.pdf.

Belle, Kathryn Sophia. 2020. "Interlocking, Intersecting and Intermeshing: Critical Engagements with Black and Latina Feminist Paradigms of Identity and Oppression." *Critical Philosophy of Race* 8, no. 1–2: 165–198.

Council of Europe. 2001. *Common European Framework of Reference for Languages: Learning, Teaching, Assessment*. Cambridge: Press Syndicate of the University of Cambridge.

De Wit, Hans. 2011. "Globalisation and Internationalisation of Higher Education." *Revista de Universidad y Sociedad del Conocimiento* 8, no. 2: 241–248.

Firang, David, and Joseph Mensah. 2022. "Exploring the Effects of the COVID-19 Pandemic on International Students and Universities in Canada." *Journal of International Students* 12, no. 1: 1–18.

Government of Canada. 2019. *Building on Success: International Education Strategy, 2019-2024*. Ottawa: Government of Canada (last accessed August 21, 2022). https://www.international.gc.ca/education/assets/pdfs/ies-sei/Building-on-Success-International-Education-Strategy-2019-2024.pdf.

Guo, Shibao, and Yan Guo. 2021. "Combating Anti-Asian Racism and Xenophobia in Canada: Toward Pandemic Anti-Racism Education in Post-COVID-19." *Beijing International Review of Education* 3, no. 2: 187–211.

Hill, Collins Patricia. 2000. *Black Feminist Thought: Knowledge, Consciousness, and the Politics of Empowerment*, 2nd ed. New York: Routledge.

Hulko, Wendy. 2009. "The Time- and Context-Contingent Nature of Intersectionality and Interlocking Oppressions." *Affilia: Journal of Women and Social Work* 24, no. 1: 44–55.

Jones, Glen A. 2004. "Ontario Higher Education Reform, 1995-2003: From Modest Modifications to Policy Reform." *Canadian Journal of Higher Education* 34, no. 3: 39–54.

Kymlicka, Will. 2014. The Essentialist Critique of Multiculturalism: Theories, Policies, Ethos. *Robert Schuman Centre for Advanced Studies Research Paper No. RSCAS 2014/59* (last accessed August 21, 2022). https://doi.org/10.2139/ssrn.2441133.

Montsion, Jean Michel. 2018. "Resource Centre or Experience Desk? Producing Spaces for Delivering Services to Indigenous and International Students at Universities in Ontario, Canada." *Canadian Journal of Higher Education* 48, no. 1: 132–147.

Narh, Ebenezer, and Michael Buzzelli. 2022. "Higher Education Student Migration in Canada: Interprovincial Structure and the Influence of Student Mother Tongue." *Canadian Journal of Regional Science* 45, no. 1: 3–58.

Pennycook, Alastair. 2010. *Critical Applied Linguistics: A Critical Introduction*. London: Routledge.

Scott, Colin, Saba Safdar, Roopa Desai Trilokekar, and Amira El Masri. 2015. "International Students as 'Ideal Immigrants' in Canada: A Disconnect between Policy Makers' Assumptions and the Voices of International Students." *Comparative and International Education* 43, no. 3: article 5.

Shields, Carolyn, Russell Bishop, and Andre E. Mazawi. 2005. *Pathologizing Practices: The Impact of Deficit Thinking on Education*. Bern: Peter Lang Publishing.

Smith, Barbara. 1978. "Toward a Black Feminist Criticism." *The Radical Teacher*, no. 7: 20–27.

Sondhi, Gunjan. 2017. "Gendering International Student Migration: An Indian Case-Study." *Journal of Ethnic and Migration Studies* 43, no. 8: 1304–1324.

Sumner, Jennifer. 2008. "Governance, Globalization, and Political Economy: Perspectives from Canadian Adult Education." *Adult Education Quarterly* 59, no. 1: 22–41.

Tamtik, Merli, Roopa Desai Trilokekar, and Glen A. Jones (eds). 2020. *International Education as Public Policy in Canada*. Kingston & Montreal: McGill-Queen's Press.

Torres, Carlos, and Daniel Schugurensky. 2002. "The Political Economy of Higher Education in the Era of Neoliberal Globalization: Latin America in Comparative Perspectives." *Higher Education* 43: 429–455.

Walton-Roberts, Margaret 2015. "Femininity, Mobility and Family Fears: Indian International Student Migration and Transnational Parental Control." *Journal of Cultural Geography* 32, no. 1: 68–82.

Wong, Lloyd, and Shibao Guo. 2015. Revisiting Multiculturalism in Canada. In S. Guo and L. Wong, eds. *Revisiting Multiculturalism in Canada: Theories, Policies and Debates*, pp. 1–14. Rotterdam: Sense Publishers.

Woolley, Frances. 2018. "The Political Economy of University Education in Canada." *Canadian Journal of Economics* 51, no. 4: 1061–1087.

Index

256   *Index*